Wheel of Tarot

A New Revolution

○■○■○■○■○■○■○■○■○■○■○

Wheel of Tarot

A New Revolution

James Wanless, PhD

Angeles Arrien, PhD

MERRILL-WEST PUBLISHING

Carmel, California

Printed in the United States of America

10 9 8 7 6 5 4 3 2 1

ISBN 0-961-5079-7-7

This book was produced by
***Ex Libris** / Julie Kranhold, Los Gatos, California*

Tarot cards reprinted with permission from U. S. Games Systems, Inc.
Japanese crests reprinted from *Japanese Design Motifs*, Dover Publications

Merrill-West Publishing

Box 1227
Carmel, California

Contents

O■O■O■O■O■O■O■O■O■O■O■O■O

CYCLE I
STEERING WHEEL / The Eye of Tarot

CYCLE II
WHEELS OF CHANGE / Unfoldment through Tarot

CYCLE III
MEDICINE WHEEL / The Helping Hand of Tarot

Prologue

The wheel symbolizes Tarot's philosophy of life. "Rota," an anagram of Tarot, means circular rotation. Tarot affirms life's cyclical nature. Tarot cards represent experiences we encounter on the wheel of life. Each life-experience is a progression that rotates the wheel. Life is a spiral, evolutionary journey.

"Tota," another anagrammatic version of Tarot, means "total" or "whole." Every turn of life is a step toward total being. This is symbolized by the highest-numbered card in the deck, the World or Universe.

The World-Universe card symbolizes our universality. As a microexpression of the universe, we embody its characteristics and live by its principles. The wheel-like design of the World-Universe characterizes our revolutions as we move toward self-completion, the realization of our total universality.

The primary twenty-two cards of the Tarot, the Major Arcana, are numbered zero to twenty-one. The zero card, Fool, is also seen as twenty-two. This numbering implies cyclical movement, with the Fool being both the beginning and end of the cycle. The Fool as zero, symbolizing the circle and the spirit, represents wholeness. Like a fool, we must pass through the experiences on the wheel of life again and again before understanding, accepting, and realizing our total being.

Moving through life, we constantly experience revolving fortunes, the circular ups and downs symbolized by the Tarot's Wheel of Fortune card. Commitment to the realization of our Universe totality and Fool spirit-perfection ultimately brings the success and reward on all levels of being of the cornucopic fortune wheel of life.

CYCLE I, STEERING WHEEL, views Tarot as an eye that extends our circle of perception. In expanding awareness, Tarot acts as a steering wheel. It helps us navigate life's evolutionary course.

Tarot enhances self-awareness by stimulating three primary modes of cognition: superconscious intuition, subconscious dream, and ordinary conscious logic. Pictorial symbols trigger our higher intuition. They elicit visions, voices, feelings, and ideas—the forms in which intuitions arise. The subconscious is revealed through the dream world. Symbols of Tarot initiate dreams, and dreams are communicated via such symbols. Tarot symbols are also catalysts to the thinking mind. Tarot is a book of knowledge through which we can reason our way to self-understanding.

CYCLE II, WHEELS OF CHANGE, views Tarot as a revolutionary wheel that transforms us. The wheel of life, like the universe and the eye, is always revolving and adjusting. Our world and our body, thoughts, and emotions are continuously changing. Increased self-awareness through Tarot accelerates change. Awareness is like fire—the great solar wheel, the eye of the sun. The more clearly we see ourselves, the more energized we become. We are moved by the eye-opening revolutionary power of the Tarot symbol.

CYCLE III, MEDICINE WHEEL, presents the Tarot as a medicine wheel. From the hub of a wheel or the centerpoint of awareness emanate spokes or rays of light. Like spokes which are bridges and as light rays which are helping hands, the Tarot is healing.

Tarot is a counseling medium. In the joining of hands between reader-therapist-counselor, and client or friend, a healing circle is formed. The wheel of Tarot, like the original medicine wheel, is a forum for illumination and community, the foundations of psycho-spiritual health.

EDITORS of WHEEL of TAROT

Angeles Arrien, PhD, is an author, anthropologist, educator, and corporate consultant. Her teachings are based on the universality of values, ethics, and experiences as they relate to myths, symbols, and the arts. She honors her Basque heritage by lecturing internationally and teaching workshops in cross-cultural anthropology and transpersonal psychology at colleges, universities, and humanistic growth centers. She offers a year-long cross-cultural shamanic training course (The Four-Fold Way) and has a private practice in personal growth consultation. She is currently working on several new books: *Signs of Life—Five Shapes in All Art and How to Use Them* (Arcus, 1992) and *The Four Fold Way—The Paths of the Warrior, Teacher, Healer, Visionary* (Harper-Collins, 1992). She has also written *The Tarot Handbook: Practical Applications of Ancient Visual Symbols* (Arcus Publishers, Sonoma, 1987).

James Wanless, PhD, is an author, counselor, and teacher. He is co-creator of the brilliant and revolutionary *Voyager Tarot Deck.* His publications include *Voyager Tarot: Way of the Great Oracle, New Age Tarot,* and the *StarTree Correspondence Course in Tarot and Symbols.* He is the president of Merrill-West, a multimedia publisher of symbolic arts and mythology. He also publishes *The Magic and Mystery Guide Catalog.* James is a national lecturer and a tireless scholar in the field of symbols and vision-making. He also creates dynamic workshops in which he shows how signs and symbols can be used so that everyone can become their own oracle. He received his doctorate from Columbia University in Political Science in 1972.

CONTRIBUTORS to WHEEL of TAROT

Hilary Anderson, PhD, is the author of the forthcoming publication *Sri Aurobindo's Yoga of Transformation* (Pilgrims Booksellers and Publishers, Nepal, 1991); "Bringing Swords Out of Depression and Darkness" in *New Thoughts on Tarot* (Newcastle Publishing); and numerous articles and essays on yoga, self-transformation, and oracular traditions. She is currently on the faculty in psychology and human behavior at National University, Los Angeles, and is a well-known lecturer and seminar leader in East-West psychology and religion. She maintains a private practice specializing in transformation work in Tarot imagery and voice dialogue techniques for personality development and spiritual awareness enhancement.

Judith Bolinger is a poet. She believes in self-expression—anything less is life-threatening. Her writing is a quest for sound and form and rhythm. She has published *Waterchild, Poems from a Pregnant Year* and *Twelve Days of Pregnancy in a New England Summer.* Her work has also appeared in periodicals and on broadside. She lives in Marin County, California.

Susan K. Cole is a management consultant in training and development. Her early background was in education—specializing in creating innovative programs for developmentally disadvantaged children and young adults. As an independent consultant she has developed programs in stress management, supervisory training, time management, entrepreneuring, team building, meetings management, and goal setting. Her latest project is a "Family Team Building" program that utilizes concepts of team building and the development of a vision statement for families that want to be healthier and happier.

Mary C. Culberson, MFCC, PhD, has been in the mental health field for twenty years, and is currently in private practice in Los Altos, California. She earned her PhD in transpersonal psychology, her doctoral dissertation being "The Relationship Between Transpersonal Symbols: Dreams and Tarot." She has a Jungian orientation with special interest in the integration of psychological and spiritual growth; symbolic therapies such as dream work, art therapy, the Tarot, and the sand tray; and women's issues. She also does marital cotherapy and sex therapy.

Jane English, PhD, is a physicist (experimental subatomic particle physics), whose love for exploration led her to extensive investigations of consciousness. She is also the photographer/illustrator of six books, including a best-selling translation of *Tao Te Ching.* (Vintage Publishing). In 1985, she founded her own publishing business, EarthHeart.

Dori Gombold is a graduate of the University of Minnesota with studies in psychology, English, and communications. An extensive traveler, she now lives in San Francisco where, for twelve years, she has engaged in independent study of psychology, East-West philosophy, and practical metaphysics—including astrology, yoga, the *I Ching,* and alchemy. Much of this time was also devoted to studying the practical application of Tarot symbolism in the process of personal transformation, under the guidance of the BOTA Institute. She is a counselor, teacher, lecturer, and workshop leader in personal transformation. She has written articles in metaphysical publications, including the internationally circulated *Tarot Newsletter* and Book Reviews for *New Realities* magazine.

Mary Katherine Greer is an author and teacher specializing in methods of self-exploration and transformation. Each of the three books in her Tarot cycle (Newcastle Publishing) features an experiential workbook format: *Tarot For Your Self: A Workbook for Personal Transformation* (1984), *Tarot Constellations: Patterns of Personal Destiny* (1987), and *Tarot Mirrors: Reflections of Personal Meaning* (1988). She also wrote and narrated a cassette tape for Audio Renaissance Tapes, called an *Audio Introduction to Tarot* (1988), and a video for Access A/V Productions called *Healing Emotional Pain with Tarot* (1988), and is featured in the *Tarot Network News Video Magazine.* Tools And Rites Of Transformation (TAROT) is a learning center founded in 1986 and directed by Mary for the study of divination, women's mysteries, and the transformative arts. Mary leads shamanic and magical workshops in women's moontime traditions. She is currently at work on a new book called *Magical Women of the Golden Dawn* (Wingbow Press, Berkeley, Fall 1992).

Twainhart Hill has studied extensively in the areas of art, holistic health, symbols, meditation, and the Tarot. Since 1975, she has been instrumental in organizing events nationwide in these subject areas. She has a private consultation practice in the San Francisco Bay Area.

Richard Hyde is an ordained minister in the United Church of Christ. He served as Associate Chaplain of Dartmouth College and as a parish minister in Vermont. He has also performed rituals in celebration of Easter and Christmas at the Esalen Institute. He lives in Berkeley, California, where he is a writer, consultant, and bodyworker. He gives workshops on the teachings of Jesus in the Gospels of Matthew, Mark, and Luke; how to provide a drug and alcohol peer counseling program for organizations; and understanding one's psychology, spirituality, and politics through dreamwork and Tarot. His articles have appeared in the *Christian Century*, the *Oakland Tribune*, and *Matrix*. He is completing his first book, a series of reflections on higher education in America.

Karen LaPuma is the author of *Awakening Female Power: The Way of the Goddess Warrior* (Soulsource Publishing). She is a motivational, spiritual, and metaphysical counselor and has been in practice in the San Francisco Bay Area since 1979. Karen lectures, holds seminars, and is a frequent radio and TV talk-show guest. She has trained extensively in psychology, self-growth techniques, Eastern and Western mythology, metaphysics, and comparative religions. She has written a regular astrological advice column in the Marin *Independent Journal*. Karen has founded and edited a monthly newsletter entitled *Self-Growth*, and has produced local theatrical productions.

Sharon Rose Lehrer is an organizational consultant, partner in Lehrer Designs (a fine jewelry company), and a Tarot consultant and teacher. She specializes in empowering individuals and organizatons to create success through her creative approaches for aligning vision and values, strategic planning, managing change, communication and leadership. She has developed innovative methods using symbols in business for assessment, team building, and planning. Her clients range from businesses to health-care, government to religious institutions, as well as community-based programs. She has written a column: "OT: The Practice and the Art" for the journal *Vision-Action*, and gives seminars entitled, "Visionary Leadership, Personal Empowerment, and Creativity" and "Intuition at Work."

Brian McCusker, PhD, has had a distinguished academic career as Professor of High Energy Nuclear Physics at the Dublin Institute for Advanced Studies 1948-1953, University of Sydney 1958-1984, Senior Visiting Scientist Cornell University, 1965-1975, Visiting Professor at University of Tokyo 1976, and Emeritus Professor, University of Sydney, 1985 to date. He is the author of 150 scientific papers, articles, monographs, and books, including *The Quest for Quarks* (Cambridge University Press, 1983). Dr. McCusker is the author and presenter of four scientific TV series and has given many talks on TV and radio.

Cherie Sutherland McCusker has been a lecturer in the Social Work Department of the University of Sydney (1981-1986). She is now a full-time doctoral student in sociology at the University of New South Wales. She is the author of 18 articles or book chapters, almost half of which are on the topic of the near-death experience. She is a leader of workshops in personal development, women's self-awareness, and shamanism.

Ralph Metzner, PhD, has been involved in consciousness research for over twenty-five years and is the author of more than fifty articles and several books, including *Maps of Consciousness* and *Opening to Inner Light*. He is a psychotherapist, workshop leader, and core faculty member at the California Institute of Integral Studies in San Francisco. He co-founded the Green Earth Foundation, an educational organization dedicated to the healing and harmonizing of the relationship between humanity and the Earth.

David Quigley is the creator of the Alchemical Tarot, a unique set of Tarot symbols based on the New Tarot for the

Aquarian Age. He is the founder and executive director of the Alchemical Hypnotherapy Institute in Santa Rosa, California. In over fifteen years of work in the field of Hypnotherapy, he has created a synthesis of powerful therapeutic techniques called "alchemical hypnotherapy," which he has taught throughout the western United States over the past eleven years. Alchemical hypnotherapy uses techniques from *gestalt*, Jungian visualization, and hypnosis to achieve rapid clearing of personal problems and negative habits, and to recover one's full potential as a spiritual being. David is a designated examiner and certified instructor for the American Council of Hypnotist Examiners and the Hypnotists' Examining Council of California.

Gary Ross has been involved with Tarot since 1968, and has served as editor of *The Tarot Network News* since 1983. Gary specializes in esoteric Tarot research and was a presenter at the International Tarot Symposium in 1980, 1982, and 1985. Gary is also the host of *Tarot Network News Video Magazine*, a 60-minute videocassette featuring many well-known Tarot artists and authors.

Judith Rozhon, BA, MA, has studied meditation, cross-cultural healing practices, mystical traditions, Jungian psychology, Buddhist psychology, and many transpersonal psychologies. She has been teaching classes and workshops in Tarot symbolism and dreamwork for the past thirteen years. She has served as editor of the *Tarot Network Newsletter* and has organized and been a presenter at Tarot Symposia. The past several years she has spent many months in intensive Vipassana meditation practice—often practicing in complete silence for three-month periods.

Anne Stine, MA, MFCC, is a transpersonal psychotherapist providing depth therapy to individuals and couples, and specializing in life transitions with a focus on women in midlife. She is director of Wilderness Rites, which offers rites of passage in remote natural settings. Her work is a collaboration of experience and training in Jungian and transpersonal psychologies, shamanism, applied intuition, and a life-long appreciation of the natural world.

Karen Turner, MA, MFCC, is an author, teacher and therapist specializing in midlife transitions and spiritual emergence. She has been practicing for over twenty-five years and combines mysticism, shamanism, and psychology in her work. She is currently writing a book, *MidLife Transition as a Spiritual Emergence.* Her articles have appeared in the *Yoga Journal* and the *SEN Journal.* She is in private practice in Mill Valley, California, and leads workshops and lectures throughout the United States.

Charloe Wittine is a psychotherapist and Tarot counselor. She studied at the California Institute of Integral Studies in San Francisco. She has a special interest in Jungian depth psychology, meditation, past life regressions, and telepathic communications. Charloe maintains a low-fee practice for people with alternative life-styles.

Wheel of Tarot
A New Revolution

○■○■○■○■○■○■○■○■○■○

◯■◯■◯■◯■◯■◯■◯■◯■◯■◯■◯■◯■◯

STEERING WHEEL
The Eye of Tarot

Roman mosaic, 1st century A. D.

*L*ike the eye, Tarot is a vehicle for awareness. Tarot is like the various tools we
use to facilitate our sight. It is a magnifying
glass in the validation it gives to what is
apparent but undeveloped within an individual.
Tarot is akin to the x-ray in revealing what is
hidden and not so obvious. A Tarot layout is a
hall of mirrors, reflecting different views, perspectives, and cross-sections of ourselves. The
telescopic properties of Tarot enable us to see far,
all the way into the subconscious. In picturing
all the elements of the universe surrounding us,
Tarot is a comprehensive, wide-angle, fish-eye
view of ourselves and our world. Like the hour-
glass, Tarot provides time perspectives. Tarot is
microscopic in that all these perspectives can be
applied in depth to any one aspect of our lifes.

○■○■○■○■○■○■○■○■○■○■○■○

Wheel of Fortune tarot cards from **Toth, Aquarian, Classic** *and* **Voyager** *decks*

The Science of Tarot Divination

*T*he eye of Tarot, the hub of the wheel, focalizes awareness through the "reading" of the card-symbols. In the classic reading, cards are selected from the deck, which is face down. The validity of this intuitive process is often questioned by the rational mind. These doubts are allayed as science explores metaphysics. Physicists Jane English, Brian McCusker, and Cherie Sutherland McCusker describe an extraordinary statistical analysis of readings that verifies the validity of the intuitive method of card selection.

What is this intelligence that enables us to "blindly" select the appropriate card-answer for our question? In the introductory article "Synchronicity, Divination, and Psi," Ralph Metzner shows the accuracy of Tarot through the theory of "synchronicity" and the existence of psychic "psi" ability.

Mary Culberson's empirical study of "Dreams, Tarot, and Synchronicity" indicates that the consciousness with which we select cards is akin to the dream state. Just as we can "incubate" dreams and receive answers in our dreams to questions posed before sleep, we can choose cards that give us our answers.

○■○■○■○■○■○■○■○■○■○■○

Synchronicity,
Divination, and Psi

by Ralph Metzner, PhD

The concept of synchronicity was originally put forward by C.G. Jung (1960) in order to give a systematic account of certain phenomena, such as *I Ching* divination, astrology and ESP experiments, that did not accord with the causal-deterministic science of his time. In the process of developing his theory, however, Jung came to broaden it more and more, and propose that there is a *fundamental acausal orderliness* in Nature. The phenomena mentioned above, which he called "parapsychic," could then be regarded as a special case of this more basic principle (Jung 1960: 516-517). Jung was much more interested in persuading fellow scientists and scholars of the validity of the larger, macrocosmic principle than he was in the individual, human synchronistic phenomena. He felt that the theory of synchronicity could help bring about a unification of physics and psychology.[1]

Jung suggested that synchronicity in the larger sense is a formal pattern or order, based on meaning, that exists in the world as a fourth principle complementary to the three foundation principles of physics—causality, energy conservation, and space-time. Examples of this acausal orderliness known to physics are the phenomena of radioactive decay, and the properties of natural numbers.[2] These phenomena seem to point to a kind of "meaningful orderedness," similar to the Chinese concept of *Tao* and to Leibniz's *"pre-established harmony."* Jung writes, "The absolute knowledge which is characteristic of synchronistic phenomena, a knowledge not mediated by the sense organs, supports the hypothesis of a self-subsistent meaning, or even expresses its existence. Such a form of existence can only be transcendental, since as the knowledge of future or spatially distant events (in ESP studies) shows, it is contained in a psychically relative space and time" (Jung 1960).

Jung points out that the macrocosmic synchronicity principle is foreshadowed not only in Leibniz and Lao-Tzu, but also in the hermetic-alchemical *theory of correspondence*. This is the doctrine, found also in Hindu and Buddhist Tantras, in Sufism and the Kabbalah, that there is a correspondence or parallelism between God-as-macrocosm and man-as-microcosm. Jung paraphrases the Alexandrian philosopher Philo, "the great principle or beginning, heaven, is infused into man the microcosm, who reflects the star-like natures, and thus . . . contains the whole" (Jung 1960: 490). Similar formulations are found in Hippocrates, Paracelsus, Pico della Mirandola, Agrippa, Kepler, Schopenhauer, and Leibniz. In the last-mentioned, the ancient theory of correspondence "petered out," (Jung's phrase) and became diluted with the concept of "psychophysical parallelism." Leibniz compares the relationship between soul and body to that between two synchronized clocks. Since it omits any consideration of the spiritual element, one must regard this as a rather mechanical analogy.

The two clocks analogy does, however, provide a meaningful perspective on astrology. One could say that the relationship between the pattern of planetary positions at a given moment, and the pattern of forces in the psyche of the individual born at that moment, is like the relationship between two synchronized clocks. One does not *cause* the other (the planets do not cause behavior)—they are composed of quite different matter or substance—but the one (the psychic) can be inferred, or read, from the other (the cosmic) because there is a pattern of correspondence, an *isomorphism*. As von Franz puts it, "all the events which occur in a given moment of time share the same quality, because they are exponents of one and the same momentary situation, from which fact one assumes that a picture is there, which can be 'read' or 'understood.'" (von Franz, 1975: 245).

The correspondence principle points to a parallelism of *spatial patterning* between macrocosm (the world, Great Nature) and microcosm (the psyche, human nature). The synchronicity principle, on the other hand, emphasizes the equivalence or parallelism of a *temporal patterning*, a pattern across time. Jung himself stated, in a footnote to a later essay (Progoff 1973: 159), that "synchronicity . . . is an unsatisfactory expression in so far as it only takes account of time phenomena." Simultaneity, or co-occurrence in time, is *not* a necessary part of synchronicity. Precognitive dreams are examples of synchronicity, even though the psychic event (dream) and the outer event to which it is related are not simultaneous. Jung states, ". . . synchronistic is not to be confused with synchronous." (Jung 1960: 526).

Synchronistic events are meaningful coincidences between causally unrelated events. As human beings we do not cause them, nor can we predict them, although we can increase our sensitivity to them. Jung uses the term *Gleichartigkeit* (which can be translated as "similarity in nature" or "equivalence in meaning") to describe the relationship between two events. We could arrange the examples discussed by Jung in the following manner:

Inner event	Synchronistic meaning equivalence	Outer event
I Ching hexagram (based on coin throws)	———————	Reader's life situation
A dream or fantasy of similar nature	———————	A "real" event
Subject's mental image of card-symbol experiment	———————	Actual card-symbol in ESP

The two events linked by synchronicity may or may not be connected in time and space—which is the principal criterion distinguishing synchronicity from causality. The causality principle requires that if we are to say A causes B, A must precede B in time, and be connected to B in space. J.B. Rhine's experiments demonstrated that space and time contiguity are irrelevant to the ESP effect; thus, the subject can "guess" the cards regardless of physical distance, and regardless of when the cards are actually selected, shown or exposed. Thus, these experiments are examples of the relativity of space-time in the psyche, as postulated in the synchronicity principle. Jung in fact felt that synchronistic phenomena are similar if not identical to the phenomena studied in parapsychological experiments. This is a point of view that is currently coming into the foreground of theoretical discussion in parapsychology, where the trend is away from theories that posit subtle or psychic forms of energy to account for psi phenomena and towards synchronistic-type explanations (Palmer 1979).

Synchronistic and parapsychological phenomena are alike, then, in that both transcend the ordinary space-time framework of our world. They are further alike in the role played by *emotional charge* or interest. It is generally agreed that emotional interest and enthusiasm increases subjects' psi scores (Tart 1977). And in synchronistic phenomena, the activation of archetypes with a specific charge is responsible for a kind of "numinous effect" (Jung 1960: 436). According to Jung, what happens is that the activation of a powerful archetype in the psyche produces feelings (affects), which in turn bring about a partial *abaissement du niveau mental* (an expression Jung borrowed from Pierre Janet), a "lowering of mental threshold." This lowered threshold gives "the unconscious a favorable opportunity to slip into the space vacated" (p.436). This is a rather extraordinary metaphor, suggestive of the altered state kind of phenomenon. The archetype constellates the pattern (a star-pattern!); it is *wirkend* ("effective"), but not deterministic-causal.

This theory, that parapsychic events are brought about through the unconscious with emotional factors becoming stronger than a conscious mental (inhibitory) factor, is rather similar to Rex Stanford's theory of the "psi-mediated instrumental response" or PMIR (Stanford 1974). According to Stanford, a parapsychology researcher, we unconsciously scan the world constantly for cues and clues, using psychic faculties unconsciously; and we incorporate this psychically derived information into our ongoing instrumental (purposive) behavior. An everyday example would be the person who, on the way to an appointment, gets out at the wrong train station and, "by coincidence," bumps into the person he was going to see. Laboratory demonstrations have also been done exemplifying the operation of this principle. For example, students had the answers to half the questions of an exam they were writing, in sealed envelopes on the table in front of them. They did not know the envelopes contained the answers, nor did they see the contents. Nevertheless, they wrote better answers on those questions than on others; according to Stanford's view, they unconsciously used psi to scan the environment for helpful cues and clues.

To summarize the discussion so far, the theory of synchronicity postulates a non-causal ordering principle at two levels: (a) at the level of macrocosmic, physical phenomena; and (b) at the individual human level, where synchronistic phenomena overlap with parapsychological phenomena. Jung's account of how synchronistic, paraspychic phenomena occur is suggestively similar to Stanford's theory of psi-mediated instrumental response.

In a recent paper, Tart (1981) has given a useful conceptual clarification of various types of causality and synchronicity. He points out correctly that some kinds of psi phenomena may involve a casual mechanism, currently unknown. The kind of purposive process posited in this paper, involving archetypal, purposive activity at a metaphysical level, is approximately equivalent to what Tart calls *being-specific synchronistic causality*.

Three categories of the individual, psychic synchronicity can be distinguished:

1. The two events connected by meaning equivalence are both external. An example of this would be the relationship between the pattern of *I Ching* lines and the pattern of events in the person's life.

2. One of the two events is external and the other is subjective/internal. An example of this would be the person who dreams of a red bird, and then sees a red bird just as he is telling the dream; or the Rhine card-guessing experiments might be another example (if causal explanations are not found).

3. Both events are internal/subjective. An example of this would be a series of dreams on the same theme, or mutual dreams between two people.

In the following sections of this paper, I propose first to extend the application of the synchronicity theory to divinatory or mantic procedures such as the Tarot, which were not considered by Jung; and then to suggest that psi-processes along the lines of Stanford's PMIR hypothesis may be involved in many synchronistic phenomena, or may even be considered equivalent to them, in some cases.

THE SYNCHRONICITY THEORY APPLIED TO TAROT AND OTHER MANTIC PROCEDURES

The laying out of a pattern or spread of cards in a Tarot divination or "reading" is similar in character to the process of throwing coins and deriving a pattern of lines (the hexagram) with the *I Ching* . Let us suppose a person draws the "Lovers" card in a Tarot reading, and is in fact in love at the time. We say there is a synchronistic correspondence between the card-symbol chosen (apparently at random) and the psychic state of the questioner. Other cards chosen may relate to external events in the person's life; e.g. the person pulls the "Death" card, and there is, or has been, a death in the family.

In other divinatory procedures, a similar situation obtains: In geomancy, a medieval practice derived from Africa, a pattern of pebbles thrown in sand provides the design from which psychological or physical events are "read." In tea-leaf reading, the pattern of leaves in a cup is interpreted according to certain principles. In classical Greece and Rome the augurs (soothsayers) interpreted the meaning of the situation from the pattern of flight of birds; or from the condition of a sacrifical animal. A similar situation exists in divinatory star-gazing (technically known as horary astrology): here the constellation of planets and stars at the moment that the question is posed, is related by meaning to the questioner's state of mind or life situation.

Applying Jung's analysis of synchronistic phenomena to the Tarot reading, we can describe the situation of the person in love who draws the "Lovers" card, as follows: we say the archetype of love was activated in the person's unconscious, which brought about a strong emotionally charged state and a lowering of the inhibitory mental threshold; this in turn permitted the emergence of a meaningful correspondence between the card symbol and the psychic state. The whole process could be diagrammed as follows:

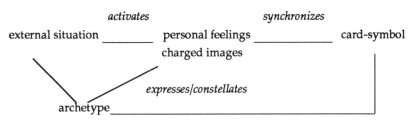

In doing this, we have not of course *explained* the occurrence of meaningful augury or divination. In fact, philosophers of science have criticized Jung's concept of synchronicity as not being an explanation, but merely another description, i.e., another word. If we limit the use of the term "explanation" to causal explanation, as most science does, then this criticism is necessarily valid: Jung explicitly states that synchronicity is acausal. On the other hand, a pattern description is also a powerful, valid and useful mode of organizing knowledge or information. One need only think of mathematical equations in physics, which are often not causal in nature, but condensed, summarized descriptions of empirical, ordered relationships. George Bateson (1979) used the term *abduction* (originally) proposed by C.S. Peirce) to refer to the vast realm of organized analogical descriptions in science and other areas of human thought.

The kind of analysis of synchronistic phenomena given above can be applied to the various divinatory or mantic procedures that involve relating a perceived external pattern arrangement to an inner state. A somewhat different situation arises when we consider natal astrology and numerology, including the use of numerological principles to derive Tarot "life-readings." Here we do *not* have a synchronistic correspondence between present divinatory elements (cards, coins, sticks, stones, birds, entrails, leaves, etc.) and present state of the individual, inner or outer. Rather, we have synchronistic, meaningful correspondence between a planetary or numerical pattern *existing at birth* , and the entire life-pattern of the individual. This would appear to be an example of a more transpersonal, macrocosmic level of synchronicity; or at least, a pattern correspondence extending over a much larger span of time.

THE ROLE OF PSI IN TAROT AND OTHER MANTIC PROCEDURES

If the above analysis of divination in terms of archetypal constellations of meaning is basically valid, it is not a very large further step also to apply parapsychological principles in this kind of situation. In fact, the process of doing a Tarot card spread is remarkably similar in its basic features to the paradigmatic "clairvoyance" experiment done in the laboratories of J.B. Rhine and others. In these experiments, a subject "guesses" which card is going to be displayed (or has been displayed) by an experimenter in another room, out of sensory range of the subject. The cards are preshuffled, i.e., randomized as to order. In Tarot readings also, the cards are shuffled at the beginning.

The main differences between a typical Tarot reading and the usual clairvoyance set-up are (1) the subject or querent in a Tarot reading is presumably in a state of heightened emotional and (hence) psychic receptivity; and (2) the subject in the Tarot reading is not expected to become *consciously* aware of what cards are coming up, as the experimental subject is. The Tarot situation in that respect is closer to the kind of situation described by Stanford's "psi-mediated instrumental response," which is unconscious.

The following hypothesis is proposed: in a Tarot reading the questioner, primed by emotional, archetypal charge and psychically sensitized, shuffles the cards; during that time his unconscious or superconscious mind (the part of his psyche capable of psi) selects the card(s) it knows or recognizes to be symbolically expressive of his inner or outer state. This is an instrumental, i.e. goal-directed, intentional, though unconscious action. It is not stretching the presumed psi ability of the average person much beyond what has already been demonstrated in laboratory situations, to think of the mind as capable of selecting the correct card in this way. The information is then transmitted, still unconsciously, to the person's brain and sensory-motor system, which "selects" the card.

Some Tarot readings involve the reader, and not the questioner, in shuffling and/or selecting the cards. In such situations, the unconscious or conscious psi abilities of the reader would also enter into the picture, as well as the degree of telepathic and/or empathic rapport between reader and questioner. It is easy to see how, with these variables, some readings are apt to be more "successful" than others; some will involve psi "hits," and some "misses." It is also easy to see the importance and relevance of relaxation and meditation prior to a reading, so as to facilitate the kind of psychic attunement, or the "lowering of the mental threshold," necessary for a meaningful synchronistic correspondence to take place, or be revealed.

If laboratory studies of clairvoyant card-guessing provide a modified paradigm for Tarot divination, other well-established parapsychological demonstrations are relevant to some of the other mantic procedures. To explain the efficacy of throwing coins or yarrow stalks (as in the *I Ching*), or pebbles (as in geomancy), we need only assume that the questioner also includes psychokinesis (PK) in his repertory of psi-mediated unconscious instrumental responses. His psi-mind, if we may use this phrase, knows and selects the relevant hexagram, and unconsciously, psychokinetically influences the throws of the coins or stalks to draw out that particular pattern.

In divination by tea-leaves, entrails, or flights of birds, the questioner selects the right time and situation by pre-cognizing when the pattern (of leaves, entrails, birds) will correspond to his situation, and then looks for it, *at that time*. This is not too different from having a dream, and then recognizing the pattern similarity in the situation that expresses it or reflects it. Our psi-mind can operate beyond the usual constraints of time and space, as has been amply demonstrated. It can know or perceive forward in time (precognition) or backward in time (recognition). Horary astrology, which is essentially sophisticated star-gazing augury, operates on the same principle: precognitively we attune our questioning to the moment and place when the stars are constellated in the pattern we can recognize.

As pointed out above, it is much more difficult to use these parapsychological concepts to account for the other class of synchronistic, divinatory phenomena, i.e., natal astrology and numerology, or life-readings based on them. Here the questioner or seeker isn't *doing* anything, consciously or unconsciously. There simply *is* a correspondence between planets or numbers on the one hand, and psychic patterning on the other. As Jung says, it is a "just so arrangement." Seen in the light of the macro/micro correspondence principle, the horoscope is a map of planetary pattern *and* a map of the psychic pattern. Using the two clocks analogy, the planetary clock "tells" the same time, in terms of the geometric arrangements of planets, as exists in the person's psychological make-up, in terms of the arrangement of traits and characteristics. Similarly, the numbers of the birthdate and the number-equivalents of the name given at birth, become a kind of short-hand equation that symbolizes certain features of the personality. I have given more details on these symbolic relationships in the book *Know Your Type* (Metzner 1979). In this sense, these procedures or principles exemplify the larger, macrocosmic sense of synchronicity discussed at the beginning of this paper.

To *summarize*, there appear to be two kinds or levels of synchronicity applicable to mantic procedures: the *first*, in which there is a meaningful connection between cosmic or abstract factors (planets, numbers) and psychic or personal events; the *second*, in which there is a meaningful connection between certain apparently random arrangements (of cards, coins, sticks, stones, leaves, entrails, flying birds) and psychic or personal events. This second kind of synchronistic phenomenon can usefully be compared with certain kinds of laboratory experiments in parapsychology. The theory of goal-directed, unconscious psi functioning can provide a conceptual bridging between scientific studies of psychic phenomena and the hitherto occult studies of Tarot, astrology, and other divinatory media. C.G. Jung's formulations of the synchronicity principle play a certain role in this kind of conceptual bridging.

NOTES

1. Progoff (1973) has given an interesting account of evolution of Jung's thinking on this matter.
2. Although Jung does not mention it, Bode's law in astronomy, which is a numerical series that partially describes and predicts the distances of the planets from the Sun, could be considered an example. There is no known physical-causal explanation for Bode's law.

REFERENCES

Bateson, Gregory (1979). *Mind and Nature: A Necessary Unity.* New York: E.P. Dutton.

Jung, Carl Gustav (1960). "Synchronicity: An Acausal Connecting Principle," in *Structure Dynamics of the Psyche* (Collected Works, Vol. 8). New York: Pantheon Books. (Original German edition, 1952.)

Metzner, Ralph (1979). *Know Your Type: Maps of Identity.* Garden City, N.J.: Doubleday.

Palmer, John (1979). Presidential Address, Annual Conference of the Parapsychology Association, Moraga, CA.

Stanford, Rex (1974). " An Experimentally Testable Model for Spontaneous Psi Events. I. Extrasensory Events." *Journal of the American Society for Psychical Research, 68:* 34-57.

Tart, Charles (1977). *PSI: Scientific Studies of the Psychic Realm.* New York: E.P. Dutton.

Tart, Charles (1981). "Causality and Synchronicity: Steps Toward Clarification. *Journal of the American Society for Psychical Research, 75:* 121-141.

von Franz, Marie-Louise (1975). *C.G. Jung: His Myth in Our Time.* New York: G.P. Putnam.

A Scientist's Experience with Tarot

Jane English, PhD

It is commonly thought that science is incompatible with Tarot, that science is totally logical while Tarot is totally intuitive. For a long time I, too, was of this opinion and, being committed to a scientific worldview, would have nothing to do with Tarot. I saw it as mere fortune-telling, as something used by the unscrupulous to manipulate and control those who were too lazy to take responsibility for their lives. However, some years after I became as interested in exploring the inner worlds of consciousness as I had been in exploring the outer world scientifically, I met and studied with people who were using Tarot in a way that appealed to me. They used it as a mirror of consciousness and as a tool for growth and transformation.

USING TAROT

I found that Tarot helped me to focus intuition and perception and to find within myself a deep and true kind of knowing. It helped me to perceive aspects of myself and of the world of which I am not ordinarily aware. I used it as a tool, a mirror for clarifying and getting new perspective on situations in my life.

As I began to use the cards, I often had a vague sense of uncanny accuracy in the three cards I chose daily as a part of a meditation. Each day I picked cards to represent body, mind and spirit aspects of myself. When I turned over the cards I had chosen face down and saw which ones they were, they usually seemed absolutely appropriate to my present situation. Often they brought into full awareness something of which I was only half aware. Sometimes the connection between the cards and my situation was very specific and sometimes more general. The following examples of dreams and Tarot cards illustrate this connection. I wrote the dream in my journal *before* choosing the day's cards. I used the Crowley-Thoth deck.

Dream: Water with green slime in it is poured over me.

Tarot Card: Seven of Cups—Cups overflowing with green slimy water.

Dream: With paper and charcoal, I am making a rubbing of a stone that has a bumblebee and an elegant lady carved in it.

Tarot Card: The Empress—An elegant lady with bumblebees embroidered on her shirt.

Dream: The water coming from a garden hose I am using slows to a dribble. I follow the hose back and discover that it is not connected to any source.

Tarot Card: Eight of Cups—Only four of the eight cups are being filled with water. The flower stems are not rooted in the earth. This is a similar image of reduced flow and disconnection from a source.

Dream: A house I have lived in and a car I have driven are both burning. I am not afraid.

Tarot Card: Princess of Wands—Swirls of fire and the fearless lady with the tiger by the tail. Flowers that symbolize aspects of one's identity that are no longer needed are burning on a pedestal.

Connection: Cars and houses are also symbols of identity. In both the dream and the card, symbols of identity are burning, and this is happening without fear.

Dream: I am with a friend who is one of my teachers. We have a bowl full of cookie dough and half-formed cookies. We meditate before starting to work on the cookies. As I start to reach for the dough, he asks that we meditate more. I close my eyes and experience light, stars, colors, and patterns of energy. I feel our unity as energy. I no longer have an identity; there is no sense of "me," just consciousness and energy. There is awareness that he and I are in this experience together. We are the experience, the awareness.

Tarot Cards: The Tower—In the "body" position of the spread. A fire-breathing dragon destroying the tower, a symbol of identity. Human figures falling from the tower, symbols of personality images being cleared away. An eye above, a symbol of clear vision of one's true self.

Three of Wands—In the "mind" position. Orange and white flames and open lotus flowers, symbols of integrity and wholeness in one's perception of self and others.

Ace of Wands—In the "spirit" position. The torch of fire, a symbol of the ability to burn out obstacles in consciousness and to go beyond conditioning.

Connections: Light, fire, vision, energy, and transcendence in both dream and cards.

"SCIENTIFIC" DOUBTS

Reconciling my experience of the cards as mirrors with my scientific training that views external things as really separate from ourselves was a slow and difficult process for me. From an orthodox scientific perspective the Dream/Tarot correlations would be seen as too subjective to be good data. Most scientists would say that the cards are separate from the person who chose them, that they were chosen randomly, and that therefore the cards could not have a meaningful connection to the person's subjective reality. Connections like those in the Dream/Tarot examples would be seen as the result of imagination and chance, and therefore not to be considered real. Scientists say the cards and the person are separate so the choices are random, and Tarot practitioners say the cards and the person are connected so the choices are not random.

Being both a scientist and a Tarot practitioner, I was intensely interested in resolving this conflict! Having experienced much that is useful and valuable in using the tools of both science and Tarot, I was interested in integrating these two areas of my experience. I decided to apply one of the tools of science to my Tarot experience. I did a statistical analysis of my records of the Tarot cards I had chosen in meditation for a period of two years. Two friends, whom I will call B and C, had followed a similar practice and had records of cards chosen over two and three years, respectively. They lent me their records so I could do a statistical analysis of their choices, too.

Statistical analysis is a tool used in science to test the relative validity of conflicting hypotheses, conflicting theoretical explanation of phenomena observed in experiments. As such, it was ideally suited to seeing which was more valid, science's claim that choosing Tarot cards is random or tarot's claim that it is not random.

I had much mental and emotional resistance to doing the statistics. I knew that I would feel stuck with the results. Either it would affirm my old scientific worldview that I was beginning to find too narrow, or it would force it to change and set me off into the unknown.

THE IMPORTANCE OF SUBJECTIVE DATA

When exploring something, like the use of Tarot, that is related to both subjective and objective experience, it is important to include subjective data along with the objective data. The following material is the subjective data associated with the records of the Tarot cards chosen.

As I did my three-card spread each day, I expected that the cards chosen would mirror my state of consciousness. I chose them after a period of shuffling that served primarily as a concentration device as I focused my awareness on myself and the coming day. The shuffle was only secondarily a way of randomizing the cards. This focusing of awareness was not a narrowing of attention, the usual thinking about or concentrating on something. On the contrary, it was an expansion, a relaxing that allowed new thoughts, emotions, intuitions, sensations, and sometimes a sense of quiet emptiness to emerge into awareness.

After the shuffle, I then spread out the cards face down in a fan. Following an inner sense of appropriateness, I chose three cards to represent body, mind, and spirit. Sometimes my eyes and hand seemed drawn to a particular card. I knew it was right when my whole being seemed to say "yes." The "yes" is the verbal component of an experience that involves thoughts, emotions, intuitive images, and physical sensations. At the time of doing most of the spreads, I had no intention either of trying to guess what cards I was choosing or of eventually subjecting the cards chosen to a statistical analysis.

Person B says that during the shuffle, she becomes very quiet and clear. She feels that everything is on hold. She sometimes shuffles for as long as five minutes before spreading out the cards face down in a fan. She has a variety of ways of choosing the cards. Sometimes, she runs the palm of her hand above the cards without touching them and at certain cards experiences a sensation that to her means "stop." At other times, she uses one of her fingers rather than her palm to choose in a similar manner. At times her eyes seem drawn to a particular card. Occasionally, instead of feeling a sensation, she notices that her breathing becomes irregular or that she feels very clear as her hand, fingers, or eyes approach a certain card. She may not immediately pick a card that comes to her attention in one of these ways. She may move on to other cards and then come back to the original card to see if what she calls the "charge" is still there. She may experience charge with several cards before deciding which three to choose.

Person C says that she chooses her cards each morning. She usually spends ten to fifteen minutes on a spread. She shuffles the entire deck, then divides it into three stacks. She then shuffles each stack individually and makes a fan of it. There is always one card in each stack that her eyes are instantly attracted to. About half the time, the cards mirror to her either what is going on in the physical world at that time, what she is thinking about, or what she is feeling. And half the time, she doesn't immediately see any significance in the spread. But she says that as the day progresses, she can see a correlation between the spread and what she is experiencing.

STATISTICAL ANALYSIS OF THE CARDS CHOSEN

The question being considered is, "Are the choices of Tarot cards done as described above random, or are they not random? The following procedure is a way of deciding that question by calculating the probability that they are not random.

Definition of e—the expected frequency: If the choices are random, the probability in any one choice of picking any one of the 78 cards in the deck is exactly equal to the probability of picking any other of the 78 cards and is equal to 1/78. When a large number "N" of choices is made, the expected number of times "e" that a particular card is chosen is defined as $e = N/78$; "e" is called the expected frequency.

Definition of f_i—the actual frequency: Anyone who has rolled dice knows that on the average, each number comes up 1/6 of the time, but that for a finite number M of rolls the actual number of times each number appears varies widely from $M/6$, even when the dice aren't loaded! Similarly, the actual number of times card "i" is chosen from the 78 Tarot cards will vary widely from $N/78$, even if the choices are random. The actual number of times card "i" is chosen is called the actual frequency and is labeled "f_i." The group of 78 numbers f_i for $i = 1$ to 78 is called the frequency distribution of the cards chosen.

Definition of X^2: In statistical work the quantity X^2 (chi-square) is used as an overall measure of the variation, in a frequency distribution, of the actual frequencies f_i from the expected frequency e. The following equation is the definition of X^2:

$$X^2 = \sum_{i=1}^{78} \frac{(f_1 - e)^2}{e} = \frac{(f_1 - e)^2}{e} + \frac{(f_2 - e)^2}{e} + \ldots + \frac{(f_{78} - e)^2}{e}$$

Finding P—the probability of nonrandomness: Statistics texts contain tables showing the probability P that a frequency distribution with a certain value of X^2 is not the result of random choice. From the records kept by myself (person A) and by persons B and C, I counted N the total number of cards chosen by that person and all 78 of the f_i the actual number of times each of the 78 cards was chosen by that person. Using these numbers, I calculated "e" and then X^2 for each person. Then by using the tables, I found a value of P for each person. Figure 1 shows these values of N, X^2, and P.

Tarot cards by person	N	X^2	P
A	1982	127.3	99.97%
B	2015	1161.0	99.999 ... % $(100-10^{-10})$
C	2395	132.4	99.99%

Figure 1

Controls: For a control, I made a pack of 78 index cards, blank on one side and numbered 1 to 78 on the other. Using the same kind of shuffle procedure I had used with the Tarot cards, I chose the same number N cards, three cards at a time, recorded them, and did the same statistical test for nonrandomness. The only difference was that I chose them all in a period of a few hours and not as part of a meditation. The results of this are shown in Figure 2.

Index Cards	N	X^2	P
	1982	85.83	53%

Figure 2

As a further check I programmed an Apple computer to perform the same process. The results of this are shown in Figure 3.

Results: In most statistical work, probabilities of either 95% or 99% are considered sufficient for an effect to be considered real. So the data in figures 1, 2, and 3 certainly constitute evidence that something other than random chance was operating in the choice of Tarot cards in meditation, and that the index-card and computer choices can be considered random.

INTERPRETATION OF THE STATISTICAL ANALYSIS

This statistical analysis exemplifies one of the positive aspects of science. You follow your doubts in a systematic way as far as you can. Then when you have finished with this, you are stuck with the reality of your results. There is no room for further doubt. I used statistical analysis, one of the tools of science, to measure the probability of nonrandomness in the choice of Tarot cards.

Apple computer	N	X^2	P
1	1410	82.5	50%
2	1680	88.5	65%
3	1821	59.2	*
4	1983	70.84	*
5	1983	66.04	*
6	1983	102.31	*
7	1983	58.64	*
8	1983	71.63	*
9	1410	66.9	*
10	1680	69.7	*
11	1821	79.8	*
12	2052	85.9	53%
13	2394	85.8	53%

* = less than 50%

Figure 3

Saying the choice is random is the same as saying that the cards are totally separate from the person who picks them. Saying the choice is not random is to say there is a connection between the person and the cards. After doing all the analysis, I was stuck with the reality of the connectedness of the cards and the person who chooses them in meditation, even though my old scientific belief system asserted that there was no connection. The statistical analysis doesn't show the nature of the connection between the person and the cards; it just shows that it is very probable that there is a connection of some kind.

This evidence of a connection can be interpreted in a variety of ways. One possibility is that we cheated in some way, that we peeked at the cards or that their backs were marked. But the fact that, except for 29% of my own data (person A), the Tarot cards were chosen without any intention of subjecting them to a statistical analysis provides a reason why we would have no motivation to cheat. It is also possible that the shuffle was not sufficient to make the choices random. However, the index-card data make this possibility seem quite unlikely.

Another possibility is that some kind of psychic or ESP process was happening. Remembering that in the process of choosing the cards, physical sensation was involved in the experience of "yes," one could say that the cards are perceived by some kind of sixth sense. My objection to this kind of explanation is that calling it psychic mystifies the experience of direct intuitive knowing, an experience that really is quite common and ordinary. Introducing an "ESP mechanism" is an unnecessary complication.

I prefer to interpret the statistical analysis and the Dream/Tarot correlations as showing that there is some kind of subtle connectedness or direct knowing involved. This is far more simple and elegant than hypothesizing more mechanisms of perception. Direct knowing is a dissolving of boundaries and a merging of identities. We experience the cards as if they were part of ourselves. The assumption that the cards are separate from us is what underlies the "scientific" belief that the choices are random. On a gross physical level the cards *can* be seen as separate. Though there is a kind of physical connection from the cards on the table through the table legs, down into the floor and up into our bodies through the chairs. But that is not the kind of connection referred to in direct knowing. The connection is more subtle, at a deeper level of reality that underlies the physical level.

The interpretation of the data as implying a deeper kind of connectedness supports the evolving worldview of Tarot practitioners, the belief that the external world and inner states of consciousness mirror and reflect each other. The Tarot cards form a microcosm in which this reflection is clearer than in everyday life. Having been created by many people over a long period of time, Tarot is a good mirror with few distortions. It is easier to see the reflection symbolically in the cards than in the complex events of life.

The next step in this evolving worldview is to go beyond the inner/outer split and find that the totality of one's experience is coherent, is based on unity of some kind. It seems that separation is an appearance, an illusion that we can play with and enjoy, rather than being something absolute.

An Experimental Test of the Basis of Probability Theory

Cherie Sutherland McCusker
and Brian McCusker

○■○■○■○■○■○■○■○■○■○■○■○

INTRODUCTION

The theory of probability underlies a great deal of modern science. In physics, for instance, the fundamental theory, quantum mechanics, deals only with probabilities. The Schrodinger wave function is itself the square root of a probability. Chemistry and biochemistry, in turn, lean heavily on quantum mechanics. In much psychology, sociology, and the social sciences, statistical methods are common. Even C.G. Jung, who was not fond of mathematics, used statistical analysis in his attempt to validate astrology[1]. However, the theory of probability itself is based on an axiom. To many people, this axiom appears trivially obvious, just as does the parallel axiom in Euclidean geometry. But, as Riemann and Lobatchevsky showed over one hundred years ago, we can have viable geometries without Euclid's parallel axiom. And indeed, as the work of Einstein and his followers has shown, in the universe at large it may well be that it is the non-Euclidean geometries that give the correct description. So, having seen one "obvious" axiom overthrown, it is common sense to have a good look at others. This is what we do in this paper. We describe an experiment to test the validity of the axiom of probability theory. It is not an original experiment but, in part, is an exact copy of an experiment carried out by Dr Jane English and her co-workers[2]. Our results confirm her findings. In easily repeatable circumstances the predictions of the axiom are grossly in error.

A BASIC AXIOM OF PROBABILITY THEORY

We will first give a non-mathematical statement of the axiom. Suppose we have a deck of 52 playing cards, and that we shuffle them thoroughly and then spread them face downwards on the table. If we nominate one particular card, say the Queen of Hearts, and then make a selection of one card from the face-downwards deck, the axiom says that the chance of drawing the Queen of Hearts is one in fifty-two and if we continue to make selections, the number of times the Queen appears will approximate more and more closely to the number of selections divided by fifty-two. If we use a Tarot deck then the chance of getting a particular card is one in seventy-eight rather than fifty-two.

Mathematically, the axiom can be stated as follows[3,4]. Suppose that we have a number of "elements": these elements might be, for instance, the results of successive throws of a die. Each element will have some property. In the case mentioned, it is the number of the die face that is uppermost. When we have accumulated a large number of elements then the number of cases in which each property occurs will approximate closely to the measure of the property. In the case of the die throws this will be 1/6, if we assume that the die is true, that is, that all the faces are of equal size, that the die is of uniform density and so on. If we accumulate n elements and the number of times that the ith property occurs is n_i then the axiom states that $\lim n_i/n = w_i$ exists and is equal to the relative measure of the property. It is called the relative frequency of the ith property. In the case of the die it will be 1/6 for all six properties. Alternative versions of the axiom exist.[5] All, however, lead to the same prediction, namely that in the case of the die the relative frequency of occurrence of any one face will be 1/6; in the case of playing cards the relative frequency of occurence of any one card will be 1/52; and in the case of Tarot cards it will be 1/78.

It will appear to most materialists (and to many others) that the axiom is obviously true. But it will not appear as such to some other sorts of people; for instance, practitioners of the Tarot. What Dr. English did was to put it to experimental test.

THE ENGLISH EXPERIMENT

Jane English, who is both a physicist and a practitioner of Tarot, became interested in reconciling, if possible, these two very different symbolic systems for understanding and manipulating the Universe. As a Tarot practitioner she was in the habit of beginning each day by, first, meditating and then selecting a card from a face-downwards spread of a Tarot deck. This first selection was a selection for body, that is, she was interested in getting a feeling from the Tarot of the state of her body. She then made a second selection, this time for mind, then a third for spirit.

She recorded these three selections each day in her journal. When she became interested in the comparison of Tarot and physics she had 1982 selections available for comparison with the predictions of the axiom. She made the comparison using a standard chi-squared test[6]. She got a value of chi-squared of 127.3 for 77 degrees of freedom. From the tables quoted, this gives a probability result being in agreement with the predictions of the axiom of 0.03%; that is, not good agreement at all.

Moreover, she had two friends, also Tarot practitioners, who had carried out the same procedure for longer periods. One had accumulated 2395 selections and had a value of chi-squared of 132.4 giving a probability of being in agreement with the predictions of the axiom of only 10^{-4} (that is, 1 in 10,000). The other had accumulated 2015 selections, had a chi-squared of 1161.0 and thus had a quite negligible probability of being in agreement with the predictions of the axiom (much less than one in ten thousand million).

It is worth noting that most of Jane's readings and all of her friends' readings had been accumulated before the idea of a statistical test occurred to her.

After making the test on her Tarot readings Jane carried out a "control" test using a pack of cards which were blank on one side and numbered 1 to 78 on the other. She made 1982 selections. The selections were made without previous meditation and all in one period of a few hours. The value of chi-squared was 85.8 giving a probability of being in agreement with the axiom of 47%.

She also made 13 runs, totalling 24,183 selections, using an Apple computer to mimic the Tarot process. This gave a somewhat ambiguous result. Overall, the resulting distribution was not in disagreement with the predictions of the axiom. However, one run had a probability of only 0.05 of being in agreement with the predictions of the axiom.

THE PRESENT EXPERIMENT

One of us (B.McC) became aware of the Jane English experiment in late 1983. In mid-1985 we decided to repeat it, and maybe, extend it. We began work on it on Oct. 1, 1985. Like Dr. English, we had three participators, namely the two authors of this paper and Eden Sutherland, the fifteen year old son of Cherie Sutherland. Cherie and Eden opted to carry out an exact copy of the Jane English experiment; Brian McCusker to carry out a slightly different experiment. This was to select, each day, one card from the major arcana of one deck and one card from the minor arcana of a different deck. Cherie and Brian made their selections each morning immediately after meditating. They were able to complete the year without missing a day. Eden was less regular, to begin with, and only completed his 365 selections on May 25, 1987.

Eden's selections give a value of chi squared of 141.3 (for 77 degrees of freedom) against the predictions of the axiom. This gives a probability of only 1.4×10^{-5} for agreement with the axiom. Brian's two selections give values of chi-squared of 15.8 for 21 degrees of freedom (probability for agreement 0.79) and 54.5 for 55 degrees of freedom (probability for agreement 0.50). However, these last two trials were for only 365 selections each. Cherie's 1095 selections gave a value of chi squared of 282 (for 77 degrees of freedom). The probability of this being in agreement with the predictions of the axiom is of the order of 10^{-24}, that is, one chance in one million, billion, billion!

Like Dr. English, we made a "control" experiment. This was to select each day a card from a deck of (52) playing cards. This selection was made casually but otherwise in similar conditions to the Tarot selection. Cherie and Brian each made 365 selections and Eden 109 selections. No considerable deviations from the predictions of the axiom were found.

Thus the results of our experiment strongly support Dr. English' results. Both of our trials that follow the Jane English procedure gave results strongly disagreeing with the predictions of the axiom.

COMPARISONS WITH SOME OTHER EXPERIMENTS

The results of many earlier experiments can be seen as supporting those of Dr. English and ourselves. For instance, in 1934, Dr J.B. Rhine reported the results in a series of tests using a deck of cards of his own devising[7]. The deck consisted of five sets (or suits) each of five cards. Each card bore one of five symbols; a star, rectangle, cross, circle, or wavy lines. The experiment involved a "subject" and an "experimenter." The deck was shuffled, cut and placed face downwards on the table. The subject then guessed to which suit the top card belonged. The top card was then removed by the experimenter, still face down, and stacked for later recording. The experimenter also recorded the guess. The procedure was then repeated for the next card until all 25 cards had been tested. Later the guesses were compared with the predictions of the axiom.

This predicts that in a large number of trials the guess will be correct close to 20% of the time.

One of Rhine's subjects in over 700 runs (that is in over 17,500 guesses) guessed correctly more than 32% of the time. Using the chi-squared test this gives a value of chi-squared of 1575 for one degree of freedom. If the axiom were true, this result is astronomically more improbable even than those already reported. The direct and simplest conclusion from Rhine's experiment is that the axiom is untrue. Many similar experiments have since been reported[6].

It is well known that Dr. Rhine considered that this experiment proved the occurrence of clairvoyance. This, we believe, is a secondary conclusion which may or may not be correct. What the experiment shows primarily is that there is an enormous discrepancy between the experimental results and the predictions of the axiom.

This is borne out by other experiments reported in Rhine's book and elsewhere. For instance, following a remark made by a young professional gambler, Rhine became interested in dice throwing. In his first test which involved 900 runs of 24 throws per run, he found that the probability of his results being consistent with the predictions of the axiom was less than 10^{-18}. He attributed this result to "psychokinesis." In other experiments, gross deviations from the predictions of the axiom have been attributed to clairvoyance, telepathy, precognitive telepathy, postcognitive telepathy, etc. While all these effects may occur, what to point out is that there is no need to make this large number of hypotheses. What all the results show primarily is that the predictions of the axiom are in error.

This interpretation is supported by the results of an experiment carried out by Robert Harvie[8], who attempted to duplicate parapsychological guessing experiments but with any possible "psi" intervention eliminated. His method was to compare a table of "pseudo random" numbers with two sets of random numbers, one set from Kendall and Smith's tables and the other from the Rand Corporation. In each case the two lists were compared number by number and the number of coincidences noted (that is, the number of cases when a 9 matched a 9, a 2 matched a 2 and so on). The expected number of coincidences, assuming the truth of the axiom, is $1/10^{th}$ the number of trials. In a total of 49,600 trials he found that the probability of agreement with the axiom was only 0.0008.

Perhaps even more remarkable are the results of the attempts to produce the tables of "random" numbers. G. Spencer Brown in his book *Probability and Scientific Inference* [9] says (p.89), "Almost all long series, from Weldon's dice data to Rand's random digits, have been found to be significantly biased when tested. Those that have been subsequently published *have had the bias removed before publication* (our italics)."

A DISCUSSION OF THE EXPERIMENTS

As noted above, in our two experiments five trials out of eleven gave results violently disagreeing with the predictions of the axiom. These five all were made using Tarot cards, after meditation, making only one set of three selections per day, and accumulating more than one thousand trials. These observations give us some idea of the necessary conditions for easily demonstrating the failure of the axiom.

Before detailing these conditions it is worth considering similar situations that have arisen in science before. For instance, classical physics was for long the backbone of science but now we know that is is a grossly incorrect description even of the material universe. Obviously, then, at least one of the axioms upon which it is based must be incorrect. If one wishes to demonstrate the inadequacy of classical physics one has a large number of experiments to choose from. A simple, cheap, straightforward way would be to observe the optical spectra from a sodium or mercury vapour lamp. Classical physics failed miserably in its attempt to account for these spectra. However, if one attempted to demonstrate the varying position of the planet Jupiter, one would need extremely expensive equipment and a very long observation time and even then one might not achieve the necessary accuracy.

So, one might expect a similar state of affairs in testing the axiom of probability theory. What Jane English has done is find a simple experiment that shows large discrepancies.

A CONNECTION WITH RECENT EXPERIMENTS
IN QUANTUM MECHANICS

The axiom of probability theory came out of the same intellectual climate as classical physics. The assumptions underlying both were realistic, materialistic, deterministic, and reductionist. As we mentioned above, classical physics failed catastrophically even to explain material phenomena. It was replaced over sixty years ago by quantum mechanics. This is a non-realistic theory (in the philosophical sense of the word "realism"); it insists on the essential role of the observer.

This non-realism and other features of quantum mechanics disturbed many people, including Albert Einstein. In 1935, he and two collaborators, Boris Podolsky and Nathan Rosen, wrote a paper purporting to show that quantum mechanics is an incomplete theory.[10] Two of his underlying assumptions in this paper were realism, that is the belief that a physical universe exists independent of any observer and, secondly, Einsteinian locality. This is a belief that action at a distance does not occur and that no influence of any kind can propagate faster than the speed of light. However, recent elegant experiments in physics[11,12] have shown that the prediction of Einstein's realistic theory are grossly in error and, on the other hand, the predictions of quantum mechanics are accurate. Aspect and his co-workers write[12] that their results "rule out the whole class of realistic local theories".

The results of the Tarot experiments also strongly contradict predictions from the 19th century view of the universe. Like quantum mechanics, the Tarot experiments emphasize the importance of the observer in the universe. And, if the observer is important, then any accurate description of the universe must include a detailed study of the observer, that is, of ourselves. This crucial point has been completely overlooked by most physicists. Fortunately, it has not been overlooked by some psychologists. Synchronistically, in the very year that Max Planck put forth his quantum hypothesis, Sigmund Freud published *The Interpretation of Dreams*.[13] Since then, psychology has progressed from Freudian to Jungian to Humanistic/Gestalt to Transpersonal. From 1977 to date a remarkable synthesis of this modern work with the older, mystical schools of psychology (Yogic, Buddhist, Zen, Christian, Jewish, Taoist, and Sufic) has been made by Ken Wilber.[14] In this synthesis the universe is no longer seen as matter, with consciousness as a very occasional by-product of electrochemical interactions in a brain, but as a consciousness structured in nine main levels, the lowest level of which is matter. In *The Atman Project*[15] Wilbur describes the levels and makes a comparison of the major schools in considerable, convincing detail. In *Up from Eden*[16] he gives a transpersonal account of evolution—seeing it primarily as evolution in consciousness and thus avoiding the many pitfalls that have trapped generations of Darwinian and neo-Darwinian theorists. In *Eye to Eye*, along with much else, he has elucidated the deep structure of the scientific method and shown how it may be applied in all three main realms of consciousness, the empiric realm, the mental realm and the spiritual realm.

The results from the Tarot experiments and from the earlier experiments of J.B.Rhine and others fit beautifully into his picture. So do the quantum experiments of Clauser, Aspect, and others. However, the

Tarot experiments have many advantages over the more physical experiments. The Tarot experiments are much less costly; they can be tried by very many more people; and they lend themselves to very considerable further development. They may turn out to be important for the exploration of higher levels of consciousness. We hope to deal with this more fully in a later paper.

DOING IT YOURSELF

Unlike many experiments in modern science, this experiment readily lends itself to checking by the reader. This repeatablility is considered by many to be one of the essentials of the scientific method. For readers who wish to make this check for themselves we offer the following suggestions.

1. If possible, work with a group of people. We notice that one person out of six failed to establish a deviation from the predictions of the axiom in one year.

2. Arrange for some of the group to follow the Jane English procedure exactly. This includes meditating for at least twenty minutes before making the selections and only making one set of three selections per day.

3. Preferably have a number of people already familiar with Tarot in the group.

4. Preferably, if the group is not balanced sexually, have more women than men.

5. Arrange for at least one member to be familiar with the chi-squared test. An excellent popular account of this appears in Moroney's book *Facts from Figures* published by Pelican.[17]

6. Preset the time for which the experiment is to run. If possible this should be at least one year.

7. Send us the results.

Finally, if you find it difficult or even impossible to believe in a breakdown of the axiom, remember the story of Galileo and the Cardinals. Galileo used the newly invented telescope to discover four moons revolving around the planet Jupiter. The Cardinals, following Aristotle, believed such moons to be impossible. Galileo invited them to look for themselves. The Cardinals refused, saying they had no need to waste time on such nonsense. The Cardinals were wrong.

ACKNOWLEDGMENTS

We are grateful to Drs. Jane English, Frances Vaughan, and Roger Walsh for their comments on our manuscript and their suggestion for its improvement.

REFERENCES

1. C.G. Jung and W. Pauli, *The Interpretation of Nature and the Psyche*, Bollingen Foundation, NY (1955).

2 Jane English, *A Scientist's Experience with Tarot*, in *The Wheel of Tarot; a New Revolution*, ed. James Wanless and Angeles Arrien, Merrill-West Publishers, Carmel, CA (in the press).

3. Henry Margenau and George M. Murphy, *The Mathematics of Physics and Chemistry*, van Nostrand, NY (1943).

4. Lazar Mayants, *The Enigma of Probability and Physics*, D. Reidel, Boston (1984).

5. R.B. Lindsay and H. Margenau, *The Foundations of Physics*, Dover, NY (1957).

6. C.S. Pearson and H.O. Hartley, *Biometrica Tables for Statisticians*, CUP Cambridge (1972).

7. J.B. Rhine, *The Reach of the Mind*, William Morrow. NY (1947).

8. Alister Hardy, Robert Harvie and Arthur Koestler, *The Challenge of Chance*, Hutchinson, London (1973).

9. G. Spencer Brown, *Probability and Scientific Inference*, Longmans, London (1957).

10. A. Einstein, B. Podolsky, and N. Rosen, *Physical Review*, 47, 777 (1935).

11. J. Clauser and A. Shimony, *Reports on Progress on Physics*, 41, 1881 (1978).

12. Alain Aspect et al., *Physical Review Letters*, 47, 460 (1981); 49, 91, (1982); 49, 1804 (1982).

13. Sigmund Freud, *The Interpretation of Dreams* (1900), republished in *The Standard Edition of Freud*, Vol 3, ed. James Strachey, Hogarth Press, London (1953 to 1956).

14. Ken Wilber, *Eye to Eye*, Anchor/Doubleday, NY (1983).

15. Ken Wilber, *The Atman Project*, Theosophical Publishing House, Wheaton Ill., (1980).

16. Ken Wilber, *Up from Eden*, Anchor/Doubleday, NY (1981).

17. M.J. Moroney, *Facts from Figures*, Pelican, London (1953).

A Transpersonal Approach to Symbolic Therapy:

Dreams, Tarot, and Synchronicity

Mary C. Culberson, PhD

oⅮoⅮoⅮoⅮoⅮoⅮoⅮoⅮoⅮoⅮoⅮo

*Symbolic language is a language in its own right,
in fact, the only universal language
the human race ever developed.*

—Erich Fromm, *The Forgotten Language*

Does the psyche speak with one voice? Is there a relationship between the symbols that come from dreams and those that come from the ancient Tarot? Is there an underlying unity operating in the universe which transcends the inner/outer split bringing a consistent totality to one's experience?

These were some of the questions that led me into an exploration of symbolic language and the Jungian concept of synchronicity.[1] This exploration developed slowly out of my own personal psychological and spiritual searching over a ten-year period. Beginning with dream work, later adding the Tarot, and grounded in Jungian psychology, I have been led step-by-step from one discovery to the next by many synchronistic events along the way. My desire to answer these questions led me into a study of the relationship between dream symbols and waking symbols.

THE SYMBOLIC LANGUAGE OF DREAMS AND THE TAROT

I became very interested in the "split-brain" research[2] of recent decades, which has begun to study the different functions of the right and left hemispheres of the brain. It has been established that the left hemisphere governs the logical, rational, verbal, analytic processing, while the right hemisphere governs the visual, spatial, nonrational, intuitive, global functioning. The left hemisphere thinks in words, while the right hemisphere thinks in symbols and images. It was the right hemisphere and this symbolic thinking with which I became fascinated. I discovered a number of writers[3] who were describing this symbolic thinking as a symbolic language, a forgotten language, a language we urgently need to reawaken.

I was convinced that dreams reveal the issues concerning an individual at an unconscious level, and I was fast becoming convinced that the Tarot operates in much the same way as dreams. I saw time and time again in my own experience and in the experiences of my family, friends, and clients how the dream symbols and Tarot symbols were communicating the same message, often with the same symbols. The Tarot seems to respond as an outer correspondent to the inner unconscious process of the individual. It is like a mirror reflecting the same images and issues as one's dream. Slowly, a hypothesis formulated itself in my thinking, and I began to gather data to test it. The hypothesis set forth and experimentally tested was this:

> *The symbols of dreams and the Tarot are archetypally[4] connected, since they come from the same unconscious domain. Therefore, the symbols of both an incubated dream and a focused Tarot spread for a given individual at a given time will reflect the same themes, issues, and contents.*

RESEARCH STUDY OF THE DREAM/TAROT CORRELATION

The California Institute of Transpersonal Psychology (CITP) in Menlo Park, California, was the setting for this research study. CITP is a Ph.D.-granting institution in Transpersonal Psychology, which distinguishes itself from other psychological perspectives by its focus on the spiritual or religious dimension of humankind. Along with this approach comes a holistic orientation that affirms each individual's development equally in body, mind, emotion, and spirit within a supportive environment or community. CITP uses a largely experiential learning model, and much of the "CITP experience" is therapeutic and growth-oriented.

Participants. All the subjects and judges and all but two research assistants participating in this experiment were CITP students. Therefore, all the participants brought a transpersonal orientation to this study. It is important to underline the selective nature of the subject population for this research project. The individuals who participated in this project were all highly sophisticated subjects. In short, this study was not conducted with a random-subject population.

Twelve subjects took part in the study—six men and six women. All twelve were selected on the basis of a questionnaire sent out to sixty graduate students at CITP. The twelve were chosen on the basis of good dream recall and their successful use of the technique of dream incubation. Six research assistants and three judges were also selected from those who returned questionnaires.

Procedure. Each subject was asked to incubate[5] two dreams over a two-week interval. The dreams were recorded along with the dreamers' "day notes" of the previous day, the incubation question, and any associations the dreamer had to the dream. Immediately after having the dream and recording it, the subject met with a dream-research assistant to do a half hour of dream analysis. The subject then filled out a seven-point dream-rating scale (with no aid from the dream research assistant), rating how well the dream responded to the incubation question. As soon as this task was completed, the subject met with a Tarot research assistant. The subject was instructed not to reveal either the dream content or the incubation question to the Tarot research assistant. The subject was then told to concentrate on the same incubation question he or she had used for the dream incubation. The subject was to shuffle the cards[6] well for several minutes while focusing upon the incubation issue in silence. After shuffling, the subject was instructed to pick three cards, leaving them all face down.[7] The subject was instructed to ritualize or view the selection process in whatever way was meaningful for him or her; i.e., by following one's intuitive or inner sense of the "rightness" of the cards chosen. The three cards were then turned up one at a time by the subject and interpreted in turn by the Tarot research assistant. Once the Tarot interpretation had been given (taking a half hour), the subject was instructed to record the three cards drawn in the Tarot spread and rate the spread on the same seven-point scale used to rate the dream in relationship to the incubated question. Again, this was done with no aid from the Tarot research assistant.

This Dream/Tarot process was performed twice by each subject, yielding twenty-four sets of incubated dreams and Tarot spreads. Once all the data were returned, they were coded, removing all identification, and typed. The three-card Tarot spread originally picked by each subject was randomly mixed with three other Tarot card sets. These "false sets" were turned up by a neutral individual who had no knowledge of the dream contents, incubation question, or original Tarot spread. A random order was used to mix the Tarot spread picked by each subject with the three "false" Tarot spread sets. The Tarot interpretation made by the Tarot research assistant was not included in the Dream/Tarot transcripts.

The twenty-four Dream/Tarot transcripts, twenty-four judges rating scales, and a Tarot Glossary[8] were then presented to a panel of three judges. The judges were instructed to carefully read each of the twenty-four dream transcripts as they came to them and to consult their Tarot Glossary as they studied the four sets of Tarot spreads that went with each dream transcript. They were then to rank and rate each of the four Tarot spreads in relationship to the dream transcript on the seven-point judges' rating scale. In addition to their rating and ranking, the judges were requested to write their subjective comments as to why they rated and ranked each Tarot spread as they did. They were instructed to make their rating and ranking evaluation on the basis of facts of the dream transcript and the Tarot cards, not on the basis of intuition and hunches not based upon facts. Finally, the judges were instructed not to discuss the research project with each other or anyone else. Nor were they to get any help in making their choices from anyone.

Once all the rankings and ratings were returned by the judges, the judging data were then statistically analyzed in two ways. First, a chi square was applied to determine the significance of the rankings of the correct and incorrect Tarot spreads in correlation with the dream for each of the three judges. Then a "t-test" was employed three times to compare the mean ratings of the correct and incorrect Tarot spreads for the first and second trials of each of the twelve subjects and, finally, for the combination of the two trials. The statistical results of both the judges' rankings and ratings showed the P values to fall at or beyond the .05 level. These data constitute evidence that something other than chance is operating in the judges' ability to correctly match the Tarot spread chosen with the dream and incubation issue for the subject.

Results. I have concluded that this statistically significant evidence supports the hypothesis that was tested by this research study. This conclusion maintains that the judges were able at or beyond the .05 level to perceive the symbolic connection between the themes, issues, and contents of the dream and the Tarot for a given individual. If there is a coherent inner process, which this hypothesis maintains; if symbols reflect it; and if dreams and the Tarot both use these symbols, then it logically follows that an incubated dream and a Tarot spread on the same inner theme should give similar symbolic responses. The .05 level indicates that real similarities exist in the symbolism of themes, issues, and contents of the dream and the Tarot spread.

This does not speak to the correctness of the "answer" by the dream or Tarot spread to the incubation question, but rather says that the inner dream symbols and the outer Tarot symbols that are selected are objectively consistent and communicate the same response. This is the case, even though dream symbols are selected by an inner process and the Tarot symbols are selected apparently randomly from a limited set of external images.

SYNCHRONICITY AND THE DREAM/TAROT CORRELATION

In exploring this interpretation of the Dream/Tarot correlation and the statistically significant judging results, it seems appropriate to examine the Jungian concept of synchronicity. Jung observed many cases of what he called "meaningful coincidences" between dreams reported by his patients and external events occurring in their lives. He came to the conclusion that these meaningful coincidences or synchronistic events, as he came to call them, seem to rest on an archetypal foundation.

Underlying the development of his principle of synchronicity was Jung's conception that the psyche carries all the necessary answers within itself. Jung held a microcosmic/macrocosmic concept of the human psyche. He felt that at its depth, the psyche contained reflections of the larger universe and that the images and symbols contained within the individual psyche reflect the universe in miniature. In like manner, Jung saw, through the many examples of meaningful coincidences he witnessed, that the external world of events reflects the inner psyche, that matter becomes a mirror of mind. This seems to be how the Dream/Tarot correlation operates. The Tarot cards that occur in the spread for an individual become the outer correspondents of the inner psychic pattern of the moment. Thus, the primary issue or life situation the individual is attempting to resolve at any given time will be reflected in their dream images and mirrored in the Tarot cards they pick. Jung described this process as:

> ... a kind of "atmosphere," a state that is more than psychological, an
> "aura that sets up the feeling of the situation that ... comes together to
> form patterns, at once transcendent and immanent, and constellating
> situations that draw physical as well as psychological phenomena into their
> field .... within the pattern of the moment ... these events always corre-
> spond to each other in some meaningful way.[9]

This explanation of the "atmosphere of the moment," which draws psychological and physical phenomena into its field in a meaningful way, seems to me to apply to the Dream/Tarot correlation for a given individual attempting to resolve a particular incubation issue or life situation.

The concept that the external world of events is a reflection of the inner psyche, that matter is a mirror of mind, speaks directly to the concept of the inner/outer split, the notion that there is no relationship between mind and matter. The concept of synchronicity goes beyond the inner/outer split and affirms that the totality of one's experience is consistent, coherent, and based upon a unity of some kind. This notion of a unity between the individual and the universe lies at the heart of the principle of synchronicity. It implies a connectedness with oneself and the universe. It is in this unity that the illusion of the inner/outer split and the subject/object dichotomy is transcended and the individual is able to see the relationship between and integration of the inner and outer. What seems separate really is not.

This line of thinking leads one into the transpersonal realm. Eighty years ago, Dr. Richard Burke called this "cosmic consciousness." [10] He saw then that this unity or harmony was a special phenomenological state in which the individual can somehow perceive the whole cosmos or at least the unity and integration of it. There is a sense of belonging, or being "a part of," in contrast to the sense of isolation or aloneness. Once an individual has this sense or an experience of being inside or a part of the universe, he or she is then open to see the interconnection with all things and has that perception apparently permanently. Frances Vaughan[11] describes this sense as a mystical experience, "in which the individual transcends the subject/object dichotomy, feeling him- or herself to be at one with everything. In this experience there is no separation between inner and outer, knower and known."

To illustrate how the same themes, issues, and contents appear in both the incubated dream and the Tarot spread for a given individual, I will now present one of the twenty-four dream transcripts and four Tarot spreads that were rated and ranked by the three judges in this study.

EXAMINING THE DREAM/TAROT PROCESS: AN ILLUSTRATION

Resistance to Work

This illustration comes from a female subject, age 30. Her incubation issue was stated: "What is my resistance to work in the world?" Her day notes follow:

I worked my last day at the restaurant where I have been a cook. With my birthday coming in two days, I planned to spend the next day focusing on the issue of my work in the world. I thought some about my friend, Ann, who would not be able to be with me the next day, on my birthday. I felt our strength as friends.

In her day notes, she mentioned her friend, her feelings of the strength of their relationship, and her intention to spend the next day focusing on her incubation issue. The day of her dream happened to be her last day of work at her current job. Also, her birthday was to be two days later. So the background of her waking life held the theme of endings and beginnings. This is often an ideal time to take stock of one's life. It seems this is what this subject intended to do. Henry Reed[5] discovered with his dream incubation experiment, that this kind of reflection is an important part of effective dream incubation. Given the timing of this subject's birthday and ending of job, one might anticipate the presence of an "atmosphere of the moment," which Jung defined as the milieu around which both physical and mental paranormal events tend to cluster. Here is her dream:

Dream: *I dreamed that Ann and I are at some kind of music festival or game, and we are walking away from it together in the crowd after it is over. We are walking outdoors, down a highway in a rural area where everyone has parked their cars in a big field. I have driven us there. The crowd is thick, and moving too slowly for our pace. A few people are leaving the main road to take a path up a hill into the woods. This path also leads to the field where the cars are parked, but it takes longer. Ann says, "I think I'll go up that path. See you at the car." And she walks off up the hill. Because I have driven, I feel a responsibility to get back to the car as soon as possible, so, although I could have walked up the hill with Ann, I stay with the crowd. Initially, I feel a little resentment that Ann has left me to walk alone in the crowd to the car. Then I think to myself it is okay; Ann needs to take a different path than I do, and when we separate, we only come back together again with more resources and stories to tell one another later. So, as I walk along in the crowd, I feel as though I am driving in slow traffic on a freeway. I keep trying to pass people, and getting boxed in. I feel very impatient, and just have to settle back into myself. At this point, the scene changes and I am walking alone on an empty highway in the southwest. The day is bright and clear. Mountains ring the horizon. I am leading a beautiful chestnut-colored horse, with my right hand holding his halter. He is too overheated to ride, so he has to be walked. I reach up to pat his neck and he jumps back. We are new to each other and he doesn't know he can trust me yet, but I know he will in time. A little beagle is trotting along beside us on the road.*

Now and then, he stops to sniff things in the brush beside the pavement. I wonder what he is doing with me. I walk up and tie my horse outside a coffee shop on the road. Ann is waiting for me there. We have a peaceful reunion. When it comes time to pay the bill Ann tells me that I should pay for her, too. I am okay with that, although money feels tight to me now. I ask her why I should pay, and she explains that since she is doing a lot of spiritual work for both of us, I need to take care of the material side of things for us. That sounds reasonable to me as a way of sharing responsibility. End of dream.

Associations and Possible Meanings

Music Festival . . . the world, life. CITP?

The crowd . . . Society, my sense of social restrictions and demands.

Ann . . . Herself; the spiritually-oriented part of me (asocial).

The Horse . . . My work; productivity; strength and joy; reward.

The Beagle . . . unassuming curiosity; playfulness.

The Southwest . . . open freedom, spaciousness.

Coffee Shop scene . . . union of spirit (Ann) and work (me). I am supposed to work to support my spirit (I pay for Ann's lunch).

Dreamer's Comments

The dream is set up in two parts: the first being in the crowd, and the second being on the open road with my horse.

In part one, I experienced the impatience and fear of losing my essential self (Ann), which I associate with working in the world. I also came around to a sense of acceptance that it is my responsibility and choice to remain in society (the crowd), and to a feeling of trust that my essential self (Ann) will not desert me, even if it seems to separate temporarily from my social self.

In part two, I experienced the potential freedom and strength to be realized through my work in the world. This followed upon my acceptance of remaining on the road with other people. I notice that I saw myself as alone on the road, i.e., in my work, but with the strong friendship I have with Ann to support me in my journey. This feels both literally and figuratively true, with Ann being both herself in the dream and a symbol of the deeper spiritual pull in my life. It was Ann, personifying my spirit, who told me why I must work in the material world, that is, in order to support the work of my spirit. We work together, even when it would appear that we are separate.

The dreamer has done a very helpful job of identifying the different symbols in her dream and has given us her associations to each one. It seems clear, in reading her interpretation of the dream, that she sees a strong correlation between the dream and her incubation question. On her Dream Rating Scale, she gave the dream in relationship to the incubation question a 2 rating of Great Correspondence. In her subjective statement of this rating, she said:

I didn't check 1 above, because the dream didn't illustrate to me the source and the sense of dread I can feel about needing to work. Something about fear isn't clear to me. Or maybe it is so clear and simple in the dream that I'm missing it!

It seems to me in reading the dreamer's transcript that her dread is related to her fear of losing her essential self as she chooses to stay with her work in society (remain with the crowd). While this rating is not the highest rating, it is, nevertheless, a high rating of correlation between the dream and incubation question.

The next step in the Dream/Tarot process was for the subject to pull the three-card Tarot spread. The four Tarot spreads presented to the three judges follow:

TAROT SPREADS

Body	Mind	Spirit
1. The Fool	The Priestess	Nine of Swords—Cruelty
2. The Magus	Ace of Wands	Five of Disks—Worry
3. Six of Cups—Pleasure	Three of Swords—Sorrow	Two of Disks—Change
4. Knight of Disks	Eight of Swords—Interference	Nine of Disks—Gain

The Tarot Spread. The Tarot spread, chosen by the subject, is the fourth spread, with the Knight of Disks in the body position; Eight of Swords—Interference in the Mind position; and the Nine of Disks— Gain in the Spirit position. The three randomly chosen Tarot spreads were given with the correct spread, in the order they were listed for the judges. All three judges ranked this Dream/Tarot set in exactly the same way. The correct Tarot spread was ranked number 1 by all three judges with a number 2 rating of Great Correspondence. On her Tarot Rating Scale, the subject gave the Tarot spread in relationship to the incubation question a number 1 rating of Very Great Correspondence.

In looking at this Tarot spread for a comparison of symbols, themes, and issues with the dream, one is immediately struck by the identical symbol of the horse which appears in both the Tarot spread and dream. The horse as a symbol appears on only four of the seventy-eight cards in the Thoth deck of the Tarot, with each of the four knights. The chances of choosing a Tarot card with the symbol of the horse is about one in nineteen. All three judges noted and underlined the horse in their subjective comments: Judge No.1 said of the Knight of Disks, "*Horse* in the field"; Judge No.2 said of the Knight of Disks, "The journey-work is with the *horse* traveling alone but committed to the crowd"; Judge No.3 commented, "Health-harvest? *Horse*!"

The symbolic interpretation of the Knight of Disks in the Tarot tradition is that he is the "Healer," the doctor, the diagnostician, one who has a deep commitment to health. He carries the thrashing tool, ready to bring in the harvest, so he is the "harvester." His sun disk is a symbol of health and *financial* well-being. The sun disk also contains the symbol of Leo, which represents both creativity and leadership ability. The horned animal on his helmet is also a symbol of guidance or leadership, cross-culturally the horned animal (deer, antelope) is seen as the inner guide.

In her subjective statement the subject said of the first card, the Knight of Disks, "My body gives me the clearest guidance as to handling my resistance." She seems to be recognizing the leadership/guidance quality associated with this card and the position in the spread of this card, the body position. It seems appropriate to insert here that this subject has devoted a great deal of her time and energy during the past six years to the body discipline of Aikido and that the development of the relationship of her good friend who appears so significantly in this dream has come about largely through their contact in Aikido. Her friend has a black belt in Aikido and was also her Aikido instructor.

The second card in the spread is the Eight of Swords—Interference. In the Tarot tradition, this card means mental interference, and since it appears in the second position of mind, there is a double emphasis on the mental aspect of the interference. This card symbolizes the tendency to overanalyze a situation, going over and over two choices, directions, or issues in doubt and confusion. There is a quality of paralysis in this situation with a tendency toward indecision. The subject said of this card that she often felt like this is relationship to her work and making money: "My mind 'interferes' with the solution to this problem by overanalyzing." The three judges said of this card: Judge No.1,

"analyzing about Ann's going off on hill trail; being left with the crowd."
Judge No.2 comments, "I see interference (concern about Ann's leaving,
frustration with the slowness of the crowd) being overcome by the *gain*
of settling back into herself." Judge No.3 states, "overanalyzing two
choices, crowd-hill." Clearly, all three judges saw the parallel of the same
theme of two choices to stay with the crowd (society) or to stay with her
essential self (Ann), and the theme of the dreamer mentally analyzing,
"mulling over" the decision to stay with the crowd versus staying with
her friend/essential self.

The third card in the spread is the Nine of Disks—Gain. This card is
physical profit, benefit or gain. It represents gain on all levels, mentally,
emotionally, spiritually, and particularly physically and financially,
since disks is the physical suit. This card more than any other of the
seventy-eight in the Thoth deck is associated with gain or loss in
relationship to money and weight. This card fell into the spirit position,
thus linking the spiritual dimension with the physical dimension of life.
The dream also links these two dimensions of life together.

The subject said of this card: "My spiritual purpose is to work and
gain things in the material world, in the areas closest to my heart
(therapy, Aikido, art)." Judge No.1 said, "Gain from relationship; gain
from working/finances/spiritual work." Judge No.2 underlined the
word gain in her comment on the second card, interference, and went on
to say, "Gain card is on every level, including spiritual and financial—the
two primary concerns of the dreamer." Judge No.3 comments: "*Gain* in
relationship to Ann; concern over money." All three of the judges related
this card to the issue of making money in relationship to work and saw
a parallel between the Tarot and dream on this theme.

SUMMARY

In summarizing this Dream/Tarot illustration, it seems clear that the
themes of indecision or mental overanalysis, work and spiritual direction, and concern for money were recognized by all three judges in both
the dream and the Tarot spread. Also, all three judges saw the common
symbol of the horse in both the dream and Tarot. It was precisely these
kinds of common themes, issues, and symbols that I hypothesized would
appear in both the dream and the Tarot spread at the outset of my
experiment.

All three judges rated the remaining incorrect Tarot spreads in the
last five categories of the seven-category rating scale, noting some

similarities between the dream and the Tarot spread, but none so strong or clear as between the correct Tarot spread and the dream.

In terms of the therapeutic value of the dream and the Tarot spread, the subject responded in the follow-up questionnaire as follows:

I found the incubation dream/Tarot experience was very positive and useful, and both the dream incubation and Tarot spread were equally effective for me. In particular, my first dream about Ann and my work in the world was a preview of developments over these past four months. She and I have recognized the extent of our partnership, so to speak, as co-workers on the spiritual level, in the world. To the degree that we complement and support one another individually, we double the strength of what we give to others as teachers and healers. This incubation about my work opened both myself and Ann to the worth and purpose of our connection.

It is my hope that this presentation will aid in the affirmation of the worth and purpose of the Tarot as a valid symbol system and underline the importance of continued exploration and research in the area of right-brain symbolic language.

NOTES

1. The concept of synchronicity maintains that there is a fundamental acausal order in nature—a meaningful order. Synchronistic events can be defined as meaningful coincidences between causally unrelated events.

2. Split-brain references:

Tony Buzan, *Use Both Sides of Your Brain.* New York: E.P. Dutton, 1974.

Daniel Goleman, "Split-Brain Psychology: Fad of the Year." *Psychology Today*, October 1977, pp. 81-92.

Robert Ornstein, *The Psychology of Consciousness.* New York: W.H. Freeman & Co., 1972.

3. Symbolic language references:

Leopold Caligor and Rollo May, *Dreams and Symbols: Man's Unconscious Language.* New York: Basic Books, Inc., 1968.

Erich Fromm, *The Forgotten Language: An Introduction To The Understanding of Dreams, Fairytales and Myths.* New York: Grove Press, 1951.

Carl Jung, *Man and His Symbols.* Garden City, N.Y.: Doubleday, 1964.

John Sanford, *Dreams: God's Forgotten Language.* New York: Paulist Press, 1968.

Edward Whitmont, *The Symbolic Quest: Basic Concepts of Analytical Psychology.* New York: G.P. Putnam's Sons, 1969.

4. Jung defined archetypes as the contents of the collective unconscious. The word *archetype* means an original model after which other similar things are patterned. A synonym is *prototype*. Just as there are basic patterns, or archetypes, of biological form, so there are also basic structural patterns to the human psyche.

5. Dream incubation is an ancient technique used in many ancient cultures. Perhaps the most well known is the classic Greek dream-incubation technique temples of the god Asklepios. This technique of asking guidance and healing from one's dreams has witnessed a revival in modern psychology. The pioneering work of Drs. Henry Reed ("Dream Incubation: A Reconstruction of Ritual in Contemporary Form." *The Journal of Humanistic Psychology*, 16(4), pp. 53-70) and Gayle Delaney, *Living Your Dreams*. San Francisco: Harper & Row, 1979 has been drawn upon for this study.

6. The Thoth deck of the Tarot was used for this study largely because of its abundance of symbols and because it was the deck with which the author and the judges were most familiar.

7. The Actualization Spread—a three-card spread representing body, mind, and spirit, developed by Angeles Arrien, was the spread used for this study.

8. The Tarot Glossary was compiled from class notes given by Angeles Arrien in the beginning, intermediate and advanced Tarot classes at CITP.

9. Quoted in Ira Progoff's *Jung, Synchronicity, and Human Destiny: Noncausal Dimensions of Human Experience*. New York: Dell, 1973, p. 92.

10. Richard Burke, *Cosmic Consciousness: A Study in the Evolution of the Human Mind*. New York: E.P. Dutton & Co., 1901.

11. Frances Vaughan, *Awakening Intuition*. Garden City, N.Y.: Anchor Press/Doubleday, 1979, p. 64.

WHOLE SELF MANDALA

A Symbolic Portrait of Yourself and Your World

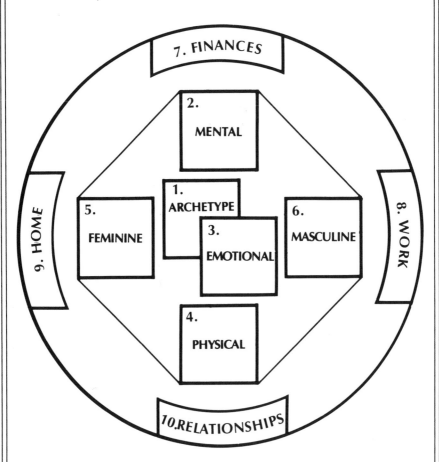

Your Inner Self

1. **Spirit: Archetypal Personality**
2. **Head: Mental State**
3. **Heart: Emotional State**
4. **Legs: Physical State**
5. **Left Side: Feminine**
6. **Right Side: Masculine**

Your World

7. **Finances**
8. **Work**
9. **Home**
10. **Relationships**

Whole Self Mandala Layout from **Voyager Tarot Guidebook**

The Tarot Layout:
Mirror, Changes, and Choices

*A*fter the cards have been chosen in a reading, they are placed in certain positions that have predetermined meaning. Cards are interpreted in relation to this positional meaning. The arrangement of these positions forms what is known as a layout or spread.

A layout is a mandala, a circular conceptual framework that mirrors realities and proposes ideals. Tarot readings through mandalic layouts are centering. They provide a sense of personal order, unity, and wholeness through their symmetrical portrait of the psyche.

Life is not still; it is always changing, and so are our parameters of choice. The popular notion of Tarot is that a reading shows what is and will be with fatalistic certainty. For the serious seeker of self-knowledge, Tarot is a sophisticated, non-deterministic tool for reflecting and revealing changing realities and possibilities. Readings are subjective, inevitably influenced by the consciousness of the interpreter. As consciousness changes, cards in a layout naturally take on different meaning.

Tarot gives us the temporal awareness of the sundial. A reading defines us at a given time; but as time changes, so does the reading. Like a compass, Tarot gives us spatial awareness and dimension. It defines where we are and where we are moving.

We update our situation not only by new readings, but by the ingenious method proposed by Mary Greer in "Permutations: On The Celtic Cross Spread." She views Tarot as a movie camera revealing the movement of life. Greer examines the oldest and most popular mandalic layout in Tarot, the Celtic Cross. Just as the individual is multidimensional and ever-changing, this layout through "permutations" or rearrangements presents different perspectives and perceptions.

The Celtic Cross becomes a whirling wheel of cyclic change. By turning the Cross around, the layout shows the variables of our life for the past, present, and probable future. Instead of a single-framed, flat picture, the Tarot reading is holographic, portraying different facets of personality and circumstance simultaneously.

Hilary Anderson in "The Destiny Spread" presents a crystal-like structure for seeing the archetypal facets of the human being. This master layout based on the Tarot's twenty-two Major Arcana, reveals, like a crystal, the pattern of personal transformation at the deepest levels.

Permutations

On the Celtic Cross Spread

Mary Katherine Greer

O█O█O█O█O█O█O█O█O█O█O█O

Although the Tarot did not appear exoterically until the 14th century in Italy, the oldest method for reading the Tarot is not an Italian but an Irish one known as the Celtic (or Keltic) Cross Spread. It continues to be used today and is, with occasional minor variations, the single most popular method of "spreading" the cards. Referred to first by A.E. Waite in 1910 only as an "ancient celtic method," not much is known about the origins of this pattern for laying out the cards, and I have been unable to find any myths or legends pertaining to its development. This lack of information makes it all the more extraordinary that through the years the Celtic Spread has maintained essentially the same form and significance, while the Tarot cards themselves have evolved, been reinterpreted, and occasionally radically changed.

There are many styles and ways of reading the Tarot. The fact that most seasoned and professional Tarot readers are still using the Celtic Cross Spread after years of experience testifies to its broad applicability, practicality and meaningfulness. This article demonstrates what makes this spread so versatile and archetypal, and at the same time expands upon its capabilities for use as a mode of personal and spiritual growth.

Permutations are, according to Webster, "changes, alterations, rearrangements; the combinations or changes in position possible within a group." In this context, permutations refers to the many possible ways of reading a single Celtic Cross Spread. Some are true permutations (rearrangements of the order and position of the cards). Others are alternative ways of viewing the reading or of applying the information. Each permutation gives a different perspective on the whole. The truth? Well, that lies somewhere in the spaces between them all.

Many of these permutations have been taught or suggested to me by

---

* From Mary Katherine Greer, *Tarot for Your Self*, 1984. Newcastle Publishing, North Hollywood, CA, pp 61-73. Reprinted with permission.

other people. Through the years, I have combined them into my own method of reading the Tarot. I have used material especially from Angeles Arrien, who has devised a brilliant conceptual framework for the use of the Thoth deck, and Joanne Kowalski, whose short pamphlet *The Psychic Tarot* presents an excellent modern, psychological method for reading the Tarot with the Waite deck. I use both of these decks in my readings and work with the Tarot.

Permutations should be used when you seek a deeper understanding of the energies and forces with which you are currently dealing. They emphasize an understanding of yourself perceptually, mentally, emotionally, physically, and archetypally. Any current situation has developed out of past actions (including previous lives) and influences future behavior. The more clearly you see the flow and effect of these patterns in your life, the more you can transform yourself into the individual you want to become.

THE ORACULAR DILEMMA

We all seek quick answers to our problems, hoping that someone will appear with an answer that will resolve all conflicts, give us a sense of security in the future, fulfill our hopes, and allay our anxieties. Out of this human desire have sprung the oracular methods common to all cultures—a way to know the future, to predict events, to divine what the gods and goddesses have in store for us. Oracular knowledge represents a way to escape the anxiety of risk. We want to be winners, to bet on a sure thing, to achieve fame and fortune, and by avoiding the errors, the risks, the failures, we hope to find ourselves on the straight road to success.

But the wheel turns. That everything changes is the only thing we know for sure.

It is through your own individual, personal encounters with life, with chance, that you test yourself and try things that will eventually evolve into the personality you are. Through the quality of your own perception of the events around you, you achieve greater heights of self-awareness and personal ability. How do you use the circumstances that come your way? Do you value your own strengths and use them effectively? That means, do you effect change in a way that is beneficial to yourself, the planet Earth, and all living beings. What are the options for you to express your individual free will in any given event?

UNLOCKING THE DOORS OF OPPORTUNITY

The Tarot encourages you to look at life symbolically — not so much by means of omens but as simultaneous levels of meaning. For instance, in a reading, the Devil card may denote a power struggle in your job or personal relationships, but with an underlying recognition that the wheel has turned; the struggle itself now controls you. Obsessed and bound by your own greed and lust, you have created a monster which has limited your freedom of choice. A bleak interpretation, perhaps, but in the Devil card itself we also find an option—another mode of perceiving the situation. The Devil card advises "mirth," that is, learning to laugh at yourself, seeing the humor and absurdity in a fixed and stubborn view of reality. It is difficult to get embroiled in a battle for power and control when you recognize the absurdity of the whole structure and can laugh at yourself, your own pompous power games, and even the cultural value system which created this. The Devil card thus urges you to see the existing situation as an inversion of reality. Rather than give in to guilt and anxiety because all is not as you thought it to be, you can use this new awareness as an opportunity to create, structure, and build a new order out of chaos, putting together the "absurd" fragments into a new transcendent order. Will you choose to see and act on your opportunity? Your rewards are commensurate with the level of chaos into which you have plunged and the energy you exert in creating a new understanding. It is the way to the top via the bottom. It may mean the reversal of all your values. And for the obsessed struggler, bound by the lust for control and power, it points the way to freedom from a self-created bondage. The Devil offers opportunity!

Only by looking closely at the cards, by spending time with them, arranging and rearranging these symbolic keys to your growth and development, can you begin to understand what opportunities are being presented. The interrelationship of the cards before you can help you see how the different parts of life are interconnected, how actions in one aspect of life are manifestations of concerns in another.

THE HISTORICAL AND SYMBOLIC BACKGROUND OF THE CELTIC CROSS

The Celtic Cross is a form of cross found throughout Ireland. Many of these crosses, like the famous Muireadach's Cross at Monasterboice, Ireland, served in the tenth century A.D. as visual aids in open-air sermons. These stone crosses, up to 21 1/2 feet tall, are typically carved with spiral motifs and scenes from the Bible and the life of Jesus. "The deep relief scenes fitted into panels all over them were used for teaching the scriptures to peasants."[1] Muireadach's Cross is covered with scenes from the Old and New Testaments that culminate in the center with Christ at the Last Judgment. These crosses are unusual in Christianity in that the four arms are linked in a large wheel, representing the unity of Spirit in Matter.

Never far from these Christian structures, the Celtic and pre-Celtic monoliths of the Old Religion can be found. Variously known as cairns, megaliths, or omphali (navels), these upright stones seem to connect the sky and the earth, often actually pointing out particular stars, and the earth turns in its yearly cycles. In the ancient Pre-Druidic fertility religions, the monolith represents a generative, creative phallus. It also stands for a single, unified vision (like the Wand of the Magician). As monolith, it is a pathway or ladder through which one can aspire to the spiritual heavens above—wo/man's eternal attempt to attain God(des)hood. As omphalos or navel, it is the connecting link with Mother Earth—the way to eternal comfort, protection, and nurturance. Either way is toward unity with the Whole. It is interesting that the ladder motif is found again at Monasterboice in a legend about its founder, St. Buithe, who is said to have climbed his way to heaven at his death on a ladder provided by the angels.[2]

It is possible that these joint Christian/Celtic objects inspired the Celtic Cross Spread, for the cards here are laid out in the form of the archetypal cross, together with an adjacent ladder monolith of cards, usually to the right of the cross. Symbolically, the horizontal bar of the cross represents the positive and negative duality of the material plane, the earthly self. The vertical bar represents the spiritual impulse descending into (involution) and ascending out of matter (evolution), impregnating the earth, creating consciousness in physical form. It is the world axis forever pointing to its own center, wherein lies the sense of self. Here, all duality—light/dark, above/below, spirit/matter, conscious/unconscious, logic/intuition, masculine/feminine meets. J.E. Circlot, in his indispensable book *A Dictionary of Symbols*, identifies the cross as a "magic knot binding together some particular combination of elements to form one individual."[3] That individual, most often identified as the Christ, aptly reflects the Celtic Cross layout, in which we seek our own highest selves, the Christ within us. As a sign of crucifixion, the cross represents suffering, conflict, agony, pain, death; and contrariwise, rebirth, hope, love, unity and forgiveness. We can recognize ourselves in either or both perspectives. The cross represents the way in which we deal with a problem (the cross we have to bear). The ladder is a way in which we can surmount barriers and overcome limitations.

THE SPREAD, AND THE SIGNIFICANCE OF TEN

Made up of ten cards (not counting Significators, Daath packs, Wish cards, and other additional appendages to basic form), the Celtic Cross spread represents totality, perfection, completeness. With the number 10 we return again to the 1, but a 1 which is now, having experienced all other numbers, conscious of itself. The 10 is sometimes pictured as a dot or a line within a circle:

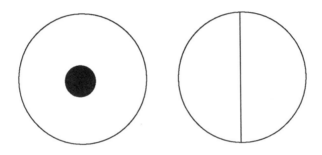

The masculine and feminine duality (or left and right brain) merge into consciousness of the whole. We begin with a 1 and end with a 1. The cycle of events is complete but only to start on another cycle. It reminds us that every point on the Wheel of Fortune (Arcanum X) is a starting and an ending point. So each spread is, therefore, complete unto itself. For this reason I personally do not find it necessary to use any other cards in the Celtic Cross Spread and will not be covering the above-mentioned supplemental cards. The complete meaning and the total picture, for a particular moment, are to be found within the ten-card spread—now it is up to you to decipher them.

The first six cards form a cross consisting of the four directions: North, South, East, and West (with which we are familiar) and the two additional directions (represented by the center cards) of Sky and Earth, the above and below which are found esoterically within our heart-centers, known by the Native Americans as Father Sky and Mother Earth. Therefore, there are actually six directions. These six cards (not counting a significator) form the basic cross of the spread.

NORTH
Above
The Head
The Astrological Midheaven
Consciousness, Aspiration

WEST	Center/Duality	EAST
The Left Hand	The Heart	The Right Hand
The Setting Sun	Life Energy	The Rising Sun
The Descendant	Dynamic Tension	The Ascendant
The Passive, Receptive		Aggressive, Action
Past-Oriented		Future-Oriented

SOUTH
Down, Below
The Feet or Base of the Spine
The Lower Heaven
The Basis or Subconscious

EXPERIENCING THE CELTIC CROSS SPREAD

The best way to get a sense of the Celtic Cross spread is to sit cross-legged on the floor or upright in a chair. With elbows relaxed, hold your hands out to either side, palms up. Imagine a Tarot card in the center of your head, one in each hand, and a fourth at the base of the spine.

Spend a little time sensing each of these parts of your body and each Tarot card that you now find there. How do you feel toward each card? Can you see them clearly? As you picture them in their respective positions on your body, which specific cards from the deck come to mind: In your head? In your left hand? In your right hand? At the base of your spine? Now add two cards crossing at the center of your being, over your heart and just above your solar plexus. Feel the tension and the balance of these two cards. What cards are they? Uncross them, putting one directly on top of the other. Now put the bottom one on top. Do you feel shifting, gliding energies as one predominates, and then the other, as they mesh and merge and cross? The two center "heart" cards are truly the heart of the reading—often you need go no further; ultimately, you must return. The rest of the reading is only a further elaboration on this central theme. Gather these six imaginary cards together and put them back in their deck.

Besides the six cards making up the basic central cross, there are four cards placed in a vertical line to the right. The four cards represent the

Way, the Path, or the Ladder on which one travels, the direction one *might* take. It is a probability line: the action you will probably take based on who you are, what you have learned, your past, your expectations, and so forth, at the moment of the reading. Paradoxically, because you are doing this reading, becoming conscious of the energies at work in your life, you now have the option of changing this probability line. These four cards represent the four elements and the four suits of the Minor Arcana: the perceptual, emotional, mental, and physical aspects of yourself. Occasionally, you will find them placed at the four open angles of the cross, much like the symbols of the four fixed signs of the Zodiac: the Lion, the Eagle, the Man, and the Bull that appear on the Wheel of Fortune and the World cards in the Waite deck.

Rituals of the reading vary. They can be used to concentrate your energy, get in the mood, and become attuned to the moment. The kind of reading described here takes a significant amount of time and a commitment to delve deeply into your own (or a friend's or client's) motivations, fears, hopes, plans, concerns, strengths, and weaknesses. The more you can center and relax yourself, establishing a direct link with the four elements, asking for inner direction, and focusing your energies on the task, the better.

Thus, if you like to spend a long, leisurely evening with yourself or a friend exploring all the nuances of the latest situation in which you find yourself enmeshed, then I would like to recommend the following "permutations," to be used singly or occasionally in combination.

You will not be able to master all of these permutations at once. Select one permutation to become familiar with, using it every time you do a Celtic Cross Spread and exploring its nuances and possibilities. To understand the following permutations, it is best to look at the illustrations and actually follow along with your own deck of cards. Eventually you will develop a pattern or sequence of permutations that works for you. Create your own permutations to express the insight you have gained into the interrelationships of the cards.

READING THE CELTIC CROSS SPREAD

Permutation 1: Maintaining Ambiguity

Everyone reads the Celtic Cross Spread slightly differently, and the order in which the cards are laid out varies somewhat. You do not have to use my numerical sequence, although the relative positions should be somewhat similar. The "problem" can actually become a strength. Test your sense of ambiguity and read the same cards using all the various perspectives at once. This helps to keep you from remaining fixed and dogmatic about what you see. For instance, the left hand card (4) is your natural, creative talents *and* it represents what influence is passing away. Thus the abilities and talents you have now came from past experiences, possibly even past lives. Whatever strengths you are developing now (mostly cards 5, 6, and 10) will serve you in the future, and eventually become cards of the past. This concept is developed further in Permutation 2: The Turning of the Wheel.

The following are a selection of variations in the meanings of the Celtic Cross positions adapted from books on the Tarot and from friends who have helped me to see the Tarot in many different ways—simultaneously. The meanings are identified by the originator's initials. They are *A.A.*: Angeles Arrien; *J.K.*: Joanne Kowalski, with assistance from Rick Nemick; *JUNG*: Jungian style developed from several sources; *TRAD*: Traditional; *OTHR*: A conglomeration of sources, including me.

The first two cards actually give the essence of the whole reading. They create an expression of dynamic tension which is the impetus for future actions and has been created by the person you have been in the past. As your heart, core, or center, these cards tell you what your inner, true self wants you to know. By seeking to understand this basic energy tension through the rest of the cards, you have the opportunity to become conscious of the dynamics behind your actions so that events do not just appear to "happen" to you.

CARD 1:

A.A.: Your heart in the past. Karmic relationships.

J.K.: The way to self-development. What you must work on. Strengths you can use, trust, count on.

TRAD: The general environment or atmosphere. That which covers you.

OTHR: Where you put your energies previously, your habits, past lives. What is developed and manifested. The focus of your energies. What you are aware of. Commencement. What you want to create.

CARD 2:

A.A.: Your heart in the present. Visionary in outlook.

J.K.: Impediments that prevent your self-development.

TRAD: The conflicts, obstacles. That which crosses you.

OTHR: *What is developing and manifesting. That which deflects or that which augments the focus of your energies. An imbalance, causing the potential for change, growth. Reaction. What you want to preserve.*

CARD 3:

A.A.: The subconconscious mind. The legs. The ability to earth, ground, and express your natural energy.

J.K.: Internalization of past attributes.

JUNG: Your shadow. What you cannot or do not want to look at in yourself. The Collective Unconscious.

TRAD: The foundation or basis for the situation. Something which is already a part of your experience. That which is below you.

OTHR: The base of the spine. First- and second-chakra energy. Your subconscious desires, and physical and emotional needs. What you do not yet know or are not yet consciously aware of. Roots. Unconscious habits. Balance. Subconsciously known integration of 1 and 2. Resolution.

CARD 4:

A.A.: The left arm (or side) of the body. Ability to receive and structure situations and opportunities. What you bring toward you or receive. Creative talents, skills, and abilities.

J.K.: The Anima. Your receptive, feminine nature.

TRAD: The Past. What is passing out of influence. What is behind you.

OTHR: Opportunities presented which you may or may not take. The aesthetic, visual, image-producing part of yourself. Things which you "know" without knowing how you know —your intuition. Your ability to relate with others. What you have realized or accomplished through experience. Past resolutions.

CARD 5:

A.A.: The conscious mind. The head or center of human awareness. Awareness of your own power.

J.K.: What you should strive to incorporate within yourself.

JUNG: Your Higher Self or Guide.

TRAD: Your goals. The best that can be accomplished. What is above. Purpose. Aim. Ideals.

OTHR: What you are consciously aware of. What you strive for, or are aspiring to. That for which you are always reaching. The Freudian Superego: what you think you "should" or "ought to" do. Recognition: how or for what you will be recognized. That which you are guided by or in which you place authority. A new direction or new talents which you need to develop. Contrast to what you have already developed (card 4), and which will help you resolve the tension between cards 1 and 2.

CARD 6:

A.A.: The right arm (or side) of the body. Ability to give and execute situations and opportunities. What you cause. Your ability to make decisions.

JUNG: The Animus. Masculine, directive, outgoing energy.

TRAD: That which is before you. The future. The next turn of events.

OTHR: Your ability to take action. What you put out into the world. The outer expression of your self and needs, especially through action. How you will use your abilities.

CARD 7:

A.A.: Status, work, creative possibilities.

J.K.: Your source and level of energy, motivating force, individual perspective.

JUNG: The Persona or Mask.

TRAD: Yourself as you see yourself.

OTHR: Your condition and attitudes at the time of the reading. Personal strengths and weaknesses. Self-concept.

CARD 8:

TRAD, OTHR, etc.: Your environment. What is Not-You. Your home, work, family, friends, lovers. That which surrounds you. Influences, attitudes, emotions of those near to you toward the situation. The world. Your attitude toward, or influence on, others. How other people see you.

CARD 9:

A.A.: How you confront and handle the polarities within your being.

J.K.: Something unresolved which is creating an energy block. That which must be resolved for further development to take place.

TRAD: Hopes and Fears in attaining the goal. (I always read this card as both).

OTHR: The way to integrate yourself with the environment. Inner, hidden emotions and secret desires. Anxieties. Secrets kept from other people. The lesson to be learned.

CARD 10:

A.A.: Your individual expression in the future—based on your thoughts and energy expression in the present. Or, blocks and obstacles that you are determined to release.

TRAD: The outcome.

OTHR: Culmination. Resolution. The result of the path taken. The quality or tool which will help you achieve a breakthrough. The end of one cycle and the beginning of another. An additional element which you may or may not have considered. The reward. What you will gain from this experience.

REARRANGING THE CARDS FOR FURTHER UNDERSTANDING

Once you have read all the cards and have a basic understanding of what they mean, you can begin rearranging these same ten cards into new and different patterns and relationships. The numbers throughout will refer to the original, archetypal Celtic Cross layout positions.

Permutation 2: The Turning of the Wheel

I have adapted this from a "Tai Chi Chuan" spread designed for one of my classes by Marcia Church.

When trying to understand yourself and your motives, it is sometimes helpful to look at how you have acted in the past or at how you might act in the future after you have internalized the new lessons. The situation you are currently involved in can be put in the larger perspective of shifting, turning, ever-changing patterns in your life.

The Celtic Cross is a cross with a circle around it connecting the four arms. It corresponds with the *Tao* and the Wheel of Fortune: everything travels in a circle eventually returning to itself. Rotate the four arms of the cross (Cards 3, 4, 5 and 6) clockwise. Card 5 will then be in position 6, Card 6 in position 7, etc. Now read these cards in relation to each other. In this way you can have a look at what will happen when what you are currently conscious of (the old Card 5) becomes your next action (when moved to position 6). At the same time your outer expression of self (the old Card 6) will become a subconscious habit (when moved to position 3), and the unconscious basis (the old Card 3) will be a creative talent from a past life (when moved to position 4), and your past life knowledge (the old Card 4) will become a conscious directing force (when moved to position 5). Rotate the cards a second time and begin again. Continue rotating the cards clockwise and reinterpreting them until they are back in their original positions. Can you better understand what these four cards mean now?

As you move the cards clockwise around the wheel, you sometimes find yourself looking at the past, perhaps the experience you went through last week or a realization of a year ago. You may find yourself describing a previous lifetime and how you acted based on your knowledge then—and what you were then not conscious of that caused you to make some particular decision.

Similarly, future possibilities for action become apparent when you no longer hide your needs in your subconscious but have moved them into conscious thought (when Card 3 moves to position 5). You can actually watch the wheel of events turn before you and see how the past becomes the present, and how the future is another way of seeing the past. How do you know whether you are reading what is past or to come? Read the cards in both ways! But your intuition will tell you. It is almost always obvious.

Permutation 3: Past, Present, Future

This permutation is adapted from a method Hilary Anderson once taught in her class in the "Oracular Dimension of Creativity" at the California Institute of Integral Studies in San Francisco.

Put the cards back into their original Celtic Cross positions and then sort them into three separate groups as follows:

The Past: Cards 3, 4, and 9. These cards all relate to the past. Hopes and fears are included in this category, since your expectations of future success and failure are based on past experience—this helps you to see where these expectations come from.

The Present or Now: Cards 1, 2, 7, and 8. These cards represent yourself—7, in your environment—8, dealing with the basic situation—1 and 2. They pretty much tell you where you are at now.

The Future (in the Process of Manifesting or Eventuating): Cards 5, 6, and 10. These are forward-looking, visionary, active, conscious. They show you where and how you are manifesting your energy which *may become* the future. Eventually, what you think and what you surround

mes your reality. Move the cards around within their
nay tell you more and suggest future interactions.

Whole-Person Summary Spread

n is taught by Angeles Arrien as a further develop-
'erson Spread.
ds into five groups by suits and the Major Arcana.
rizontal line beginning with the Court Cards and
numerical order from ace to 10. The Major Arcana
and should also be placed in numerical order.
e the other to create a visual structure.

creative, perceptive forces at work within you.
nitiator.

Cups: Your emotional nature. Your ability to love, relate, dream, imagine.

Swords: Your mental/rational thoughts, your ability to discriminate. Sometimes where you struggle or find conflict.

Pentacles or Disks: Your physical concerns, how you ground and earth yourself, how stable and secure you are. Your ability to utilize your energies for work and study.

Major Arcana: Archetypal forces at work in this situation. Qualities within you that are being called forth and tested. Aspects of yourself involved in the situation.

Cards that are seemingly negative show the areas in which you need work. Remove these cards, and you can see the person you can become once you are able to deal with your fears, hang-ups, and insecurities. If a suit is not represented, it is usually not an area of major concern in the matter. But occasionally it becomes obvious that you are avoiding the real issue (the missing suit). For example, I did a reading about a love affair, and no cups came up. The emotional aspect could have been strong and not needing attention. In this case, it became apparent that that's exactly what the relationship was lacking. The relationship was based on security needs and convenience, not feelings. Individual egos were being bruised, not hearts being broken. It became clear in discussion that the people were actually avoiding accepting the fact that they were not in love.

Permutation 5: *Yod He Vau He*—The Path of Hermes

This permutation is based on the work of Papus in his book *Tarot of the Bohemians*. He describes the structure of the Minor Arcana as a series of three triangles symbolizing a dialectical process of Thesis (commencement), Antithesis (reaction or opposition), and Synthesis (resolution), followed by a new Thesis. Cabalistic mysticism states this same idea in the Tetragrammaton, the four letters that spell the name Jehovah or Yahweh—*Yod, He, Vau, He* and which represent the process of manifestation.

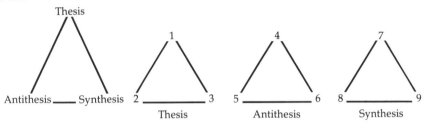

Each new thesis represents a birth, new order, or new action emerging out of the center of the previous dialectical triangle:

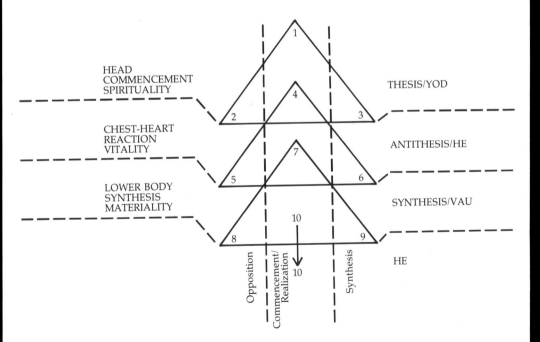

Your Celtic Cross Spread can be rearranged and laid out in this pattern, in order by number, and interpreted according to the following meanings:

CARDS 1, 4, 7, 10 and TRIANGLE 1 (YOD):

Thesis, action, creation, commencement, beginning, root, seed. It is initiatory and relates to Spirit and consciousness.

CARDS 2, 5, 8 and TRIANGLE 2 (HE):

Opposition, reaction, reflex, obstacles, contradiction, doubt, preservation. This is the emotional, astral level; it seeks to maintain order or preserve the status quo and is fixed. Inertia.

CARDS 3, 6, 9 and TRIANGLE 3 (VAU):

Synthesis, integration, equilibrium, transformation, resolution, transition, passage. It relates to the Body and is mutable. A merging of opposites.

CARDS 4, 7, 10 and 1 (HE) (and the new YOD):

Realization, seed, new action, new order, birth. The stabilization of one triangle and the commencement of the next. The reward or result of your actions.

The following meanings are not to be taken as absolutes but as examples of how to view the sequence of cards.

CARD 1:
The commencement of the commencement.

CARD 2:
The opposition to the commencement.

CARD 3:
The integration of the commencement and opposition.

CARD 4:
The commencement of the opposition.

CARD 5:
The opposition to the opposition.

CARD 6:
The integration of the opposition and commencement.

CARD 7:
The commencement of the integration.

CARD 8:
The opposition to the integration.

CARD 9:
The integration of the integration.

CARD 10:
The reward, result, or seed of new action.

This can be one of the most significant permutations. A whole new understanding of how each card relates to the other, evolves out of the others, and influences the others can be gained through study.

A thought about using this pattern: turn the pattern upside down and you have the Cabalistic Tree of Life—another permutation perhaps. I'll leave this variation to those interested in the Sephiroth and their Paths.

Permutation 6: Variations Through Time—The Journal Approach

Write down all your readings and date them with notes on the significance of the cards to you at the time. Append significant readings you have done to your journal if you have one, or note on the reading itself what is happening in your life—quick thumbnail sketches. Four to eight weeks later go back to these significant readings. Note the progress of events. Can you now identify persons more specifically? Who was the mysterious Knight of Wands? How were you yourself actually manifesting this masculine, Knight energy? What was that argument about (the 5 of Wands)—or was it something other than an argument? What did you have to let go of (Death)? What was the final impetus that made you let go? Can it be identified by another card in the reading? I always use different color pens, writing my new comments next to the old. Date them. Then come back about six months later and add a third series of notes in a third color of ink.

Usually by the third overview you can begin to see your own personal pattern evolving. The layers of self-deception begin to thin out. You can start recognizing the games you play with yourself—your inability to "see the facts." But also the evidences of your intuition peep through —the hints, those places where you already recognized what was happening. Your own inherent wisdom and words of advice come back at the most appropriate times. It often "happens" that I pick up a particular notebook on a day when it is especially meaningful. Note particular themes that keep reappearing. What aspects of your life never seem to appear in your readings? Why not?

Since you won't be able to follow all of your Tarot readings over the next several years, set aside particular readings to represent milestones and turning points in your life. Some recommended "moments" to save: the commencement of anything—such as a new job, new home, new relationship, your birthday. The ending of anything. Every new moon or every full moon. For women, during the first day of your Moon (menstrual period) is an excellent time to focus on yourself and your own needs. Men might want to ritualize their own cycles in a similar way — try the day every month when the moon returns to the natal position in your astrological chart.[4]

Permutation 7: A Composite Relationship Spread

This permutation is different from the others. It is actually a variation on the use of the Celtic Cross Spread in which two people select cards and the reading is for that third entity which is the relationship between the two.

Have both persons shuffle the deck. Designate one person as the male principle (Person A) and the other as the female principle (Person B). Person A cuts the deck in two stacks. Person B chooses one of the stacks using his or her intuition, Person A taking the other. Both shuffle their individual stacks and then make a large fan and intuitively select the following cards, placing them in the traditional Celtic Cross layout:

CARD 1:
Person A's heart in the relationship.

CARD 2:
Person B's heart in the relationship.

CARD 3:
The basis of the relationship. What the couple is not yet consciously aware of. (To be selected by Person B, who should be more feminine and/or passive, receptive.)

CARD 4:
The karmic past of the relationship. The talent, skill, creative ability of the relationship. (Selected by Person B.)

CARD 5:
The conscious goals and ambitions of the couple in the relationship. (Selected by the more aggressive, masculine, outgoing Person A.)

CARD 6:
Decisions before the couple and their ability to act on them together. (Selected by Person A.)

Taking turns, the couple then shuffles the remainder of the cards. Make one large fan.

CARDS 7 and 8:
Each person draws a card to represent "themselves as they see themselves." Their self-image in the relationship. Therefore, there is a card of the Self and a card of the Other.

CARD 9:
That which must be overcome or resolved to develop the relationship. (Can be drawn by either person.)

CARD 10:
That quality or tool which will help you achieve a breakthrough to a new depth in the relationship. (To be drawn by the person who did not draw Card 9.)

Both persons should read each of the cards since the individual interpretations can be even more important to the two people doing the reading than the objective meanings of those cards. Ideally, the couple will synthesize a picture of their interaction, coming to some realization of how they each help to create that entity consisting of the relationship between them.

SUMMARY

I have presented many possible ways to look at a single Celtic Cross reading. If you do all of them at once you risk being overwhelmed by too much information. Therefore, I recommend that you choose one permutation at a time to work with until it becomes comfortable and "second nature." Eventually, you will work out a sequence or pattern of permutations that works for you. Permutation 4 (The Whole Person Summary Spread) is perhaps the most basic variation and one that can be used with any other spread design.

These seven permutations (including the expanded and sometimes contradictory list of position meanings) can help you delve below the surface indications of the cards. Maintain paradoxes, seek ambiguity. The resulting creative tension will help you to see everyday events from different points of view, thus increasing your perspective. What appears as a "heavy" card with a bleak outlook can be something to be faced eagerly as it spurs you on to new horizons, opens a closed door, or yields an exciting opportunity, and perhaps stimulates you into action and taking charge of your life.

NOTES

1. Brendan Lehane, *The Companion Guide to Ireland*. New York: 1973. p. 87.

2. Lehane, p. 86.

3. J.E. Cirlot, *A Dictionary of Symbols*. NY: Philosophical Library, 1978, p. 68.

4. This information and the new and full moons can be found in astrological calendars and almanacs such as the *Celestial Influences Calendars*, the *Daily Planet*, and *Witches' Almanacs*.

Destiny Spread

A Process for Self-Transformation

Hilary Anderson, PhD

The Tarot is a remarkable language of inner knowing, and in whatever pictorial formulation it is found, it can be deeply revelatory. Like most of the oracular traditions, it is dependent upon the interpreter's depth of life experience as well as his or her ability to express creatively through its profound archetypal symbology. Psychic talent is useful in the handling of impressions coming to mind as suggested by focusing on the graphics, but the profundity of the tradition lies fallow when merely predictive measures are engaged. Arts of prediction there can always be, but the deeper underlying wisdom influencing how the process of time is to be experienced must be evoked through an interpretive work of the spirit. This order of work comes from one who can read through such a tradition oppportunity for others to see themselves transformatively rather than merely fatalistically. The Tarot is one of the world's such languages which provides an invitation to its interpreter to continually embody the work of transformation, and thereby impart such guidance for others along the way.

The Tarot is by nature flexible and adaptive in its usage and therefore evokes in the devoted student of the tradition occasion to express his or her creativity. Whether it be in the devising of new layouts, procedures and rituals or in the creating of updated artistic and/or new mythological perspectives, it can often provide additional archetypal interpretations of the cards themselves. One such newly created method for the use of the cards is hereby offered in the *Destiny Spread* which works with the tradition from the perspective of transformation of consciousness.

First of all, multi-dimensionality is emphasized through the use of two different-size decks. The 22 Major cards or archetypal Trump images of the larger-size deck are used to form the arrangement or layout pattern (see page 70). Then, the regular-size full deck of 78 cards is shuffled and laid out on the larger Majors as they are dealt from the top of the deck.

The regular-size Major cards appearing on the large-size Majors provide interconnecting links to the archetypal symbolism and the Minor cards falling on the large-size Majors bring added depth to their interpretation within a transformational perspective.

THE DESTINY SPREAD AND THE MAJOR ARCANA

As a group of images, the 22 Majors comprise a profound story of self-discovery. The Destiny Spread divides them into stages or convenient groupings that can be utilized to pictorially demonstrate a particular pattern of individual development depicting a powerful myth of transformation. The spread contains nine developmental levels of which three of those levels are seen as pivotal points of integration. The three points form a vertically arranged lemniscate, or infinity sign, with the Fool image at the top of the spread, the Wheel of Fortune image at the converging midpoint and the World image at the bottom.

Within this dynamic arrangement, the two well-known divisions of the Majors remain intact—the lesser and the greater mysteries. The lesser mysteries group can be seen to correspond with our psychological development and cultural conditioning. They comprise the first eleven images—the Fool through the Wheel of Fortune. The greater mysteries reflect our deeper spiritual response to early conditioning, providing a proving ground that begins with the Justice image and is completed with the World.

Within this orientation, the spread can reveal with great clarity present difficulties and strengths of personal development and the interrelationships between these two poles or groupings. The connecting links can be drawn from empathetic relations between the Majors and Minors as they become recognized according to court card and suit designations as well as numerical similarities.

Radical Potential: Fool

The Fool image stands alone at the top of the spread and forms the first level of development called the Radical Potential. The Fool figure is seen to represent the author or originator of the transformational process. Having a sort of free-floating genius quality, it stands for one's essential freedom to take the radical step or leap into an entirely new phase of life. It can be understood as the self that cannot be defined or limited by any process. The Major or Minor card that happens to fall on the larger Fool image indicates the quality of uniqueness by which the

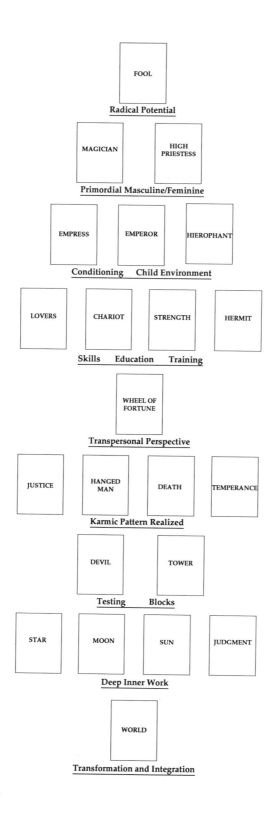

FOOL

Radical Potential

MAGICIAN — HIGH PRIESTESS

Primordial Masculine/Feminine

EMPRESS — EMPEROR — HIEROPHANT

Conditioning   Child Environment

LOVERS — CHARIOT — STRENGTH — HERMIT

Skills   Education   Training

WHEEL OF FORTUNE

Transpersonal Perspective

JUSTICE — HANGED MAN — DEATH — TEMPERANCE

Karmic Pattern Realized

DEVIL — TOWER

Testing   Blocks

STAR — MOON — SUN — JUDGMENT

Deep Inner Work

WORLD

Transformation and Integration

person receiving the interpretation can always free himself of all those areas of obstruction that may be encountered in the pattern presently projected on the spread for his or her growth and development. This quality marks the person's essential capacity to shift into the new cycle of events with abandon and spontaneity.

Primordial Masculine/Feminine: Magician, High Priestess

The Magician and High Priestess images comprise the second level called the Primordial Masculine/Feminine polarity dynamically working the individual's consciousness. The Magician image or masculine part stands for one's capacity to transmit from the universal mind source a creative intelligence which is capable of configuring new views, theories and experimental procedures through the instrumentality of the four elements represented by the four suits that usually appear on the graphic image. These configurations can be projected at will through delegation of suggested fields of expertise.

The High Priestess image or feminine part stands for one's capacity to become totally receptive to past impressions streaming in from the subconscious mind that can unify diverging and conflicting tendencies inherently functioning in the creative intellect. This placement makes available a range of psychic sensibilities to the communicative arts.

The card falling on the Magician shows the way one can presently become more aware of one's essential creativity in powers of formulation. The card falling on the High Priestess shows one's ability to reach into the depths of the subconscious and bring to awareness information that is needed upon the instant.

Conditioning/Child Environment: Empress, Emperor, Hierophant

The Empress, Emperor and Hierophant images are a three-part series of archetypes making up the third level called Conditioning/Child Environment. This refers to aspects of early cultural patterns and perspectives gained from the mother, father and socio-religious values expressed through a variety of demonstrable responses to the demands of life experience personally and professionally. The Empress figure expresses one's generative abilities to bring to birth through available material resources new creations, be they physical children or the offspring of one's life in a more universal sense. The placement suggests one's capacity for nurturing and providing a material base for love, beauty and creativity to flourish.

The Emperor figure expresses the function of consciousness that sees the administrative possibilities whereby these "children" can be ordered, established and perpetuated in the larger arena of society over time. The placement indicates one's ability to put into operation the ideas configured by the creative intelligence, setting up workable, pragmatic systems for personal, corporate or civic survival.

The Hierophant figure gathers these two above functions and through an internalization of the meanings of these births and establishments, sanctifies them in ritual and celebration for their right relation to deity. The placement indicates one's capacity to enter into a teaching and express through one's own person the unification implied. Cards falling on these placements describe our capacities to generate, perpetuate and sacralize new applications from old patterns of stability.

Skills, Education, and Training: Lovers, Chariot, Strength, Hermit

The Lovers, Chariot, Strength and Hermit images form a level of personal development called Skills, Education and Training. The Lovers figure seems to have proved the most ambivalent in its artistic rendering down through the centuries. This ambivalence is probably due in some part to western culture's sexual attitudes that have expressed an uneasy balance between erotic impulse and sensation on the one hand and intellectual decision-making on the other, the old body-mind split. Therefore this placement attempts to deal with the immediacy of creative choice between factors of tradition and new possibilities inherent in changing attitudes energized by erotically harmonizing tendencies available in relationship.

The Chariot portrays the mobilizing of one's intellectual powers to articulate particular gifts and talents through a chosen field of endeavor, thus defining and armouring oneself to carry out strategies of movement in the life process.

The Strength figure stands for one's capacity to harness charismatic qualities through the restraining influence of disciplining natural vitality, or libido. Through proper cultivation of available energies, potency of personality can be developed and focused at will.

The Hermit figure reveals an ancient wisdom available to us from above and beyond the ordinary turmoil of mundane activities and serves as a vertical alignment with the larger purpose of life through the light of understanding.

Cards falling on this grouping define qualities through which one can find harmony in love and choice, martial acute articulation of talents, tame vitality to fortify strength of will power and bring the light of wisdom upon current issues of concern.

Transpersonal Perspective: Wheel of Fortune

The Wheel of Fortune image stands on its own at the mid-point of the spread and designates the level called the Transpersonal Perspective. This view affords an expanded consciousness of time, change and evolution in an individual's life as it must synchronize with that of society, bringing increasingly to awareness an unfolding pattern of his own destiny in time. Time can now be seen as an energy to serve a life rather than to bind it to a fate that is merely time-bound. In this view, time becomes an instrument for one's own revolutions, in which one begins to see life and world not only from outside in but also from inside out so that one's perspective can be entertained from the true center of the movement of consciousness, at the hub of the wheel. The card that falls on this placement gives the quality by which one can most creatively shift his or her consciousness into this total perspective.

Karmic Pattern Realized: Justice, Hanged Man, Death, Temperance

The Justice, Hanged Man, Death, and Temperance images form the level called Karmic Pattern Realized. This level provides an opportunity for one to come to terms with the quality of life that past actions have thus far configured, and therefore one can begin to undergo the individual changes and adjustments that this might imply. The Justice figure reveals the ability to carefully weigh past actions, take total responsibility for them, and through the performance of right action bring present activities and relationships into alignment with the life direction being presented to awareness and decided upon.

The Hanged Man figure represents one's capacity to undergo the transforming visionary experience of the deity through which the life is transfigured. At this point, one has the opportunity to envision the real meaning of his life in image, in symbolic form, and by the process of visualization begin to effect the transformation his or her destiny requires. One can now willingly sacrifice, and through a conversion or reversal experience, offer up all his energies to the way upon which the transformation vision guides him.

The Death figure depicts the natural process of change by which all that does not conform to the vision simply falls away. The dissolution of the old arrangement of energies and activities is often experienced as a kind of dismemberment or disembodiment. Only the true structure of reality remains.

The Temperance figure suggests the work of balance, adjustment and experimentation in reconfiguring in oneself an ability to work with vibratory levels at intensities the new challenges of the path present. This placement emphasizes cultivation of the art of handling life from its totality of experience, thus enriching one's capabilities of efficiency and competence in a chosen vocation.

In this grouping, one's life energies literally become judged, reversed or converted to the way, changed and tempered. Therefore, those cards falling on these placements show the character by which the work of transformation may be more firmly carried out in the patterns of one's current life process.

Tests and Blocks: Devil, Tower

The Devil and Tower images comprise the level called Tests and Blocks in which one has the opportunity to experience a kind of proving out, through meeting the challenges of alternating shocks and insights, and a deep penetration into instinctual, unregenerated areas of consciousness. The Devil figure provides for excursions into areas of self-seduction in which one is tempted to perceive the apparent for the real, and to reach out through projection on the desired object for self-gratification. It is therefore a testing for that which can be materialized or grounded for oneself through sensual experience from outside oneself to within oneself.

The Tower figure brings insights often experienced as catastrophic shocks to consciousness and reveals what has truly been realized or manifested from identifications built in the name of reality. This position can be seen as the iconoclastic perception that shatters the illusion, bringing an enlightenment of what truly is the case.

The card falling on the Devil placement indicates the way in which one can most easily misperceive in the projective experience the reality needed for deep satisfaction, but if correctly perceived can be the occasion for natural satisfaction in spontaneous sensuality. The card falling on the Tower placement shows the quality through which one can receive profound insights and enlightenments concerning what has or has not been gained or materialized.

Deep Inner Work: Star, Moon, Sun, Judgment

The Star, Moon, Sun, and Judgment images form the level of Deep Inner Work into which one plunges after experiencing the ordeals of the level above. The Star figure affords an opportunity for total vulnerability when one is stripped of all the mantles of role-playing and is open to receive inner guidance from within one's own embodiment. Here one becomes the "body of light" from which pours the inspiration of one's own life experience.

The Moon figure brings one into direct contact with the subconscious realms in their raw realities unprotected by the veil of the High Priestess at the second level. Here cultivation of far memory, lucid dreaming and psychic communication is conducted in much yet unmapped areas of consciousness. Such delving can be experienced as an inundation, confrontation, merging and uncovering of the personal and collective reservoir of supportive energies upon which one can reflect for creative activities of all kinds.

The Sun figure depicts the new being born of oneself wherein a new face emerges from the depths of the life experience. It is the face bearing the essence of individuality, self-luminous and revealing a new collectivity of identity lighting up the entire life process with a clear signature. From this new face radiates an intensity generated in the crucible of the transformation process itself.

The Judgment Card portrays the immediacy of a resounding call of spirit to all levels of consciousness to participate in an altogether new dimension of experience. All past experience is now unified and regenerated, and through a sharp clarification is raised to its new order of functioning. This new order becomes the context that bears the unmistakable seal of one's personal destiny upon it.

In this grouping, one's life receives and gives inspiration, recalls and communicates from the depths of subconscious knowledge. It configures a new identity and regenerates all energies into a new orientation ordained by spirit. Cards falling on these placements indicate the qualities which can usher one into the depth of this interior work promising total transformation.

Transformation and Integration: World

The World image stands alone and marks the level of total Transformation and Intergration completing the vertical lemniscate, or infinity sign, at the bottom loop formed with the Fool and Wheel of Fortune images. The World figure brings into administrative operation all of the experience and knowledge gained through all of the levels of psycho-spiritual development and stands for solidarity of creative self-expression in the universal flow of energies. At this level, these energies are experienced as strong, recognizable and self-perpetuating. The integration implies that the integrity of a work developed through personality transformation carries its own unique and distinguished stamp. This placement can truly be called "the dance of life" in which the individual dances to the rhythm of the world, giving freely from his or her own life and work. The card falling on this placement suggests the quality through which one might best experience the goal of the current process of transformation.

SUMMARY

The rationale for developing such a spread was to offer to the Tarot tradition a way of using the archetypal depth dimension of the 22 Major Cards that carry a pattern for self-transformation as a structure upon which personal process selections of the cards could be projected. This multi-dimensional use of the cards has opened up an entirely new depth of interpretation by which a given personal process can be seen graphically, bringing an immediacy of recognition of the totality of possibility as provided through the language of the Tarot. An additional shuffling of yet smaller Majors can be added to bring even more complex readings of the images with more interconnecting links to recognize and develop themes of discovery.

NOTE

1. There are several decks that are available in varying sizes, including Troth and Rider-Waite. Any two variant-sized decks may be used, as long as the imagery of the underlying Major card remains somewhat visible.

The Big Picture:
Tarot, Astrology, Numerology, Mythology, Nature

*T*arot provides a comprehensive, holistic view of an individual or situation by combining with other symbolic, diagnostic media. Tarot cards picture mythological and archetypal characters with components of the natural world such as animals, elements, numbers, and places. Tarot teaches us to see metaphorically, to view the external world as symbolic of our inner worlds, states, and processes. It teaches us to become one with the external universe.

Astrologer/Tarotist, Karen LaPuma, in "Charting the New Age by Astrological Tarot," shows how the planets and constellations interface with our archetypal nature as symbolized by the mythological figures in theTarot cards. By connecting the transpersonal and transformative energies of Uranus, Neptune, and Pluto to Tarot, Ms. LaPuma provides insight into the revolution of the new Aquarian Age.

Twainhart Hill's "Life Cycles, Numbers, and the Major Arcana," shows the correspondence of the mathematical formulation and structure of the world—with the number appellations of the cards forming our numerological wheel akin to natural growth rings of a tree.

Gary Ross, in "The Court Cards: Nature's Archetypes," views the Court or Royalty cards as symbols of our elemental or natural archetypology. This relationship between Tarot and nature helps us harness the natural forces within ourselves.

O▪O▪O▪O▪O▪O▪O▪O▪O▪O▪O▪O▪O

Charting the New Age by Astrological Tarot

Karen LaPuma

○■○■○■○■○■○■○■○■○■○■○■○■○

Tarot and astrology, as maps of consciousness, are two of the many keys to the human journey of evolvement. Both are tools for drawing us inward to the collective unconscious. Both are symbolic, metaphysical languages that communicate all of life's energies. These mediums of universal knowledge were used by the ancients as practical guides for self-awareness.

Today, in the dawning of the Aquarian Age, these intuitive sciences are being reborn. They present a constructive way of modifying our confusions and some of our natural tendencies, resulting in the positive expression of our energies. We learn from these metaphysical arts how to integrate the contents of our vast subconscious—to make an alignment between the internal and the external. Through astrology and Tarot we have an opportunity to travel the depths of our beings, purging old fears, outmoded attitudes, psychic wastes, imprints, and conditionings.

Each of us holds, within, the seeds of wholeness (as symbolized by the zodiac wheel) and we naturally strive toward it. Life is a process and, through the framework offered by the combination of Tarot and astrology, we observe our wholeness and our oneness with nature. We can discover our true selves, become more conscious, and operate at our full potential.

PLANETS, SIGNS AND TAROT SYMBOLS

The astrological symbols, rich in their meanings, draw us into the depths of the ancient hieroglyphic-like symbols on the face of each card. The Tarot deck provides a perfect fit of twenty-two Major Arcana (or trump cards) equaling ten planets and twelve zodiac signs (See Table 1.)

The planets symbolize energy patterns innate in humankind. The

Table 1: ASTROLOGICAL/TAROT

ASTROLOGY Planets (Movement of Energy Patterns)		Zodiac Signs (Description of Movement of Energy Patterns)		TAROT* Symbols of Tarot (Visual Images of Movement of Energy Patterns)
10	+	12	=	22
Uranus				0. Fool
Mercury				1. Magus
Moon				2. High Priestess
Venus				3. Empress
		Aries		4. Emperor
		Taurus		5. Hierophant
		Gemini		6. Lovers
		Cancer		7. Chariot
		Libra		8. Adjustment
		Virgo		9. Hermit
Jupiter				10. Wheel of Fortune
		Leo		11. Lust
Neptune				12. Hanged Man
		Scorpio		13. Death
		Sagittarius		14. Art
		Capricorn		15. Devil
Mars				16. Tower
		Aquarius		17. Star
		Pisces		18. Moon
Sun				19. Sun
Pluto				20. Aeon
Saturn				21. Universe

*Crowley-Thoth designations

Sun and Moon are included as planets to simplify, even though they are luminaries. The zodiac signs represent how that energy is manifested, thus describing the energy movement. The Tarot symbols, as pictorial mythologies that have come down to us through history, are the visual humanistic images of these energy waves.

These three categories—planets, signs and Tarot symbols—interact with each other within a gestalt.* Each feeds, blends, and intensifies the other. Through interfocusing these disciplines, the process becomes like

*A gestalt is a system where parts come together to form another viewing of the whole, which is more powerful than any part separately.

a camera lens, illuminating life. The camera operator or reader has the opportunity to choose from a reservoir of symbolic meanings. The individual's interpretation can be a projection of one's personal experiences, thoughts, feelings, and intentions in order to mirror the energy patterns.

THE ROLES OF URANUS, NEPTUNE AND PLUTO
IN ASTROLOGY AND THE TAROT

It is my contention that Uranus, Neptune and Pluto simultaneously rule the metaphysical disciplines of astrology and the Tarot. These planets, like astrology and the Tarot, awaken us to the universal unconscious and break down our personal barriers.

As a species, we had to evolve before we were ready for the energies of these "transpersonal" planets, since they are beyond the sight of the human eye. We had to develop telescopes. These energies are extraordinary, beyond everyday existence and the personal. They appear to have some connection with what modern depth psychology calls the "transpersonal unconscious." The power and strength offered to humanity through these planets belongs to a larger psychic unity. They represent the dynamic quality of change in life and prompt us to transform within ourselves. They awaken us out of our ego-centered lethargy. They force us to realize that we live in a world of metamorphosis from which we are not exempt, a world in which we have a transformative function to perform. These energies symbolize the ongoing revolution of our planet into the Aquarian Age, signifying the trends of the generation. We can receive some very important insights as well as project visions of the new age by studying these transpersonal energies represented by the symbols of the Tarot and astrology.

Astrologer Dane Rudhyar refers to Uranus, Neptune and Pluto as the "ambassadors of the galaxy," as they are beyond conscious human control. All we can do is control our attitudes toward their influence. They symbolize the cosmic forces that impel humankind to grow in consciousness.

Uranus

Uranus was discovered in 1781, during the times of revolutionary cries of freedom, liberty, and justice for all. This planet represents the need for freedom and independence, and the need to express oneself without restraint—individualization, yet with an eager awareness of universality. It is the vehicle through which new ideas are born, revolutionizing one's way of being. Uranus rules Aquarius and wants to seek and share ultimate truths as well as help others evolve. As the great awakener and illuminator, it symbolizes the universal mind, the creative mind—a mind beyond reason and the establishment (a higher octave of Mercury).

Uranus follows Saturn in the planetary sequence, which symbolizes reality boundaries and the law; Uranus is everything Saturn is not. Uniquely unconventional, it breaks with tradition and experiments. Once something is accepted, it is no longer Uranian. This powerful vibration is as electrical and rapid as lightning, and symbolizes sudden changes of life patterns, sudden alterations of consciousness, and flashes of insight. It cuts away the old as though dispensing with nonessentials. It is the perception of the genius, a master at manipulating symbols, a rapid-fire synthesizer.

Traditionally, Uranus is connected with the Fool and, through Aquarius, the Star, with the Five, Six and Seven of Swords, and with the Prince of Swords.

Uranus is androgynous, having both male and female characteristics within it. The new age brings more balance of male and female energies along with a common awareness of our being both male and female within. It is a creature of yin and yang as it combines action with intuition and sensitivity.

Fool: The Fool is probably the best known of all Tarot cards. His greatest assets are freedom from limitation and the absence of fear. Uranus links the Fool to those intuitive channels where powerful forces flow into awareness with electrical rapidity. He deals with what ought to be, situations where rules don't apply. His realities are our ideals. He's ready, willing, and able to embark on new territory—his own path. He sparks the mind into new creativity, beyond reason or the established view of what is possible. He is capable of finding new ways of achieving. Sometimes a feeling of uprootedness and unsettledness can occur, because Uranus symbolizes reversals and surprises. The Fool is ready for the unexpected: he creates opportunities and opens doors, and represents switches in life patterns as well as consciousness. He crumbles, shatters, makes fragments of our egos, and gets to the truth of matters.

Because of the symbolism on the card, the Fool is also associated with Aries, and suggests the quality of initiation and the vast potential for new growth. The beginnings and potentials are the pervading life force about to enter into a particular experience. We need to get past the fear of our own power and challenge the old system with the spontaneous, ever-changing energy of the Fool. As astrologer Robert Hand says, "True liberation involves coming to the point where all structure is taken by choice and life is self-created."

Star: The Star, connected to Aquarius, is a main concept, since it has a symbolic link with our new age. The Aquarian Age is a time for individuals everywhere to get in touch with their own personal power. Power is the ability to act, to express what we are, and to take responsibility for our decisions and our actions. Real power, too, is the balance between the masculine and feminine. Frequently, that power is given away. The more we become aware of our personal power, the more we realize that the channel of the universe flows through us. The Star, as the symbol of the Water Bearer, holds the bottomless urn and is a distributor of wisdom. She carries the water of life, filled with spiritual nourishment. She sees all things as truth, broadcasts her perspective, and has something original to contribute.

The Star, like Aquarius, is a law unto herself, wants freedom as a principle, but wants to help or serve others. This energy doesn't go along with the rules of society and experiences pain if concerned with valida-tion. When we seek validation, we give our power away. She represents the concept of self-respect and self-esteem. No one can give this to us; we have to develop it from within. The only security is an inner security. The Star symbolizes new recognitions to the inner self and an awakening of consciousness—a new recognition that we do it ourselves. We create our own life. We create our own reality. We can individually have whatever we want by believing in the self and getting in control of our thoughts. Everything is a manifestation of our thoughts; thoughts are energies that shape our existence.

The Star has the ability to change emotions into perception and let the creativity flow through her from divine sources. An intuitive, sensitive strength, she expresses a detached, humanitarian, brotherly/sisterly love.

Neptune

Neptune is a highly sensitive influence, for it represents natural attunement to other levels of awareness. It is the universal feeling level, the instinct to transcend the self, to break down barriers, and to escape the limitations of the self and the material world. It is a deconditioner.

Expansion happens by dissolving the limitations of our personal and social conditions. Neptune is the sea and the collective unconscious, endless, formless, flowing, boundless, controlled power. It is the urge to go higher in consciousness and thus can rule spirituality as well as drugs. It is those feelings of obligation to society and to others, and the idealization that prompts us to give without desire or expectation of payment. Neptune is the sympathetic and compassionate vibration that allows one to tune into the needs and feelings of others telepathically. It is beyond boundaries, blending and flowing with the cosmic tides around and through, merging into others' spaces. Neptune dissolves the ego and any structure, connects with the subconscious and the subtle currents of the universe. It represents those forces beyond reason or anything comprehensible to the logical mind. It can be highly inspired, refined, and imaginative; or confused, deceptive, and spaced out. In the strong, it represents spiritual enlightenment; in the weak, it brings out the desire to avoid responsibility. It rules dreams, phobias, illusions, mysticism, psychic phenomena, the Tarot, much of astrology, and the sign Pisces.

Neptune traditionally is connected to the Hanged Man, and through Pisces, to the Moon, to the Eight, Nine and Ten of Cups, and to the Queen of Cups and the Queen of Wands.

The Hanged Man: The Hanged Man, symbolized by Neptune, suggests breaking through blocks by dissolving them and escaping limitations by facing them. He represents disintegrating and dispersing with highly ordered patterns of the consciousness, and demands an inevitable breakdown of some aspect of one's personality. He is hung up, suspended, and being made aware of the limitations of his normal perceptions. There may be a sense of confusion, because Neptune fogs over and conceals. Idealism, fantasy, and the imagination always play a role in this energy. It is an urge to transcend the material and the self by surrendering the self to some greater awareness. There is a tendency to relinquish to others, dissolving the ego and sacrificing the self for something greater than the personal. The Hanged Man can represent an attunement with the collective unconscious, seeking some form of refinement, discovering insights that come from within.

The Moon: Pisces, the sign where Neptune naturally resides, is represented in the Moon card. Here, we deal with karmic relationships, and the illusions and delusions connected to our idealistic models. The

Moon card deals with the world of intuition and fantasy, and those who perceive a different reality. One needs to bring in the aspect of concentration, because there are lessons to learn, there is work to be done. Fears connected to the unknown, old habits, and old patterns need to be broken through. There is a romantic, dreamy quality to this energy that intrigues and beguiles, and wants to escape. We need to break down the barriers, go deeply into the self, and pierce through our illusions. We will be forced to face the things that do not work in our lives. Our challenge here is to be able to enter into feelings with another and share. Strong heart connections open up painful areas that must be clarified through communications. The two Ra kings on the Moon card hold two keys: one is Mercury; the other, Pluto. These can mean the ability to make changes through communication and our thought patterns. The symbols reveal perception in relating and an awareness of mind power—an intense, stimulating ability to probe into the secret depths. Psychological powers and mental resourcefulness have cleansing and healing effects.

Pluto

Pluto is a subtle, yet powerful and concentrated energy pattern. It is so complex and so deep that an aura of mystery surrounds its meaning. It rules the underworld and the unconscious. It is the desire to penetrate to the depths of an experience, to delve into the core of a meaning—the desire to go inward. It rarely operates entirely on the surface. Thus, it is very difficult to judge these energies by their appearances. Pluto reveals the work we have to do at deep levels of our being and what habit patterns we have carried over from the past that manifest sometimes as compulsions and obsessions. Pluto is death and regeneration, breakdown and reconstruction. Something must die—something must consciously be let go of, eliminated, or rejected to have a rebirth. Pluto destroys old ego—those patterns, attitudes and attachments that prevent our achieving a more universal consciousness. Jung states that there is no coming to consciousness without pain. Pluto symbolizes the snake shedding its skin: he is vulnerable for awhile, but then he grows a much stronger skin. Pluto can bring crisis (which in Chinese has two characters—one meaning opportunity and one meaning danger; in Greek, *crisis* means "to decide"). Plutonian energy can be greatly transforming and healing, because it is an outgoing power force coupled with a receptive sensitivity.

This energy can also be very manipulative and possessive, and it does not mix well with the personal ego. This great energy comes from a transcendental force. We can usually only understand this abstract term in polarities. Thus, Pluto manifests in terms of opposites, bringing in both the old and the new, the light and the dark. Its force can evoke a spectacular display, then later produce an incredible negative backlash. Nuclear energy and chemical pesticides are examples of this phenomenon. Pluto therefore symbolizes a kind of influence that has the highest potential for constructive or destructive action. Its power should be spiritual, for spiritual evolution is the only aspect in which the potentiality doesn't have a backlash.

Pluto is a drive that needs intensity and passion, and it is impelled by the need for renewal and cleansing. It represents getting in touch with one's personal power. The lessons of Pluto involve learning to let go smoothly.

Aeon: Aeon is symbolized by Pluto. Looking at this card as portrayed in the Crowley-Thoth deck, one can see the old forms in the background that must be eliminated, the new births at the bottom forming. Inwardly, this card represents a time to let go of old psychological patterns, old conditioning of the past. It is a need to open up to the subconscious, return to the collective roots and to the foundation of one's being. One needs to open the inner self and recognize it, know it again, and penetrate deeply into the self, rummaging around and tossing out everything that clutters the way. It is a passionate and intense energy, always dealing with the light and the dark, the old and the new. This card is called Judgment in other decks, and some of the old renditions have the dead rising from graves for the Last Judgment. The Aeon means expansive time; it presents deep, intense changes, reforms and transformations, cleansing through self-mastery.

The goddess, Nuith (Nut), also on this card, represents the need to go into the darkness to see the light and forms the symbol of Leo, which expresses a need for recognition. Creativity is displayed through the quality of love. It shows our need for a centered interior as well as the awakening of the ego. Pluto says, "Let go of the ego."

Death: Death represents Scorpio, probably the most complex astrological sign, and the least understood. This card often frightens those who turn it up, but it is such a beautiful concept! It represents profound and intense change cutting through limitation at a deep level. It is our opportunity to let go of old habits, patterns, physical addictions, and safety and security attachments that get in the way of usable power. It is the passage through the dark door, facing a dragon that must be slain. This tremendous psychological power can be a purging and cleansing experience. Death means letting go. "It is often necessary to advance through retreat"; "Triumph through surrender"; and the ultimate, "Gain and victory come from loss." These are all voices of Scorpio. This card represents all eliminative functions that bring a transformative experience or a total turnabout in life.

SUMMARY

We are leaving the age of Pisces with its duality, its emotionality, its repression of women, and its fanatic devotion to religious beliefs. The watery symbol of fishes and its polar-opposite sign of the Virgin were apparent throughout that age. We were urged to surrender to God. To be holy or spiritual meant to be an ascetic. It started near the time of the crucifixion of Christ and ends in a very expansive state, with the exploration of space, as well as a volatile state, with inventions like the atomic bomb, capable of destroying our planet Earth.

Elizabeth Haich, in *Initiation*, tells us that the new age will know no limitations, eliminating all obstructions from its path. This new age and its technical achievement will operate with waves of energy patterns. The boundaries between religion and science will disappear as the same truths and the same God will be at the center of all religions. The Aquarian Water-Bearer is a symbol of pouring water from divine sources, nourishing life with spiritual enlightenment.

No one knows exactly when the new age starts, since the transition between these two overlaps, allowing the new to flow into the old. The new age is dawning. We have to find new tools and rediscover old ones to deal with this transformation. It will be unpredictable, erratic, and even shattering to those who hold onto the past. Don't be disillusioned as the old regime is crumbling. Prepare yourself for the new.

There is much hope for our planet. Neptune and Pluto have been in sextile since about 1940 and will continue for 100 years. This symbolizes imaginative solutions to our problems such as our energy crisis. Science has already worked out how we are going to build space stations all around the Earth to utilize the magnificent power of our Sun. Our problems are predicaments for helping us learn something. We see a better life for all and much beauty within.

Astrology and the Tarot have their place in the growth of our consciousness. They are more than tools for divination; they are maps of potentialities as well as pictorial representations of our journey toward evolvement—personal as well as global. Within these symbols lies a wealth of knowledge. It is our role to reclaim this knowledge and use it to deepen our understanding.

BIBLIOGRAPHY

Arroyo, Stephen. *Astrology, Karma and Transformation.* Vancouver: CRCS Publication, 1979.

Arroyo, Stephen. *Astrology, Psychology and the Four Elements.* Vancouver: CRCS Publication, 1977.

Allen, Marcus. *Astrology for the New Age.* Berkeley: Whatever Publishing, 1978.

Crowley, Aleister. *The Book of Thoth.* New York: Samuel Weiser, 1969.

Greene, Liz. *Relating.* New York: Samuel Weiser, 1978.

Greene, Liz. *Saturn.* New York: Samuel Weiser, Inc., 1976.

Hand, Robert. *Planets in Transit.* Gloucester, Mass.: Para Research, Inc., 1976.

Hickey, Isabel. *The Cosmic Science.* Watertown, Mass.: Fellowship House Bookshop, 1970.

Hickey, Isabel, and Bruce Altieri. *Minerva or Pluto, The Choice is Yours.* Watertown, Mass.:Fellowship House Bookshop, 1972.

Haich, Elizabeth. *Initiation.* Palo Alto: Seed Center, 1974.

Mayo, Jeff. *The Planets and Human Behavior.* London: L.N. Fowler & Co., Ltd., 1972.

Moore, Marcia, and Mark Douglas. *Astrology: The Divine Science.* York Harbor, Maine: Samuel Weiser, 1982.

Soric, John. *The New Age Astrologer.* San Antonio, Texas: Star Astrology, Inc.1976.

Wing, R.L. *The I Ching Workbook.* Garden City, New York: Doubleday and Co., Inc., 1979.

Life Cycles, Numbers, and the Major Arcana

Twainhart Hill

O▮O▮O▮O▮O▮O▮O▮O▮O▮O▮O▮O▮O▮O

Tarot cards have varied applications. The old concept of Tarot as a method of fortune-telling has limited its application. Currently, a new perspective is being explored. Jack Schwartz explains this point of view:

> These twenty-two cards are symbolic of all the laws operating in our lives. As symbols, they are not the truth in themselves; rather, they are intended to guide the mind toward the attainment of truth. Remember that this system is merely a tool; the ultimate objective is to express the energy that we are.[1]

In my own Tarot research, I associate three modalities that help determine a person's self-expression (or energy) and bring meaning to the changes that occur in every person's life. The modalities are (1) numbers (numerological procedures), (2) cycles, and (3) the twenty-two Major Arcana cards of the Tarot deck. This association gives the individual an opportunity to learn about his or her own energy (self-expression) and how this individualized expression integrates with Universal Life Cycles. This integration will be discussed later in the article.

LIFETIME PROGRESSION CHART

The association of numbers, cyles, and Tarot cards helped me in developing a chart I call the *Lifetime Progression*. The chart was designed to enable me to view the yearly events of my life in a more meaningful context. I needed to understand why things were occurring at particular times in my life, and the chart evolved to aid this process. The meanings revealed themselves through the archetypal symbols pictured on the Tarot cards, and I related these symbols to the cycles that appeared after making the mathematical calculations.

Symbolism and the Lifetime Progression Chart

Because studying Tarot symbolism and numerological procedures led me to the discovery of the Lifetime Progression Chart, an explanation of how a symbol (a picture, an abstract symbol, or a number) conveys knowledge is important in understanding how meaning is extracted from it.

My training in art and design taught me to graphically convey a thought, idea, or concept by presenting shapes, lines, and colors in various ways. For example, one thinks of blossoms, growth, fragrance, bees, beauty, pollination, sun, photosynthesis, spring, flower boxes, fields, and so forth, when looking at the flower drawn here:

This single symbol conveys many meanings. Another application of a symbol is a company logo. These logos are designed to graphically establish a public image for the company (most people are familiar with the logo for IBM). Another type of symbol is a street address. Houses have numbers to locate them on the street. These pictures, logos, and numbers are ways to help identify a particular object and all the functions associated with that object. For example, the picture of the flower represents, externally, how it looks and, internally, how it grows; the company logo represents, externally, who the company is and, internally, what they do; and the house number represents, externally, the house that is built there and, internally, who lives there, and so on. These examples illustrate that one picture conveys both external appearances (structures) and internal happenings (functions). In the Lifetime Progression Chart I use the Tarot cards (Major Arcana cards numbered 0-21) to represent an individual's life:

Cards 1-9 represent the internal meaning. These cards symbolize how the individual relates to him/herself emotionally, mentally, perceptually, and physically.

Cards 10-18 represent the external meaning. These cards symbolize how an individual relates to the external, material, physical world.

Cards 19, 20, and 21 represent the mergence of the internal and the external. Card 19 symbolizes manifestation on a material level (body). Card 20 symbolizes manifestation on a conscious level (mind). Card 21 symbolizes manifestation on the universal level (spirit).

Studying the Major Arcana cards taught me to recognize that there is a Universal System of Cycles that supports our efforts as individuals to manifest self-expression. These universal cycles have been recorded in various ways for the movements of our planet in time (e.g., calendars, clocks, tide tables, celestial navigation, etc.). It seems natural that we as individuals fit into this scheme. For example, when a flower's seed is affected by earth, sun, and water, the interaction stimulates the flow of a life-giving force. If conditions are favorable, the flower grows. In like manner, our thoughts, emotions, or perceptions can stimulate the flow of this life-giving force (growth), or obstruct it, causing stagnation (disease).

The union of the external and the internal is a merging that creates growth (Life Force). The sun, water, and earth (the external) invites the buried seed (the internal) to grow. For us, our life events (the external) invite our thoughts, emotions, perceptions (the internal) to know, feel, and sense our ability to learn and grow. Thus, this chart is used primarily to foster an individual's awareness that his/her external life-events are directly associated with what he/she is thinking, feeling, or perceiving internally. Each of us has unique creative abilities and, through learning what these are and integrating them into our lives, we can begin living according to our natural expression (our internal creative abilities being externally applied).

Concept / Numerological Procedures of the
Lifetime Progression Chart

The Lifetime Progression Chart was inspired by the innovative perspective on Tarot developed by Angeles Arrien. She discovered what she calls the Personality, Soul, and Growth Cards which are explained below:

Personality and Soul Card(s): Arrien took the *Date of Birth* (month, day, and year), added those numbers together, and associated the reduced total (see below) with the corresponding number(s) of the Major Arcana card(s) (0-21) of the Tarot. This calculation reveals to the inquirer his/her creative abilities and natural expression. These qualities are for the inquirer to discover, utilize, and draw energy from. They are what Jack Schwartz was speaking of in the opening quote. When referring to this card or cards here, I use the term *Lifetime Cards*.

Sample Calculation:

$$\begin{array}{l} 6 \text{ Month} \\ 12 \text{ Day} \\ + \underline{1916} \text{ Year of Birth} \\ 1934 \quad = \quad 1 + 9 + 3 + 4 = (17) = 1 + 7 = 8 \end{array}$$

Add vertically, then horizontally. Calculate each year in this manner to determine the Growth Card (discussed below).

Personality Card:	(17)—the *Star* card
Soul Card:	8—the *Adjustment* card

Growth Cards: Arrien took the month, day, and *present* year, added those numbers together, and associated the reduced total with the corresponding number(s) of the Major Arcana card(s) of the Tarot. The Growth Card(s) represents the present year bringing a new life-event (Growth) that will open an awareness to the inquirer of his/her Personality and Soul Card(s).

Sample Calculation:

$$\begin{array}{l} 6 \text{ Month} \\ 12 \text{ Day} \\ + \underline{1980} \text{ \textit{Present} Year} \\ 1998 \quad = \quad 1 + 9 + 9 + 8 = (27) = 2 + 7 = 9 \end{array}$$

Add vertically, then horizontally, as above. The Growth Card for 1980 for this person is the *Hermit* card, number 9.

Because there is a direct association between the number and the Major Arcana card, when I use a particular number, I am also referring to the card, and vice versa. For example, the number 16 refers to the qualities of the *Tower* card, just as the number 7 refers to the qualities of the *Chariot* card, and so forth. On the following page is a list of Major Arcana cards (using the Aleister Crowley Tarot deck) and the possible combinations that can occur when making the above calculations.

The number in parentheses is called the *Principle* number, and the number following is called the *Support* number. When a year is represented by both a *Principle* and a *Support* number, e.g., (16)-7, the major

0 - The Fool 0-4	11 - Lust (11)-2
1 - The Magus 1, (10)-1, (19)-10-1	12 - The Hanged Man (12)-3
2 - The High Priestess 2, (11)-2, (20)-2	13 - Death (13)-4
3 - The Empress 3, (12)-3, (21)-3	14 - Art (14)-5
4 - The Emperor 4, (0)-4, (13)-4	15 - The Devil (15)-6
5 - The Hierophant 5, (14)-5	16 - The Tower (16)-7
6 - The Lovers 6, (15)-6	17 - The Star (17)-8
7 - The Chariot 7, (16)-7	18 - The Moon (18)-9
8 - The Adjustment 8, (17)-8	19 - The Sun (19)-10-1
9 - The Hermit 9, (18)-9	20 - The Aeon (20)-2
10 - The Wheel of Fortune (10)-1, (19)-10-1	21 - The Universe (21)-3

emphasis is (16)—the *Tower* card, the external, letting-go of old patterns, purification — and it is being supported by 7— the *Chariot* card, the internal, the ability to restructure, expand, move ahead.

In consultations, I have had a variety of comments from clients about their Lifetime Card(s). Some individuals identify with them; their life situations have been moderately harmonius, but they feel a need to use more of their potential as symbolized by the Major Arcana card(s). From other responses, it appears that the individuals are not living according to the symbolism of their Lifetime Card(s) and are having a difficult time experiencing their individualized self-expression. Those who are having difficulties and who choose to make some changes more consistent with their card(s) tell me that, after understanding the personal application of these symbols, events in their lives have begun to turn in a more positive direction. And others reply, "Yes, that's me."

Creating the Chart

After learning the Arrien method, I made a calculation for each year, starting with *Date of Birth* and extending through the year 2000. For very young children, the chart needs to extend much further into the future. In doing such year-by-year progressions, I noticed patterns of numbers forming, and started studying them. For a given individual, certain numbers did not appear at all, others appeared once or twice and did not appear again, some numbers appeared throughout the chart, and so forth. This study revealed cyclic patterns in the numerical sequences, the most evident being a 9-year cycle (representing "Completion") and a 10-year cycle (representing "Growth and Regeneration").

On the next page you can see how the Lifetime Progression Chart looks after the calculations are completed. Note that a year is represented by one, two, or three numbers. The 9- and 10-year cycles are also indicated. (An explanation of these two cycles follows the chart.) Each year is interpreted by the card that symbolizes that year. For example, when a 6 appears (The Lovers) it means there is an opportunity to learn about relationships; when a 7 appears (The Chariot), there is an opportunity to move ahead and to be independent.

CYCLES

Each human being has a cycle of existence (birth to death). As Spencer Lewis states:

> Everything that is in the Universe is existing and manifesting in accordance with a cycle of rhythm distinctly its own, and everything that has had a beginning or a start whereby it became a distinct entity moves forward in time in accordance with a cycle of progression distinctly its own.[2]

My observation of the 9-year cycle and the 10-year cycle in the Lifetime Progression Chart is a representation of this thought. Each year provides an opportunity to learn more of one's self.

Nine-Year Cycle—Cycle of Completion—The Hermit

Since the number 9 corresponds with the Hermit card (the card of completion), I have entitled this 9-year cycle the "Cycle of Completion." The Hermit suggests qualities of introspection, study, clarifying or completing one's own self-expression or creative abilities (being true to one's self). Starting with the date of birth, the Lifetime Card(s) repeat

LIFETIME PROGRESSION CHART

INQUIRER: Woman Born 6/ 12/16	PERSONALITY: SOUL:	17 -THE STAR 8 - ADJUSTMENT
1916 - (17)-8	1959 -	6
1917 - (18)-9	1960 -	7
1918 - (19)-10-1	9 yr 1961 -	8
1919 - (20)-2	1962 - (18)	9
1920 - (21)-3	1963 - (19)	10-1
1921 - 0-4	1964 - (20)	2
1922 - (14)-5	1965 - (21)	3
1923 - (15)-6	10 yr 1966 - 0	4
1924 - (16)-7	1967 -	5
9 yr 1925 - (17)-8	1968 -	6
10 yr 1926 - (18)-9	1969 -	7
1927 - (19)-10-1	9 yr 1970 -	8
1928 - (20)-2	1971 -	9
1929 - (21)-3	1972 - (19)	10 -1
1930 - 0-4	1973 - (20)	2
1931 - -5	1974 - (21)	3
1932 - (15)-6	1975 - 0	4
1933 - (16)-7	10 yr 1976 -	5
9 yr 1934 - (17)-8	1977 -	6
1935 - (18)-9	1978 -	7
10 yr 1936 - (19)-10-1	9 yr 1979 -	8
1937 - (20)- 2	1980 -	9
1938 - (21)- 3	1981 -	(10)-
1939 - 0 -4	1982 -	2
1940 - -5	1983 -	3
1941 - -6	1984 -	4
1942 - (16)-7	1985 -	5
9 yr 1943 - (17)-8	10 yr 1986 -	6
1944 - (18)-9	1987 -	7
1945 - (19)-10-1	9 yr 1988 -	8
10 yr 1946 - (20)-2	1989 -	9
1947 - (21)-3	1990 -	(10)-1
1948 - 0-4	1991 -	(11)-2
1949 - -5	1992 -	3
1950 - -6	1993 -	4
1951 - -7	1994 -	5
9 yr 1952 - (17)-8	1995 -	6
1953 -(18)-9	10 yr 1996 -	7
1954 - (19)-10-1	9 yr 1997 -	8
1955 - (20)-2	1998 -	9
10 yr 1956 - (21)-3	1999 -	(10)-1
1957 - 0 4	2000 -	(11)-2
1958 - 5		

every 9 years. If you were born with the Lifetime Cards (17)-8 (the Star, Adjustment), these cards would repeat (or the Supporting Number would recur) every 9 years. For example, in the previous chart, it occurs as follows:

```
1934—(17)-8
1943—(17)-8
1952—(17)-8
1961—    8
1970—    8 (and so forth)
```

Reports from clients have shown me that every 9 years, experiences occur in their lives to bring them closer to understanding their creative abilities as symbolized by the card(s). It is in the year when these Lifetime Card(s) appear that the opportunity comes for an individual to focus on him/herself. Paradoxically, clients have reported guilty feelings during this year because they thought they were being selfish or nonsocial. What was actually happening was self searching.

One example is a man born with the Lifetime Cards (18)-9, the Moon and the Hermit. The Moon (18) symbolizes romanticism, reflection, karmic relationships, fantasies, and making choices. The Hermit signifies studying, being true to one's self, introspection, completion, aloneness (privacy), and/or significant relationship.

The Data: He reported that, for him, relationships are very important, but he needs his independence within the framework of the relationship. He has an active imagination, but has a tendency to leave projects unfinished, an area he is working on. His first 9-year appears on his chart as an (18)-9. He remembers that at age 9, he did not want his schoolmates to know that his parents were divorced and that his mother worked. He was attending an exclusive school and was embarassed that he was from a broken home and did not have a Cadillac like the others. He created stories not true to his situation at the time. His second 9-year appeared as a single 9. The 18 (the Moon) did not appear. During these 9 years (ages 9-18), his mother sent him to live with his father and, since his father was a car dealer, his dream of having the newest car in town was fulfilled. The disappearance of the Moon card (18) reflected his ability to drop the fantasies and false impressions or deceptions. He now had what he wanted. He was now experiencing more of his Hermit (9) qualities. At the completion of the second 9-year cycle (age 18), he began flying lessons. It was a time to enjoy being alone. His flying career is bringing him much satisfaction.

The system of Lifetime Progressions reveals this kind of information and provides a framework for the individual to find meaning in cycles or progressions of past events and to see their possible effects in the present. Another short example:

> **The Data :** *A woman at the completion of her second 9-year cycle graduated from high school, married, and became a secretary. At the completion of her third 9-year cycle, she divorced and decided to move to California to start a new career. Her Lifetime number is 7—the Chariot, symbolizing independence, change of living environment, free choice, career changes, self-expansion, and restructuring."*

All these changes were very positive for both people. Now they can understand the rhythm of these events, and know more of why they were compelled to follow these natural expressions of themselves.

Ten-Year Cycle—Cycle of Growth and Regeneration— The Wheel of Fortune

The number 10 corresponds to the Wheel of Fortune card. The Wheel of Fortune brings change, abundance, prosperity, and the ability to stand steady through cycle changes. It is the first card that offers an external awareness, and is another expression of number 1, The Magus (because 10 = 1 + 0 = 1), which represents internal awareness. The number 10 reveals to us the great Pythagorean truth that all things in Nature are regenerated through the decade. Pythagoras also taught that the number 10 is the archetype of the universe, and that it encompasses all arithmetic and harmonic proportions.[3] Thus, I call these 10 years the "Cycle of Growth and Regeneration."

By starting with the *Date of Birth* and counting 1 through 10, beginning with the first birthday, every tenth year the number increases by 1. For example, if the Lifetime Card is 5 (the Hierophant), the first 10-year cycle will end on a 6 (the Lovers) and the second 10-year cycle will end on a 7 (the Chariot), thus indicating a progression. Therefore, the 10-year cycle (the Wheel of Fortune) teaches self-realization on all levels, reveals new skills, shows how to handle change, and increases awareness and desire to turn our experience in more positive, prosperous, and fortunate directions. The card that corresponds with the last year in the 10-year cycle symbolizes the type of experience that is bringing this awareness of growth.

The basic 9- and 10-year structure of the Lifetime Progression Chart demonstrates there is a need to complete projects, ideas, concepts, (9—the Hermit) for growth and expansion (10—the Wheel of Fortune) to occur. Another use for the chart is to help objectify certain qualities or aspects (such as relationships, work, etc.) of life.

The Individual Years

An inquirer was interested in looking at her relationship patterns. We decided to look at the years in which the 6 card (The Lovers) appeared. We discovered the following:

The year 1957 (age 2) was too early for any recognition of what was happening at that time. She remembers that in 1966 there was group or peer pressure in the form of a group of friends putting her down, and in 1975 (age 20), she had been in a love relationship that was ending, while at the same time she began therapy, turning her attention to her own internal (feelings, thoughts, perceptions) relationship—how she saw herself.

Each of the number 6 years (the Lovers) expressed some aspect of her awareness of relationships that was following a natural state of maturity or growth. All the other cards can also be used in this way to observe the progression of a particular aspect of one's life.

INTERPRETATION OF LIFETIME PROGRESSION CHART

The chart on pages 98 and 99, "Qualities or Aspects of Life Symbolized by the Major Arcana Cards," is used to interpret the Lifetime Progression Chart. The chart defines what the cards symbolize. It is a compendium of my research and that of others; as more research is completed, the symbolism will reveal more qualities consistent with the changes of society.

Techniques for Using the "Qualities or Aspects of Life" Chart

1. Select a year you want to look at on the Lifetime Progression Chart.
2. Note the number that is calculated for that year.
3. Find that number on the Qualities or Aspects of Life Chart.
4. Read the qualities or aspects represented by the number/card.

The Lifetime Progression Chart maps out when these qualities or aspects enter and leave. Study the sample chart: note that in 1932, the

QUALITIES OR ASPECTS OF LIFE
SYMBOLIZED BY THE MAJOR ARCANA CARDS
(Using Aleister Crowley Tarot Deck)

No.	Card	Qualities or Aspects of Life
0	Fool	Starting a new adventure, courage, manifestation, breakthrough on fear, peak experiences, state of consciousness before birth and after death.

INTERNAL

No.	Card	Qualities or Aspects of Life
1	Magus	Communication, developed skills and gifts, the need for expression.
2	High Priestess	Desire for balance, intuition develops, independence, self-nurturing (taking care of oneself).
3	Empress	Emotional clarity, love of creative expression, motherhood issues, heart-mind union.
4	Emperor	Establish foundation for self, new direction, authority (either giving or receiving), leadership, fatherhood issues, major move.
5	Hierophant	Learning/teaching (either school or life situations), music, resolving family issues, application of creative projects or ideas.
6	Lovers	Relationships, individual or group, awareness of relating patterns and polarities.
7	Chariot	Change of living environment, independence, free choice, career changes, self-expansion, restructuring.
8	Adjustment	Balancing opposing forces, fairness issues, legal matters, sensory awareness, health, finances.
9	Hermit	Introspection, completion, being true to oneself, studying, significant relationship or privacy.

QUALITIES OR ASPECTS OF LIFE
SYMBOLIZED BY THE MAJOR ARCANA CARD
(continued)

EXTERNAL

10	**Wheel of Fortune**	Changes, learning to stand steady through cycle changes, brings abundance, prosperity, awareness toward more positive direction.
11	**Lust**	Handling the beast within (being in control of mind, emotions, and body), inner strength, seeing the multi-faceted creativity in life.
12	**Hanged Man**	Past unresolved experiences revealed to be resolved, desire for new perspectives, surrender.
13	**Death**	Rebirth, transformation, metamorphosis.
14	**Art**	Creativity, integration, consummation, relationships.
15	**Devil**	Developing a sense of humor, sensuality and sexuality issues, creating more stability.
16	**Tower**	Purification, cleansing, self-realization, letting go of old patterns, health.
17	**Star**	Self-esteem, self, and external recognition.
18	**Moon**	Karmic relationships, fantasies, making choices, romanticism.

MERGENCE

19	**Sun**	Co-partner situation, money issues involved, expressing creativity, body awareness.
20	**Aeon**	Past understanding creates new future, breakthrough on judgment issues, mental awareness, birth.
21	**Universe**	Completion, major move in consciousness, applying knowledge of universal awareness (i.e., solar energy, wind energy, etc.).

numbers (15)-6, the Devil and the Lovers, respectively, appear. Then, in 1941 (9 years later—the Cycle of Completion), the 15 (the Devil) disappears and the 6 (the Lovers) appears alone. By studying the significance of the number/card which appears each year, the inquirer then learns what experiences are benefiting him/her the most in that year, which ones have already entered and left, and which ones are coming into his/her life.

TAROT'S SEVEN STEPS TO MANIFESTATION WHEEL

Thus far, I have described a system that reveals to an individual his/her natural expression and creative abilities, and have introduced the concept that each year brings an opportunity to learn more about one's self. To integrate the knowledge learned from the Lifetime Progression Chart and the Qualities or Aspects of Life Chart with the universal cycles, I developed the following chart, called "Tarot's Seven Steps to Manifestation Wheel." It maps out the step-by-step universal laws of the Major Arcana cards 0-21. This wheel symbolizes an order that promotes the manifestation of a creative act. My main belief is that the actions we perform (Lifetime Progression) are based upon an act of creativity (Tarot's Seven Steps to Manifestation Wheel). The actions may be completed (manifestation); they may be aborted; or they may be blocked, creating difficulties (lessons) to overcome. The Major Arcana cards as shown in this wheel are one way to symbolize this act of creativity.

The wheel illustrates the Seven Steps to Manifestation[4] and the three numbers/cards corresponding with each of the seven steps. Each step is represented by the three number/cards. Then each one of the three number/cards has its own focus, which is listed on the Qualities of Aspects of Life Chart.

1. Asking, Seeking	1—Magus	4—Emperor	7—Chariot
2. Receiving, Knowledge	2—Priestess	5—Hierophant	8—Adjustment
3. Deciding, Choosing	3—Empress	6—Lovers	9—Hermit
4. Transforming, Clarifying	10—Wheel of Fortune	13—Death	16—Tower
5. Self-recognition	11—Lust	14—Art	17—Star
6. Testing	12—Hanged Man	15—Devil	18—Moon
7. Manifestation	19—Sun	20—Aeon	21—Univers

The wheel also illustrates the type of energy cycle for each number/card: active, passive, or union.

Active	Passive	Union
1	2	3
4	5	6
7	8	9
10	11	12
13	14	15
16	17	18
19	20	21

The triad principle (active, passive, union) is a reminder that when the world is perceived in a three-step manner (actively, passively, and from a point of union—active and passive combined), it allows an individual to move through changes in a balanced way, knowing all alternatives.

When used as a reference, the Seven Steps to Manifestation Wheel indicates what type of change is occurring (one of the seven steps) and how that change can best be experienced (active, passive, union).

Technique for Using the Tarot's Seven Steps to Manifestation Wheel

1. Select a year you want to look at on the Lifetime Progression Chart. Note the number.

2. Find the number/card on the Qualities or Aspects of Life Chart. Review the symbolism of the number/card.

3. Find the number/card on the Tarot's Seven Steps to Manifestation Wheel. Note which of the seven steps corresponds to that number/card. This represents the type of change that is occurring (i.e., asking, seeking; testing, experimentation; transforming, clarifying; and so forth). Next, note which energy cycle is best suited for the number/card (i.e., active, passive or union).

I use the two charts described above as tools to move into and out of experience. the following is a sample interpretation from a consultation session:

Data: A woman is feeling frustrated. We looked at the current year, which was a number 5. She reported that she was doing a lot of teaching and being very active. We looked at the Tarot's Seven Steps of Manifestation Wheel to see what type of change the number 5 symbolizes. We found that it represents a year where an individual would be experiencing receptivity and knowledge. We discussed this and found that even though teaching takes a dynamic action (giving instruction), the basic structure behind that is a receptive one (first, studying and research provide the knowledge that is needed to teach). Then we noticed that the energy cycle most beneficial to the number 5 is a passive cycle. She then mentioned that she would focus on the receptivity of this experience (number 5) and see if it would lessen the frustration she had been feeling.

Another example follows:

Data: *A woman was laid off from her job. We looked at the Manifestation Wheel to see what type of change was present. She was moving from a (10)-1 year into an (11)-2 year. She was leaving an active cycle, where she had been transforming and seeking.*

Situation: *She had changed jobs, moved to a new apartment, and had stopped therapy.*

She was entering a passive cycle, (11)-2, that was to emphasize self-realization and receiving knowledge.

Response: *She was laid off from her job, but she realized she was not suited to that type of work. She had chosen not to seek employment but to be independent (the number 2, High Priestess energy) and to take a few months to explore new creative areas she found interesting (the number 11, energy of the Lust card).*

After the consultation, the inquirer seemed relieved to know the type of change and cycle she was experiencing. She also felt she could take advantage of making this change. The change seemed natural for her, and she was looking forward to it.

A NEW PERSPECTIVE

Research on Tarot led me to study the culture of Ancient Egypt, and I found that Egypt's basic philosophy was one of growth, change, and enrichment.[5] I feel that by making the necessary changes in our lives to find balance and harmony, our life experiences teach us the extremes; and by knowing the extremes, we are able to center ourselves again. I have presented this material to provide a tool for recognizing change and accepting its advantages. This acceptance of change provides the opportunity for an individual to learn about self-expression and to know that he/she is integrated with the Universal Life Cycles.

A blank Lifetime Progression Chart follows for you to calculate your Lifetime Progression. See the Qualities or Aspects of Life Chart and the Tarot's Seven Steps to Manifestation Wheel for interpretive guidance.

LIFETIME PROGRESSION CHART

1900 =	=	1946 =	=	1992 =	=	1997 =	=
1901 =	=	1947 =	=	1993 =	=	1998 =	=
1902 =	=	1948 =	=	1994 =	=	1999 =	=
1903 =	=	1949 =	=	1995 =	=	2000 =	=
1904 =	=	1950 =	=	1996 =	=		
1905 =	=	1951 =	=				
1906 =	=	1952 =	=				
1907 =	=	1953 =	=				
1908 =	=	1954 =	=				
1909 =	=	1955 =	=				
1910 =	=	1956 =	=				
1911 =	=	1957 =	=				
1912 =	=	1958 =	=				
1913 =	=	1959 =	=	Date of Birth:_____			
1914 =	=	1960 =	=				
1915 =	=	1961 =	=				
1916 =	=	1962 =	=	Personality:_____			
1917 =	=	1963 =	=				
1918 =	=	1964 =	=				
1919 =	=	1965 =	=	Soul:_____			
1920 =	=	1966 =	=				
1921 =	=	1967 =	=				
1922 =	=	1968 =	=				
1923 =	=	1969 =	=				
1924 =	=	1970 =	=				
1925 =	=	1971 =	=	**Calculation:**			
1926 =	=	1972 =	=				
1927 =	=	1973 =	=	_____ Month			
1928 =	=	1974 =	=				
1929 =	=	1975 =	=	_____ Day			
1930 =	=	1976 =	=				
1931 =	=	1977 =	=	_____ Year			
1932 =	=	1978 =	=				
1933 =	=	1979 =	=	_____ Total			
1934 =	=	1980 =	=				
1935 =	=	1981 =	=				
1936 =	=	1982 =	=	___+___+___+___=___			
1937 =	=	1983 =	=				
1938 =	=	1984 =	=				
1939 =	=	1985 =	=				
1940 =	=	1986 =	=				
1941 =	=	1987 =	=				
1942 =	=	1988 =	=				
1943 =	=	1989 =	=				
1944 =	=	1990 =	=				
1945 =	=	1991 =	=				

You will find other similar theories based on 7: the Seven Rays, the Principle of Creativity, seven days of creation, Pythagoras' seven celestial beings, and more as you research the significance of 7.

An interesting correspondence which I discovered when last reading about Egypt was the close similarity of each dynasty to each of the Major Arcana cards. Was Ancient Egypt following the path of The Fool (0) to self-discovery?

NOTES

Schwarz, Jack. *Human Energy Systems*, N. Y. Dutton.

Lewis H. Spencer. *Self-Mastery and Fate with the Cycles of Life*, Jan Jose, CA: AMORC, 1986.

Hall, Manly P. *The Secret Teachings of All Ages*, Los Angeles: Philosophical Research Society, 1978.

The Court Cards

Nature's Archetypes

Gary Ross

O■O■O■O■O■O■O■O■O■O■O■O■O■O

The Court Cards of the Tarot traditionally represent various human personality types, in keeping with their zodiacal assignations. But above and beyond this, they are *elemental archetypes* ; they are linked to a broad spectrum of natural forces.

It was Aleister Crowley, in his masterful *Book of Thoth,* who first identified certain of the Court Cards with elemental forces such as lightning and rain. But, as usual, he was content to merely drop a few casual hints and leave his readers to work out the correspondences on their own. This article attempts to spell out these correspondences in greater detail, to rescue these vital and compelling aspects of the Court Cards from their dismal history of oblivion and neglect.

Each of the Court Cards represents several distinct facets and manifestations of Nature. These are the elemental archetypes: the lightning, the rain, the river, the sea, the mountain, the cloud, the desert, and the wind. Seeing the cards in these terms brings them to life. It opens up new levels of meaning and allows them to mirror the elemental aspects of our own natures.

Ever wake up in the morning feeling languid as a lagoon? Fresh as a flower? Dry as a desert sandstorm? With the drums of the jungle pulsing in your blood? Ever talk to someone whose head was in a cloud? Who was surrounded by "mist-ery"? Who had thunder in his voice and lightning in his eyes? Just as the mythic and religious archetypes of the Major Arcana define the human psyche and allow us glimpses of our higher selves, so do the elemental archetypes of the Court Cards reveal to us our *natural* selves—the parts of us that partake of the powers of the elements, and are rooted in the prehistoric harmonies of primitive life. The Court Cards are the cauldrons in which the human psyche and the forces of Nature are blended. They provide deep insights into our own connectedness to the natural work.

Think of the Tarot as a campfire, ablaze in a clearing in a dark forest. At first it is only a light seen from afar. As we draw closer, it captures our interest more fully. It warms and stimulates us. There is a world of fascination in the flickering flames. The wind shifts. We are obliged to approach from a different perspective to avoid being blinded by smoke screens. Now at last the flames have subsided to a bed of glowing coals, and we may harness their power, grill a fresh trout, and wash it all down with cold mountain water (or a cool Chardonnay, if we have come prepared).

The four elements—Fire, Water, Air, and Earth—appear in the Tarot as Wands, Cups, Swords, and Disks, and manifest their individual powers and properties through the deck as a whole. The Tarot has the power to illuminate, to shed light (Fire). Its pageant of shifting patterns and parade of emotional imagery partakes of the fluidity of Water. Its lofty abstractions, its symbols and smokescreens, its power to "blow your mind" are all Airy qualities. Finally, Tarot has the power to enrich us, to affect our lives. It feeds the mind and nourishes the soul. This is its Earthy quality.

In giving a Tarot reading, the truths symbolized by the cards (Fire) are filtered through the perceptions and emotional nature of the individual reader (Water), producing a material (Earth) result—the reading—and an ethereal (Air) result—the effect that the reading has on the thought processes of the persons involved. In putting out a campfire, the blending of fire and water is far less harmonious, but the end results are the same—material (ashes) and ethereal (a cloud of smoke). In going on a honeymoon, the union of male and female principles often produces a material result, delivered nine months later, and an ethereal result—love—which is enjoyed immediately. All of these examples illustrate a basic process of Nature: the union of an active seed principle with a receptive energy field will produce twin offspring—a material result and an ethereal result. This, in simplified form, is the formula of Tetragrammaton.

The Court Cards of the Tarot are the result of the blending of the formula of Tetragrammaton with the traditional symbolism of the zodiac and the four elements. The relationship of Knight to Queen to Prince to Princess is based wholly on the Tetragrammaton. Thus, some knowledge of this formula is essential to a complete understanding of the Court Cards.[1]

TETRAGRAMMATON AND THE FOUR ELEMENTS

Each of the four elements represents a specific energy field. Fire refers to spiritual energy, Water to emotional energy, Air to the mental realm, Earth to the Physical realm. But to see the elements in these terms alone is to see them only as static and inert *nouns*. In their dynamic and creative aspects, the elements also function as *verbs*, and each represents a specific activity: Fire, initiating; Water, receiving; Air, spreading out; Earth, stabilizing. These dynamic aspects (activity-receptivity-diffusion-stability) describe *patterns of relationship*; the static aspects describe the *realms of energy* in which the relationships occur.

The ancient Hebrew Qabalists devised a simple and useful formula to sum up these relationships. This is the formula of Tetragrammaton, made up of *four* (tetra) Hebrew *letters* (gramma): YHVH or *Yod-He-Vau-He*. These letters represent the ideas of Father, Mother, Son, and Daughter, which personify the dynamic verb-aspects of Fire, Water, Air, and Earth.

Father and Mother represent the active-passive, yin-yang, plus-minus dichotomy— the basic duality underlying our existence on this planet. The union of plus and minus is a *perfect* union, because Plus One and Minus One cancel out and equal Zero the Fool, which contains all dualities in latent form, and is thus the womb of all Creation, possessed of unlimited potential for manifestation.

For this reason, the union of Father and Mother can also produce a third thing unlike either of them—but this issue will also have two aspects, ethereal and material, thus restating the original duality in altered form. This is the advance into manifestation and matter—the Son and Daughter, corresponding to Air and Earth. The Son and Daughter are personified as Twins. This is an apt commentary on the interfacing of the world of thought (Air) and the world of physical reality (Earth).

It is also significant that the Mother and the Daughter are represented by the same letter, *He*. This implies that the Daughter will herself become a Mother, so that the entire system will be a self-sustaining cycle rather than a sterile dead-end progression.

The noun-aspects of the four elements are represented in the Tarot as Wands, Cups, Swords, and Disks. The formula of Tetragrammaton deals with the dynamic verb-aspects of the elements by calling them Father, Mother, Son, and Daughter. When these ideas are added to the four suits of the Tarot, they become Knight, Queen, Prince, and Princess—the Court Cards.

On a purely elemental level, the four Court titles are associated with the fiery, watery, airy, and earthy aspects of the element associated with their suit. For example, Knight of Wands represents the fiery part of Fire, the flames which transmute and destroy. Queen of Wands, the watery part of fire, its fluid motion, its power to create images, its colorful and hypnotic quality. Prince of Wands, the airy part of Fire, the *fuel* of fire, source of its warmth and heat.

By examining these subdivisions of the four elements in light of the formula of Tetragrammaton, and considering any relevant zodiacal correspondences, we are able to discover many fascinating aspects of these complex and multi-faceted cards.

THE ELEMENTAL ARCHETYPES

1. *Knight of Wands* is Aries; he rules the last decan of Scorpio and the first two decans of Sagittarius (Nov. 10-Dec. 10). He symbolizes lightning—a blast of raw power that vanishes as quickly as it appears, leaving conflagration in its wake. He embodies the initiatory aggressiveness of the Ram of Aries. He is a revolutionary, a "firebrand," the spark that touches things off. Yet, on the Tree of Life, the Aries Path of the Emperor is the path of Vision. Thus, the Knight of Wands is a visionary. His aggressive powers are brought to bear in the spiritual realm of Sagittarius. The result is spiritual illumination and high visionary experience. The lightning flash has long been a symbol of this type of spiritual insight.

The Knight of Wands is closely linked to Trump XVI, the lightning-struck Tower. Both are symbols of fire in its most destructive aspect. But destruction here is also purification. Outmoded structures are being torn down at the behest of a new vision, and obsolete deadwood now feeds the flames of a higher endeavor.

In the natural world, the violent and fiery nature of the Knight finds expression in landscapes such as lava flows and the burning Sahara. The essence of this Knight is a violent and short-lived burst of powerful energy, such as an explosion or a volcanic eruption. For this reason, it can also symbolize the explosive feeling-energy of the moment of orgasm—another form of spiritual illumination—and the releasing of the spark or seed of a new life.

2. *Queen of Wands* is Sagittarius; she rules the last decan of Pisces and the first two decans of Aries (March 10-April 10). The Queen of

Wands is a dancer, relaxed and graceful, sleek and supple as a leopard. She is completely tuned into her growth energies and completely at home in her body.

If the Knight of Wands is orgasm, the Queen of Wands is afterglow. She is a crimson cloudbank resplendent in the last rays of the setting sun. She embodies all of the hypnotic fascination and colorful beauty of dancing flames, while yet remaining aloof and apart from them. One might say that she is the fluid grace of motion and color that fire exhibits, rather than fire in any of its other aspects.

As the watery part of Fire, the Queen of Wands symbolizes the rainbow, a traditional Sagittarian emblem and spiritual signpost. Also, she rules the vernal equinox, and thus symbolizes the secret fires of growth energy—the energy of plants and trees, shooting forth in the electric Queen are manifested at the autumn equinox as well, in dazzling clouds of rainbow foliage, delighting all who see.

The Knight and Queen of Wands represent the powers of the desert. In its harshness and violence, the desert exhibits the powers of the Knight—in darkness, when the sky is split by multiple bolts of lightning, or in daylight, when the parched earth shimmers in feverish mirage. In its soft colorful beauty, the desert exhibits the powers of the Queen: the rainbow after the midday storm, the glorious conflagration of sunrise and sunset, cacti blooming in the spring—all exemplify what the Queen represents. She is ruler of the windswept oceans of sand, the frozen seas of color and mud, where power sleeps in silent cities sculpted by wind and time, and walks the night in deserted valleys.

3. *Prince of Wands* is Leo; he rules the last decan of Cancer and the first two decans of Leo (July 10-August 10). He represents the sunlight, a steady balanced energy which sustains our world. He is Photon, the prime mover, light of every star. He represents life energy in its finest and most pervasive form. We are all luminous beings, and the Prince of Wands represents the primordial orgone energy that illuminates and enlivens us.

If the Knight of Wands is the raw blazing Sahara sands, the Prince is the more mellowed magnificence of the African veldt, basking in regal splendor under the noonday sun. He is the power of the lion and the light. Therefore, he is brilliant, daring, courageous, headstrong and hot-tempered. Creativity and power are the hallmarks of the Prince of Wands. Activity and effectiveness are his essence.

4. *Princess of Wands,* like the other Princesses, has no zodiacal assignation. She represents the final issue of the energies contained in the Knight, Queen and Prince. She is the Queen in a fertilized and more concrete form. Like the Queen, the Princess rules the transition between seasons, but partakes of the seasonal energies of her Prince. Thus, the Princess of Wands represents summer giving way to autumn.

As the earthy part of fire, the Princess of Wands represents the fuel of fire. She feeds the flames through her willingness to combine and freedom to become involved. Her nature is warmth, her essence is heat, and the field of natural activity that she symbolizes is sex.

Leaping force, fire, and languid luxury are combined in the character of the Princess of Wands. She is ruler of the jungle, where power pads softly through the lush and fragrant night, eyes blazing yellow in quest of blood. She is Amazon, beautiful and terrible, obeying no laws but her own. She is Congo, pulsing in ancient rhythms, wild and untrammeled. As the Knight and Queen represent the desert, so do the Prince and Princess represent the jungle. Yet here, the color and beauty, the pomp and magnificence of animal and tribal cultures are the domain of the Prince. The violence and mystery and primitive savagery are the domain of the spitfire Princess.

Yet, in counterpoint to the unbridled jungle blood ferocity of heat, the Princess embodies equally the tenderness of warmth, manifesting in Nature as naked bodies entwining on furs near roaring fireplaces. The common denominator in these seemingly disparate domains of experience is *depth of involvement.* Love and fury are linked thereby, and are worlds removed from apathy and indifference. Thus, love and death are united in the character of the Princess of Wands.

5. *Knight of Cups* is Cancer; he rules the last decan of Aquarius and the first two decans of Pisces (Feb. 10-Mar. 10). The Knight of Cups is the fiery part of Water, which is manifested as sunlight sparkling on a watery surface. He is an expression of the surface, whereas the Queen is an expression of the depths. The fiery part of Water is also manifested as *water in motion.* The Knight represents the following aquaticisms:

A. Waves—The swell of the surf, sparkling in the sunlight, breaks into a roaring, hissing avalanche of charging white horses. This is the prime oceanic expression of the Knight of Cups, patron saint of surfers. The power and turbulence of the surf is embodied in the Knight as the power of emotional stimulation. The surf's ebb and flow is governed by the Moon, ruling planet of Cancer, the cardinal

Water sign, which in turn rules Trump VII, The Chariot of the body. In corporeal terms, ocean waves become waves of pleasurable feeling streaming through the organism. Thus, where the Knight of Wands represents the explosive quality of orgasm, the Knight of Cups represents the waves of sensation triggered by such release. Surf's up!

B. *Waterfalls*—Anyone who has visited the mountains during snowmelt knows the thunderous power of the swollen rivers, sweeping away the accumulated debris of winter. This is the power of the Knight of Cups, who achieves emotional cleansing through turbulent expression. A concentrated and individualized form of the power of the surf, waterfalls occur in the directed channel of a river's flow. In loftier waterfalls, the river expands into comet-like streamers and innumerable droplets of spray, creating, especially when fired by sunlight, a riveting spectacle analagous to the charisma of that scintillating peacock, the Knight. The tumultuous chargings and giddy plummetings of waterfalls are expressions of the intense purifying power of emotional stimulation symbolized by the Knight of Cups.

C. *Rain*—Each droplet a charging horse and rider, the rain washes away impurities and nourishes the Earth. In corporeal terms, raindrops are the equivalent of teardrops. This refers to the power of a good cry—a healing and purifying emotional catharsis. Like rain, the ability to experience and express one's sadness is "a grace descended from Heaven." This is the soft and gentle aspect of the Knight of Cups.

D. *Springs*—The bubbling up of water from subterranean sources is analogous to *inspiration*, an essential ingredient of the activity of the Knight of Cups. His emotional reservoirs are continually replenished by the free-flowing wellsprings of his link with the Queen, guardian of the deeps.

6. *Queen of Cups* is Pisces; she rules the last decan of Gemini and the first two decans of Cancer (June 10-July 10). The Queen represents the depth and stillness of water, its tranquil receptivity and power of reflection. She is the lake that mirrors the ever-changing patterns of sun and sky. She is a starlit mere that mirrors the depths of the Universe in profound and breathless waters.

Because she is Pisces, guardian of the deeps, the Queen of Cups is sovereign of dreams, those phantasmal reflections of our emotional lives. The dreamlife, acting as a mirror of the psyche, is sometimes the source of great creative inspiration. Thus, it too exemplifies the qualities of receptivity and reflection, hallmarks of the Queen of Cups.

Pisces is, of course, the sign of the fish, which alone can explore the deeps of ocean or lake unaided. The fish is thus a metaphor for the psychic *voyageur*, and the Queen of Cups is a symbol of psychic power: telepathy, clairvoyance, and other functions dependent upon a high degree of receptivity.

Another aspect of the fish is that it has free access to the bottom of its lake. This is significant because the holy lotus flower has its roots in the mud at the bottom of its pool. The fish who feeds from this level immerses itself in the Primal Pain Pool (another aspect of the Queen)— a reservoir of suppressed emotion that colors the self-expression of the consciously functioning human. This stagnant water breeds hordes of psychic mosquitoes and webs of Piscean illusion—but "still waters run deep," and the submarine muck below may also harbor the "Pearl of Great Price," a treasure lying dormant in the watery deeps, disclosed by well-placed depth charges.

Pisces is ruled by the Moon, and the reflection of this celestial pearl in lakes and ponds is a direct experience of the mystic beauty of the Queen of Cups. Moonlit waves express the blending of this beauty with the oceanic power of the Knight.

The landscape most representative of the Queen of Cups is the Boundary Waters canoe country of Southern Canada and northern Minnesota, the "Land of 10,000 Lakes." The largest lakes, such as the Great Bear and Great Slave Lakes of Northern Canada and our own Great Lakes, are inland seas and are more properly the domain of the Princess. All of these lakes are glacial remnants—and the glacier, possessed of the power to move mountains, is another expression of the fiery, active part of Water, the Knight of Cups.

7. *Prince of Cups* is Scorpio; he rules the last decan of Libra and the first two decans of Scorpio (Oct. 10-Nov. 10). The airy part of Water is expressed as the *flow*, as of a river, and also as the fog, composed of minute droplets. The character of the Prince of Cups is that of a mighty river flowing under cover of fog and darkness. This is entirely in keeping with the secretive nature of Scorpio.

More than any other form of water, a river is an analogy for the course of a human life. It is a journey through calm tranquility and turbulent uproar, culminating in a final union with the sea. This is exactly the position of the Prince of Cups. Yet there is an added dimension of mystery and ethereal power—the Fog. This represents the human capacity for mystical experience—the transmutation of corporeal experience into archetype and abstraction. It is as though one were at once conscious of the totality of the river, from beginning to end, instead of journeying down it bit by bit.

Eagle, Snake, and Scorpion—the three aspects of Scorpio—lend their powers to the Prince of Cups. The Eagle is exaltation; the Snake, passion; and the Scorpion, death—the latter manifesting as the deeps of autumn and the ghosts of Halloween. Death is also the point at which totality of the river becomes visible. Eagle and Snake allude to the human capacity for transcendent exaltation through fully experienced sexuality—the experience of oceanic merging and bliss.

8. *Princess of Cups* is Xeno, Goddess of Mystery. She represents the Ocean, final repository of all the waters of the Earth. She is mysterious because of her vast scope, and infinitely beautiful in her variety. All of the lands that fringe the sea are expressions of her essence. But the earthy part of Water is also expressed several other ways:

A. *Icecaps*—The energies of Water and Earth are combined in solidified water, or ice. Thus does Xeno partake of the otherworldly beauty of the Antarctic. Hers is the beauty of the icebergs aglow in twilight oceans, of blue and green caverns under mighty glaciers. Hers is the power of *crystallization*, giving form and substance to the flow of feeling, freezing the flood of time into crystals—the jewel-like essence of a single moment. Thus, Xeno is inspiration to the poet or visionary artist seeking to capture the essence of what is perceived. Her icy aspect is also in keeping with the part of the year she rules—autumn giving way to winter.

B. *Rainforests*—The earthy part of Water is expressed by the lush coastal rainforests and redwood jungles, dependent upon the fog and the sea for their life's blood. Their verdant, overpowering beauty is another expression of the oceanic nature of Xeno.

C. *Dew*—The freshness and beauty of dew is the very essence of Xeno, whose "eyes are the dewdrops sipped from the lawn by the songbirds that warble her songs to the dawn." Hers is the dewy-eyed rapture of the eternal romantic.

D. *Lagoons*—The Princess as a fertilized and irradiated form of the

Queen. While a landlocked lagoon is properly in the Queen's domain, a lagoon that is fed by the sea, as is the case on many tropical islands, partakes of the larger oceanic life of Xeno. "Lagoons" also imply the shallow reaches of the ocean, as opposed to the dark depths represented by the Queen. This includes the kelp beds, undersea gardens, and coral reefs—all forms of the earthy part of Water, all partaking of the strange and exotic beauty of Xeno.

E. *Islands*—Hundreds of thousands of islands punctuate the monotony of the sea, and each is unique in some respect. The smaller the island, the more it is merely an earthy part of the surrounding waters, ruled wholly by the sea. In their great variety and exotic beauty, islands are expressions of Xeno, ranging from balmy tropical gardens to wavelashed and weatherbeaten rocks. Most are visited chiefly by birds rather than humans, and all are more or less mysterious.

F. *Dolphins*—Dolphins and all other forms of marine life are solidifications of water for the purpose of the full expression and experience of the variety and beauty of Xeno.

G. *Humans*—The human body is made up chiefly of water, and although "no man is an island," there are certain similarities. Humans are mysterious, and each one is unique. Xeno is humanity, both individually and collectively. Think of the vast ocean of dreaming organisms that cover the surface of our planet. Think of the cities of concrete and coral on land and on sea. Look out over the land and see the vast populated sprawl—hills and valleys inundated with a flood of living, dreaming protoplasm. Xeno is the ocean of humanity, the Sea of Dreams. Xeno is oceanic consciousness, finding expression in millions of variegated and dreaming aspects. Some are islands, some are dolphins, some are humans—and some are birds.

9. *Knight of Swords* is Libra; he rules the last decan of Taurus and the first two decans of Gemini (May 10-June 10). As the fiery part of Air, the Knight of Swords represents air in motion—the wind. He is especially symbolic of the North Wind—cold, relentless, and powerful. The fiery part of Air also manifests as the comet, and as the aurora borealis or northern lights.

The realm of Air is the realm of the mind. The power of the wind is the power of Air that is moving in a given direction. Thus, the Knight of Swords represents directed mental power. He is persistent and penetrating, fresh and invigorating. His is the purity and intensity of the strong cold wind that banishes all traces of atmospheric haze until the world shines forth in sparkling clarity. His consciousness is a web of icy diamonds glittering high in the stratosphere. His is the power and the mystical beauty of the high cirrus clouds that are splashed across the sky in tenuous and rarefied arabesques, alight with the fires of brilliance. But the power of the Knight is a *directed* power: the cryptic horses of his genius are harnessed by determination and purity of intention, resulting in tremendous mental strength—power that cuts right to the bone, and is worlds removed from the airy labyrinths of abstraction to which genius is often prone.

The rarefied fires of the Knight of Swords are suitably symbolic of the realm of electronics and the awesome though limited brilliance of the computer. It may seem strange to suggest man-made electronic intelligence as a manifestation of the natural world. Yet, what is man if not a natural force? Furthermore, this galaxy may well be inhabited by certain noncorporeal electronic intelligences unspawned by human hands. Advanced research in quantum physics postulates discarnate collective mind at work on the frontiers of atomic consciousness. Now we are confronted with the Crack Between the Worlds, opening and expelling the raging winds of Nagual. At this rarefied level, the Knight of Swords represents that which infuses twilight winds with power beyond our ken (". . . in the twilight, there is no *wind* . . . [T]here is *only* power," cackles Don Juan).[2]

The Knight of Swords in its most basic form represents motion through space—the winds of becoming, as measured by time. At this level, as the fiery part of Air in its most refined form, the Knight of Swords is Electron, counterpart of Photon, the Prince of Wands. Photon illumines what Electron moves. Yet Photon and not Electron is Prime Mover; for Electron is inanimate, negatively charged primal wind, and Photon is orgone, force of life—the living light of every star. Thus, the connection between Libra and Leo, which is demonstrated by the occasional transposition of Trumps VIII and XI in the Major Arcana, is corroborated on this elemental and primordial level.

10. *Queen of Swords* is Gemini; she rules the last decan of Virgo and the first two decans of Libra (Sept 10 - Oct. 10). As the watery part of Air, the Queen of Swords represents the ocean of atmosphere (derived from the Greek *atmos*, meaning "vapor") which envelops our planet. She has been cleansed and purified by the power of the Knight. Thus, her

attributes are clarity and limitless visibility. On a mental level, this reflects the ability to see through smoke screens and perceive things as they are. But this is only half of the dual nature of the Gemini Queen. Her nature is to perceive things clearly and then to *transmit* them clearly and consciously. The watery part of Air manifests in the form of *waves* — sound waves, particularly radio waves, which show the Queen functioning as a synaptic link in the electronic networks of the Knight.

Because she is Atmosphere, the Queen of Swords contains both Photon and Electron. Irradiated by sunlight, she is an orgone ocean of life's breath. Yet she is wedded to the Knight, Electron, creator of the inorganic oceans of the atom. The complex interrelationship of the Prince of Wands and the Knight and Queen of Swords is a metaphysical spiderweb of great subtlety, one that can shine forth in full beauty only when jeweled by the dew of the meditation of each individual mind. A further clue to the relationship between the Knight and the Queen (atmosphere and atmosphere) is to be found in analysis of the root words *atom* (derived from the Greek *atomos*, meaning "uncut") and *atman*, the Sanskrit "breath of soul," meaning the *individual* soul; or, as *Atman*, the Universal Soul, *source* of all individual souls.

11. *Prince of Swords* is Aquarius; he rules the last decan of Capricorn and the first two decans of Aquarius (Jan 10-Feb. 10). This Prince presents paradox: he is the airy part of Air, and yet he is Aquarius, the Water-Bearer. For this reason, he represents the Cloud.

On a mental level, the cloud symbolizes the conscious, rational, logical mind, unharnessed to the promptings of the larger Self—it is the castle of the ego, drifting on the winds of fate and enmeshed in the cerebral constructs of Cloudland. The mentality symbolized by the Prince is impeccably calculating, brilliant, precise, clouded only by reason of being undirected. It is a mind cast adrift in conceptual crosswinds, like a breeze-blown spiderweb, faultless in construction but useless and unanchored. Yet redemption lies in the stainless purity of logic, which cannot fail to eventually see through its own artifices and come to awareness of the larger, nonrational dimensions of being that once integrated, anchor and empower the self. At this point, the cloud reaches critical mass, and its condensations are unloosed in the form of rain—the Knight of Cups, and all that the suit of Cups implies.

While the Knight of Swords is a symbol of electronics, the Prince of Swords represents philosophy and mathematics, the purest forms of logical reasoning. Here again, the power of mathematics is dependent upon its practical application, and the power of philosophy upon its ability to empower and enlighten the self. Nevertheless, the essence of this ethereal Prince can be said to be aesthetic rather than practical. His clouds are delightful for their beauty, not their utility.

In his most refined aspect, the Prince of Swords is manifested as starlight—the fires of the (K)night as seen through the atmospheric oceans of the Queen. This marriage of Knight and Queen is symbolized by the Prince, ruled by Aquarius, which also rules Trump XVII, the Star.

12. *Princess of Swords* is the earthy part of Air. Psychologically, she represents the materialization of idea. This can manifest as great shrewdness and efficacy on a practical, down-to-earth level, or it can denote a weighing down of the thoughts, a burden of excessive cares and conceptual baggage, and stormy and turbulent thinking or deep brooding and anger, especially self-castigation. In the natural world, the earthy part of Air has several aspects:

A. *Tornadoes and Hurricanes*—These are certainly the most earthshaking and highly materialized aerial phenomena known to man.

B. *Storm Clouds*—Black, massive, frightening anvil-heads are breathtaking manifestations of the Princess of Swords, goddess of the storm. She is also manifested in the heavy, leaden skies of winter. This is in keeping with her rulership over the transition from winter to spring. Storm clouds are an expression of the Princess as a materialized form of her brother, the Prince. These are the children of the Queen of Swords—the watery part of Air.

C. *Thunder*—The voice of the Princess can split the sky with earthshaking crashes or merely hint at stormy secrets from afar, darkening the night with somber undertones like the muttering and mumbling of distant mountains. This is the Princess as a materialized form of the Queen, who is manifested in sound waves.

D. *Sandstorms*—Like tornadoes, sandstorms are an earth-laden wind and are expressive of the Princess as a materialized form of the Knight. The link of thunder with lightning and sandstorms implies a connection between the Princess of Swords and Knight of Wands. Psychologically, the Princess represents the practical perspicacity that carries out and applies the initial revelations of the fiery Knight. Stand aside or be sandblasted! The revolution is at hand, the Weatherpeople storm the land.

E. *Meteors*—As a fiery wind that slices through the atmosphere, occasionally smashing to Earth, the meteor exemplifies the Princess as a solidified union of Knight and Queen. Furthermore, meteors rivet the attention when seen and have tremendous impact when grounded. Thus, they symbolize the materialization of powerful ideas.

F. *Dust*—This aspect is something more than housewife's bane: a mystery sleeps in every grain. Life is under constant bombardment by the invisible multitudes of dust. It implies aging and death, eternity and time. This form of earthy Air also symbolizes the thought-streams that assail us each waking moment from childhood to grave—every single thought a particle of dust that drifts through the sunray of consciousness and passes into the abysses of eternity, only to be replaced by billions of others, swirling like snowflakes, unique yet identical in substance. "Dust in the wind . . . ."

G. *Time*—The sword of the Princess cleaves the path of Electron into units of measurement—seconds, minutes, hours, years. Time is a concept so heavily materialized that it seems to be an integral part of Nature. We are all sailors lost in the vast abstract ocean of time. Our time-sense renders the "winds of becoming" apprehensible by the intellect. It is the Princess as mediator of the Knight to the Prince (a function common to all of the Princesses).

H. *Galaxies*—This is the ultimate expression of the earthy part of Air—solidification of cosmic idea in the mind of the Universe. It is the Princess as materialization of Knight, in her most comprehensive aspect. The Andromeda Galaxy is *real*, although to earthlings it is merely a concept or spot of light. The Princess of Swords represents the unfathomable reality behind the concept—reality bearing the same relation to human thought as the sum total of human thought bears to a single speck of dust. The Princesses always lead back to the *roots* (sunk in earth) of the powers of their elements—in this case, back to the infinite intelligence of supreme Mind.

13. *Knight of Disks* is Capricorn; he rules the last decan of Leo and the first two decans of Virgo (Aug. 10-Sept. 10). The fires of the Knight are the fires of Growth. A producer and protector of life, he represents agriculture and nutrition. This is analogous to Virgo. Yet his principal manifestation in the natural world is the mountain. For Capricorn, as the zenith of the zodiac, represents the highest, most barren places of the

Earth. Thus, the Knight of Disks embodies all of the exalted, colossal grandeur of the Himalayas, roof of the world.

In a more ethereal form, the fiery part of Earth manifests as the power of gravity—that which must be overcome to allow free flight into space. Thus, a certain humorless heaviness and rigidity of character is implied. At best, this is the dignity of a formidable mountain range. At worst, it is the immobilized tension of an earthquake waiting to happen.

The earthquake is another important manifestation of the Knight of Disks. In psychological terms, this aspect symbolizes the shifting or shattering of mental and emotional blocks during the more turbulent stages of the growth process.

The fiery part of Earth is also manifested as oil and petroleum, and by extension as the world of machinery—a fitting expression of the ponderous, clanking aspect of this most heavily armored Knight, and of his stability and power when properly lubricated. The massive gravity of governmental structure is also the domain of the Knight of Disks; the corresponding lubricant is money.

14. *Queen of Disks* is Virgo; she rules the last decan of Sagittarius and the first two decans of Capricorn (Dec. 10-Jan. 10). The Queen represents fertility, especially the fertility of winter—the germination of future abundance during seemingly barren times. As the watery part of Earth, the Queen also represents irrigation—both as a function of actual agriculture (ruled by the Knight) and as the reclamation of psychic deserts through introduction of the waters of feeling. The watery part of Earth has several other aspects:

A. *Snow*—This is the eternal garment of our loftiest mountains; another example of the fertility of winter, in that mountain snow-packs feed the freshets of spring and summer. A connection with the Princess of Cups (ice) is implied; also with the Princess of Swords, because they rule similar seasons and because the nucleus of the snowflake is a particle of dust (this represents the fleshing out of a thought particle by the accumulation of an emotional charge).

B. *Valleys and Canyons*—These are archetypal feminine symbols. Mountains imply valleys. Canyons add a further dimension of depth. The Knight of Disks is expressed in Nature as towering walls of rock—buildings, cliffs, or mountains. The Queen symbolizes the spaces enclosed by those walls. Thus, if the fullest expression of the Knight is Himalayan, the Queen in her fullest glory is the Grand

Canyon of the Colorado, possibly the planet's supreme interaction of water and earth. This implies another connection with the Princess of Swords (time). The Queen of Disks is also the Valley of the Nile, fertile cradle of Egyptian civilization (whose enduring pyramids express the energies of the Knight); the Vale of Kashmir, protected by snowy Himalayan heights; and the Great Central Valley of California, an agricultural wonderland. This is the Queen as an aspect of the Empress, whose function it is to provide nourishment for life.

C. *Swamps*—The Queen as Mother Nature, another aspect of the Empress, exhibits a lush variety of vegetation and animal life. The abundance of birdlife implies another connection with the Princess of Cups, but the energies of these two cards are essentially different (as a rainforest differs from a swamp). For the watery part of Earth can also manifest as *mud*, in which the soaring raptures of Xeno can never be mired. The Queen is of a somewhat less flighty disposition; yet the glorious beauty of her glowing snowfields, brooding swamps, and canyons often rivals the beauty of Xeno.

Swamps imply mosquitoes and mystic pools of stagnant water—attributes of the Queen of Cups, whose tranquil receptivity is an important ingredient in the character of the Queen of Disks as well. The link between these two Queens is corroborated by an even more pronounced link between their respective Princesses, described below.

D. *Oasis*—This aspect of the Queen emphasizes her power to provide nourishment in the midst of arid sterility—for which she is the antidote. A connection with the High Priestess, ruled by the Hebrew letter *gimel* (a camel), is also implied.

E. *Grasslands*—The oceans of rippling grass that once blanketed our Great Plains are another example of the Queen as an aspect of the Empress—an example of the plant kingdom as the flesh of the Earth-Mother. Today, this area is also intensively agricultural.

F. *Steppes and Tundra*—The Knight of Disks represents mountains; the Queen represents valleys, canyons, and plains. The High Plains of Montana and Wyoming, the steppes of Siberia, and the Arctic tundras are all realms of snow and expressions of the Queen of Disks.

15. The *Prince of Disks* **is** Taurus; he rules the last decan of Aries and the first two decans of Taurus (Apr. 10-May 10). The airy part of Earth is the flowering and bearing fruit of that element. Hence, the Prince symbolizes productivity. Taurus suggests that this productivity is the result of patience and sustained labors. Yet this Prince is a harbinger of abundance, representative of wildflowers and fruits as well as the cultivated products of agriculture. His dues have all been paid, and now he reaps a bountiful harvest.

In the natural world, the Prince finds expression in the world of flowers—a profusion of spring blossoms, or a single red rose, love's emblem (a fitting expression of Taurus, a sign ruled by the planet of love and falling during prime wildflower season). The colorful floral explosions of the Prince are also emblematic of the states of consciousness produced by marijuana and hashish, which are transformed from earth to air (smoke) in the process of activation. The festive nature of this Prince is further enhanced by the traditional association of Taurus with speech: the flowering of that function takes the form of song and music. Productive though he may be, the Prince of Disks could never be described as all work and no play. He is a child of springtime, decked in roses and greenery. His is the productivity of a truly joyous spirit.

As the airy part of Earth, the Prince of Disks finds full expression in the colorful red rock canyonlands of Utah and Arizona—a fantastic labyrinth of wind-sculpted turrets, spires, arches and obelisks, garnished and seasoned with wildflowers and juniper trees.

The Prince of Disks is the Prince of Trees: oaks and orchards express his fruitfulness. He represents individual trees rather than forests— paloverdes and cottonwoods standing proud in desert washes or dwarfed by the vastness of surrounding plains. Another aspect of the Prince of Disks is the dry and down-to-earth side of Taurus—the sagebrush country of the American West. Here the tumbleweed best captures the essence of this airy part of Earth.

16. *Princess of Disks* is Geo, secret goddess of the Earth. Like her sister Xeno, she is vast and mysterious, as variegated in her essence as the Earth itself. She includes all landscapes. In this respect, she is the summation of all of the previous Court Cards. She rules the transition of spring into summer, the time when the days are longest and the power of the Earth waxes strongest. Within the context of her global scope, certain natural forces are particularly representative of Geo, the Princess of Disks:

A. *Forests*—In general, the more landlocked and remote the forest and the less tropical, the more it expresses that essence of dark brooding mystery which is a keynote of the Princess of Disks. The

Black Forest of Germany, the Siskiyou forests of California, and the inland forests of Alaska are all very fine examples of this aspect of Geo. Perhaps the best example of all is the North Woods of Minnesota and Canada; a connection with the Queen of Cups (lakes) is illustrated. As the watery part of water and the earthy part of earth, these are the two most feminine of the Court Cards.

B. *Hills*—Smoothly rolling hills, rounded into soft feminine contours, provide contrast and complement to the blocky angularity of the Knight. Hills express the *ancient* quality of Earth. Wood nymphs and satyrs frolic in their hidden groves, in homage to Pan, god of earthly ecstasy.

C. *Caves*—The descent into the depths of the Earth and its hidden wonders are obvious aspects of this Princess. Caves are another archetypal feminine symbol.

D. *Peyote and Psilocybin*—Where the Prince represents the joyous sensual pleasures of smokable herbs, the Princess adds dimensions of mystery and colorful rapture. There is an implied connection with the deepest psychic forces of the Earth, and with Trump V, The Hierophant (Mescalito the Teacher, ruled by Taurus) is implied.

E. *Jewels*—While Geo represents all minerals and rocks, precious gems emphasize her wondrous beauty and aura of enchantment. They also illustrate an important doctrine of the Tarot: the ending of the creative process of Tetragrammaton in the densest and most material levels of the element Earth automatically implies a return to the Source—the spiritual fire of creation. This fire is symbolized by the wand and by the diamond, which is formed in the depths of the coal bed. Thus the system of creation depicted by Tetragrammaton is cyclic and self-sustaining, rather than linear and sterile.

F. *Cities*—Each city and town is a unique expression of Geo, with a character and history all its own; and each is a plasmatic dream nexus, a focal point for the creative dream-life of Xeno.

G. *Womanhood*—The Princess of Disks embodies all of the aspects of Woman, ever-mysterious, ever-beautiful. She particularly rules the functions of pregnancy, and is a hieroglyph of transformation. She incubates and is transfigured by the primal spark of the Knight of Wands, the seed of new life. She stands upon the brink of creation, presiding over the emergence of Spirit in the depths of Matter, and the emergence of jewels of new life from the caverns of the womb.

Long may she delight her children in the secret gardens of rapture. Hail, Earth!

COSMIC PROGRESSIONS

The four Princesses represent the final issue of their respective energies—Disks and Cups as the Earth and its oceans, Wands as its central fires, and Swords as its envelope of space. As the active, masculine principles, the Wands and Swords also represent the forces molding our globe. The Princess of Swords, ruling time and space, symbolizes evolution, the ongoing thought-streams of humanity and their eventual expansion into the galaxy. The Princess of Wands, ruling sex and representing the animating fires of life, symbolizes involution, the *involvement* of cosmic life energy in the patterns of terrestrial living.

The Table of Progressions on the next page illustrates the vast range of meaning contained in the Court Cards. These examples show the functioning of Knight-Queen-Prince-Princess as Father-Mother-Son-Daughter in the realms of Nature, the Psyche, and the Cosmos. Each of these progressions is a self-sustaining cycle, the Daughter returning her energies to the Father.

It is a testament to the power and intricacy of these rich and complex symbols that they lend themselves with equal ardor to the description of Nature, Psyche, and Cosmos. The Court Cards stand as mediators between the human and the Divine. They stand as mighty oaks, rooted in the fertile soil of philosophy, religion, and metaphysics. And just as the life and greenery of the oak are brought into being by sunlight and rain, so do the Court Cards find their fullest flowering as mirrors of the natural world. They are truly Nature's Archetypes.

NOTES

1. In the Crowley deck, Princes have relpaced Kings. Thus, the Royal Marriage consists of Knight and Queen, rather than King and Queen. The rationale behind this is that the wandering Knight, who actively wins his Queen, is more fit to rule than the King, who accedes to his throne by birthright, without struggle. The Princessess are analogous to Pages in all respects.

2. Carlos Castaneda, *Journey to Ixtlan*, p.89. (Emphasis added.)

3. The only real stability is in change. Thus, Geo is analogous to the archetypal Navaho myth-figure, Changing Woman. This legend of the South is nicely balanced by a corresponding legend of the North—the Alaskan myth of Fog Woman, analogous to Xeno, the Princess of Cups.

TABLE OF PROGRESSIONS

	Knight	Queen	Prince	Princess

WANDS

	Knight	Queen	Prince	Princess
Nature:	Flame	Motion	Light	Heat
Psyche:	Initiation	Adaptability	Effectiveness	Involvement
Cosmos:	Seed	Growth	Life	Sex

CUPS

	Knight	Queen	Prince	Princess
Nature:	Rain	Pool	River	Sea
Psyche:	Sensation	Sensitivity	Transformation	Rapture
Cosmos:	Birth	Image	Death	Dream

SWORDS

	Knight	Queen	Prince	Princess
Nature:	Wind	Front	Cloud	Storm
Psyche:	Direction	Vision	Intellect	Idea
Cosmos:	Electron	Space	Intelligence	Galaxy

DISKS

	Knight	Queen	Prince	Princess
Nature:	Mountain	Snow	Flower	Earth
Psyche:	Protection	Growth	Productivity	Nourishment
Psyche:	Aspiration	Patience	Joy	Mystery
Cosmos:	Pressure	Yielding	Change	Stability[3]

Tarot as Guidebook:
The Map of Universal Laws

*T*he Tarot deck is a symbolic mapping of human consciousness that is timeless and universal. In contrast, the reading is a temporal portrait of an individual, as it shows where a person is on the map for a specific time and space.

The Tarot map can be likened to an encyclopedic reference, a book of knowledge. The ancient Egyptians expressed the concepts of the Tarot's Major Arcana cards in book form. Each card-symbol represents a page, chapter, or even a book unto itself.

As a map and symbolic encyclopedia, Tarot is a guidebook. It provides the universal laws that are requisites for achieving anything. In "Mapping Consciousness: Topography By Tarot," Judith Rozhon shows the interaction between our universal or archetypal characteristics (Major Arcana) and qualities of perception, thought, feeling, and acting (Minor Arcana). She demonstrates how, through following these interrelationships, we can realize our potential and achieve wholeness.

James Wanless' "Self-Autonomy Through Tarot" demonstrates how to follow the guidelines of the Major Arcana cards to become the Emperor, a symbol of autonomy and independence. This requires adhering to the principles of all the Major cards as they relate to our self-determination.

David Quigley's "From Sex and Romance to Love and Oneness" shows how the Major Arcana is a map divided into seven stages that takes us through our sexuality and relationships into the highest state of spiritual oneness.

The value of the Tarot's maplike structure of universal laws is that it assists us to consciously determine the direction of our life. We can express any of the seventy-eight modes of consciousness and behavior depicted by the card-symbols. If we need to cultivate a certain quality, contemplation of the appropriate card-symbol will activate it. By internalizing the card symbols, we can see where moving to a place (card) in consciousness on the Tarot will lead us.

Tarot cards are signposts we can choose to follow or not. Making moves and choices in such a manner is a rationalistic way of conducting our life. There is nothing mystical in this process. The intentional use of Tarot symbolism is as integral to the practice of Tarot as the "intuitive reading."

Mapping Consciousness
Topography by Tarot

Judith Rozhon

O▪O▪O▪O▪O▪O▪O▪O▪O▪O▪O▪O▪O▪O

We live in the Age of Information—computers, transistors, DNA—the encoding of larger and larger volumes of information in smaller and smaller packages. Recent theories of neuroscientists and physicists suggest the ultimate telescoping of information: the brain may be a hologram interpreting a holographic universe. Each tiny unit of the brain may contain all the information available in the whole, and each piece of the universe may be a doorway to understanding the whole. It is often said that the ability to store large quantities of information in small packages may be of primary importance as we move into the twenty-first century. This is certainly the trend in technology. In our conscious awareness, this trend may be expressed as a reclaiming and revitalizing of the abilities of symbolic thinking and perception natural to the ancients and carried down to us through the wisdom teachings and the shamanistic traditions of all ages and cultures. Often the symbolic keys to these holographic views of the universe are encoded in various "maps" of consciousness, such as the astrological map and the Tarot.

Tarot, like astrology, is often viewed as a tool for divination. But, like astrology, the Tarot deck can be seen as a map of consciousness, in which a large amount of information is symbolized or "stored." A unique feature of these symbolic maps is that depth of understanding makes more information available, and increased information results in deepened understanding. Evidently, the volume of information expands infinitely.

If you are not familiar with Tarot cards—and even if you are—placing all 78 cards of any deck in numerical and categorical sequence in front of you can be a dramatic experience. Arranging them in proper sequence, laying them down one by one in ordered rows—Magus,

Priestess, Empress . . .; Knight, Queen, Prince, Princess; Ace through 10 of every suit—you may feel like someone first learning the game of chess. You solemnly arrange the miniature world of horses, castles, bishops, and pawns in preparation for the game about to unfold. It is an ordering process; a meditative overture. Yet chess is not so much a game as a way of training the mind. And while life may look like a game to some—a game of war, a game of peace, a game of chance—perhaps it is instead a way of training the soul.

Indeed, though there are many initiatory traditions and ways of looking at the goal of the initiate, generally speaking, that goal is to see life as a school for the soul. In Egypt (where the Tarot possibly originated) initiates used maps of consciousness (which the Tarot probably is) as tools to help in educating the soul or creative self, much as we use chess for improving the mind.

THE MAP

The Tarot deck, a 78-card map, is laid out neatly in the following order: 22 Major Arcana or Trump cards, 16 Royalty cards, and the Ace through 10 for each suit. The suits are Swords, Cups, Wands, and Disks (or Pentacles)—corresponding to spades, hearts, clubs, and diamonds in today's 52-card descendant.

This 78-card layout unveils a map of consciousness, a map of life. Symbolized and encapsulated in the four-suit breakdown are four modes of experiencing our world. The swords represent the mind, or how we think. The cups symbolize emotions—how we feel. The wands are perceptions—how we see the world. And the disks represent the physical world—how we move, what we do.

The first 22 cards of the deck are called the Major Arcana, or sometimes the Trumps Major. They are often numbered from zero to 21, rather than 1 to 22. The zero card is called the Fool, and is also considered Card 22. Hence, this numbering implies cyclical movement, with The Fool being both the beginning and the end of the cycle. These 22 cards are viewed as a "mini-map" of the journey of all human beings (who begin and end as Fools) through an evolutionary path to higher consciousness. This dual nature of the Fool card is reminiscent of the Zen story which explains that in the beginning of life's journey, to the average person, people are people and mountains are mountains. As the journey progresses, things get confused. But to the sage, after enlightenment, once again people are people and mountains are mountains.

Implied in this card is the innocence of childhood and the wisdom of the ancient sage—all things come full circle. In every deck, the Fool is a beautiful card. In the Thoth deck particularly, the Fool card and the symbols pictured on it illustrate the essential meaning of the entire deck. The card symbolizes life as a creative journey toward wholeness, and fear as the greatest obstacle to wholeness and to the manifestation of creativity. Each of the other Major Arcana cards represents a stage on this journey and lessons to be learned at that stage. The cards are traditionally divided into several paths—though the exact path breakdowns depend on which of several approaches to Tarot is used. All the paths are completed in the Universe (or World) card, card 21, and wholeness is reasserted in the Fool card as the cycle begins again, perhaps as a spiral does, moving in circles yet progressing.

When the 22 Major Arcana cards are examined in the context of the entire deck, other information becomes apparent. Though there are 22 cards, each number after 10 can also be reduced to a single digit (and hence to another card) from 1 through 10. For example, 11 is the Lust or Strength card: $11 = 1 + 1 = 2$ (the #2 card of the Major Arcana is the Priestess); 12 is The Hanged Man: $12 = 1 + 2 = 3$ (the #3 card is the Empress), and so on. This means that all the numbered cards in the deck, including the Ace through 10 of each suit, can be related numerically to one of the first 10 cards of the Major Arcana. Figure 1 on the following page illustrates this breakdown.

UNIVERSAL PRINCIPLES

The 40 numbered cards in the Minor Arcana (the Ace through 10 of each suit) may be viewed as the expression in our everyday world (a world of thinking, feeling, perceiving, and doing) of the universal principles symbolized in each of the Major Arcana cards. The precise principle indicated matches the corresponding number on the card. For an illustration of this, consider the Chariot card, which is 7 in the Major Arcana. On the card is a picture of a charioteer, chariot, and animal-like figures placed in front to pull it. The meanings of the card relate to free will, independence, choice, and motion. Because they are also numbered seven, each of the four sevens in the Minor Arcana also relates in some way to the principle of motion expressed in the Chariot card. (Figure 1 shows this direct numerical relationship.) Each seven will relate to the expressions or suppression of this universal principle of motion in the realms of thought (Seven of Swords), feelings (Seven of

Figure 1

REDUCING THE NUMBERED CARDS

1 - Magus

2 - Priestess

Major Arcana

3 - Empress

1 2 3 4 5 6 7 8 9 10

4 - Emperor

   11 12 13 14 15 16 17 18 19

5 - Hierophant

   20 21 22

6 - Lovers

7 - Chariot

8 - Adjustment

9 - Hermit

10 - Fortune

Minor Arcana

11 - Lust

(swords) Ace 2 3 4 5 6 7 8 9 10

12 - Hanged Man

(cups)   Ace 2 3 4 5 6 7 8 9 10

13 - Death

(wands) Ace 2 3 4 5 6 7 8 9 10

14 - Art

(disks)   Ace 2 3 4 5 6 7 8 9 10

15 - Devil

16 - Tower

17 - Star

18 - Moon

19 - Sun

20 - Aeon

21 - Universe

22 - Fool

Cups), sensing (Seven of Wands), and being (Seven of Disks), according to the suit in which they belong. The sixteenth card in the Major Arcana, the Tower, numerically reduces to 7 (1 + 6 = 7). While the Tower has a distinct meaning of its own—self-cleansing, transformation, and renewal—it also relates to the principles of motion and choice symbolized in the Chariot card.

As another illustration, consider the sixth card in the Major Arcana, the Lovers card. On the card a woman and a man appear to be joined together, as perhaps in a marriage ceremony, by a larger figure in the background. This is a card of balance in relationship, and it also expresses the polarity found in all of nature. Because they are also numbered six, each of the sixes in the Minor Arcana relates in some way to this principle of polarity in the realms of thoughts (Six of Swords), feeling (Six of Cups), sensing (Six of Wands) and being (Six of Disks). Card 15, the Devil, while representing principles of humor and sexuality, also reduces to 6 (1 + 5 = 6) and therefore also relates to the principle of polarity expressed in the Lovers card. Figure 2 lists the universal principles expressed through each of the 22 Major Arcana cards.

THE ROYALTY CARDS

People are pictured on the Royalty cards. There is a Knight for every suit (Knight of Swords, Knight of Cups, etc.), and a Queen, a Prince, and a Princess (or, in some decks, a Page) for each suit as well. These sixteen human figures represent sixteen different ways of mastering the mental, emotional, perceptual, and physical aspects of life. They mirror healthy and positive ways of taking action in the world and of demonstrating our natural gifts and breakthroughs in awareness. They are symbols of application. The Knight of Swords, for example, is a master of determined, committed mental action—clear thinking. The Princess of Cups has mastered the expression of emotional joy, and longevity and loyalty within relationships. Each of the Royalty cards represents the mastery of a particular way of being in the world, and almost like characters in a play, they offer inspirational models for positive, creative action. They express possibility and the direction adventure may take, as well as other individuals one may meet on the journey of life.

Because the Royalty cards are not numbered, their relationship to the other cards in the deck is not as apparent. Yet each has a tool—a cup, a sword, a wand, or a disk—that relates its bearer to each of the ten numbered cards in the corresponding suit of the Minor Arcana. And

Figure 2

UNIVERSAL PRINCIPLES EXPRESSED IN THE MAJOR ARCANA

Name of Card	Universal Principle	Name of Card	Universal Principle
1 Magus	flexibility/ communication	12 Hanged Man	sacrifice/ challenge
2 Priestess	intuition/ independence	13 Death	rebirth/ transformation
3 Empress	love/ nurturing	14 Art	alchemy/ synthesis
4 Emperor	stability/solidity leadership	15 Devil	sexuality/ humor
5 Hierophant	curiosity/teaching learning	16 Tower	restoration/ healing
6 Lovers	polarity/ relationship	17 Star	illumination/ recognition
7 Chariot	will/motion	18 Moon	mystery/ magnetism
8 Adjustment	justice/balance	19 Sun	synergy/work
9 Hermit	guidance/ completion	20 Aeon	morality/ judgment
10 Fortune	expansion/ prosperity	21 Universe	harvest/ fulfillment
11 Lust	creativity/ passion	22 Fool	ecstasy/ wholeness courage

Royalty cards are also related to many of the other cards through astrological symbols pictured on each card. The Queen of Disks, for instance, sits with a ram, and is therefore related to all the other cards in the deck associated with the sign of Aries (the ram); and also to the fourth card of the Major Arcana, the Emperor, because it is ruled by the sign of Aries.

The universal principles of the Major Arcana are demonstrated by the Royalty cards, each in a particular way (the Queen's way is somewhat different from the Prince's or the Princess' way), and each according to the suit to which it belongs. So, the Queen of Cups will demonstrate the principle of love and nurturing expressed in the Empress card (3 in the Major Arcana) through work that is service-oriented, and perhaps through family and children; while the Prince of Cups will demonstrate this same principle in the passion of a great love. The Queen of Swords, on the other hand, may demonstrate this principle of supreme caring and creative loving by cutting through the negative thought patterns that separate us from that love. Each is an adept at expressing the universal in a unique and individual way. Figure 3 shows the order of the Royalty cards as they appear in the Thoth deck.

Figure 3

ROYALTY CARDS

Knight of Swords	Queen of Swords	Prince of Swords	Princess of Swords
Knight of Cups	Queen of Cups	Prince of Cups	Princess of Cups
Knight of Wands	Queen of Wands	Prince of Wands	Princess of Wands
Knight of Disks	Queen of Disks	Prince of Disks	Princess of Disks

---

READING THE MAP

The preceding paragraphs very briefly summarize some of the qualities expressed in the Tarot map of consciousness when regarded as a whole. The map also indicates interrelationships among the different ways of being in the world. For example, according to the information given in this map, the way we think (Swords) often determines how we feel (Cups), how we see things (Wands), and ultimately what we do (Disks).

The art of reading such a map is a bit similar to reading an actual topographical map. You see elevations marked on the map; rivers, forests, major landmarks. If you're looking for water, you'll find rushing spring streams where elevations change rapidly, slowly moving rivers where the changes are more gradual. Lakes will be in valleys or flatlands. The map will tell you where to find these various features. Wandering through the terrain, you will use the map and your understanding of it to assist you on your journey, and you'll come to know a lot more about the territory than what is on the map. Some map features will help you understand the terrain a little better; some aspects of the terrain will help you understand the maps better. If you're looking for mountain goats, you won't look for them on the map—you'll check the map for the direction of higher elevations, and then head for the hills.

In our human world of thinking, feeling, sensing, and experiencing, our emotions are the water on the map of conscious awareness and are symbolized by the suit of Cups. Like water they may have the stillness of forest ponds, the energy of charging streams, the rhythm and grandeur of great rivers, or the awesome greyness of the ocean in fog. Our emotions may fall from our eyes as tears, like a summer rain. Our thoughts and the world of the mind, symbolized by the suit of Swords, are the moutains, plateaus, and high elevations on the map, where we find thin air and wisps of cloud. All the experience and furniture of our physical world, symbolized by the suit of Disks, is the earth: the fields, hills, and forests—the landed portions of the map. And our sensing and perceptions, the way we see the world, symbolized by the suit of Wands, are the lighted and fiery places on the map: the deserts, and sun, moon, and stars.

The skills involved in reading a Tarot map are similar to those involved in reading any other map, and there are as many "moves" as there are in chess, all of varying complexity. What's exciting about the Tarot is that the territory it maps is the territory of consciousness. And the moves that can be made are the motions of life.

Here is a practical example of how this "mapping" and "moving" can work using the Tarot deck. There are many other ways of using the cards. The one explained here is relatively unusual in that the cards are face up and used as a map. But this approach has the unique feature of stressing what the cards do *by themselves*, as a map, rather than what people can do with them.

In this example, consider the experience of futility—a giving-up attitude, a sentence in the mind sounding something like, "I might as well not bother anymore. What's the use?" We can probably agree that this is most often a stuck place to be. We are stopped—motionless, and not particularly happy. Imagine sitting, slumping, sighing.

In the Tarot map, this state of being is associated with the Seven of Swords: "Futility." It has an astrological association with the Moon in Aquarius, and symbolic representations on the card such as sword hilts representing various planets, meaning that the particular positive qualities of that planet are not being experienced because of this "stuckness" of mind. The Swords suit indicates that this is a difficulty in life originating in the mind—not in the sense of mental illness, but in the sense of a mistake in thinking, a *habit* of thinking that is unproductive. Hence, a stuckness. So the first thing the map has done is to give a name and category to a pattern of thinking.

The next step is to look at the map again for the universal laws or principles associated with this state of consciousness, this life experience. Because the card is a seven, it is associated with the seventh card in the Major Arcana, the Chariot. As mentioned above, the Chariot card symbolizes motion. In the physical world we might associate it with the property of inertia, the tendency of the body at rest to stay at rest or of a body in motion to remain in motion. But in this case, because we are dealing with the mind (the Swords suit), this principle of motion must be applied in the realm of thought. The futile thought pattern does not involve motion in a new direction but rather repetition of the same phrase "What's the use?" (sigh). The motion of this phrase needs to stop and something new needs to be set in motion.

One of the advantages of this map is the variety of options available for movement. Just next to the "Futility" card is "Science," the Six of Swords, indicating that objectivity is often the answer to the inertness of the mental pattern of futility. Another option for movement is below and just to the left on the "map." This is the Six of Cups, emotional "Pleasure." Often moving from circular, fruitless patterns to a pleasant emotional experience short-circuits the futile thoughts and initiates motion in a new direction. Continued working with the map in conjunction with deeper understanding of our life reveals more and more options for movement away from old habit patterns and toward positive growth.

For those who have a Tarot deck and have not worked with the particular method discussed here (using the whole deck as a map), try the following suggestion. Take each of the Major Arcana cards from 1 (the Magus) through 10 (Fortune) and place them in a row. Next, take the corresponding numbered card from each suit and place it beneath the Major Arcana card. For example, the Empress (3) would have the Three of Swords, the Three of Cups, the Three of Wands, and the Three of Disks beneath it. Now finish the exercise by applying your understanding of the meaning of the Major Arcana card, such as the Empress, to each of the levels of consciousness represented in the Minor Arcana cards. In other words, how do the principles of love, caring and nurturing expressed by the Empress card relate to thinking, and to the Three of Swords? How do they relate to the emotional world and the Three of Cups? And how do they relate to the sensing world and the physical world, the Three of Wands and the Three of Disks, respectively? Continue working in this way, and you will begin to see the interconnectedness of features on this map. Later, you may sense the locations of natural bridges and undergrounds streams not immediately apparent. The terrain just below the surface is thousands of years old, the journey is endless.

Self-Autonomy
Through Tarot

James Wanless, Ph.D.

O▪O▪O▪O▪O▪O▪O▪O▪O▪O▪O▪O▪O

In recent history, an extraordinary number of entities, including nations, ethnic groups, and lifestyle minorities, have acquired greater control over their own destinies. These obvious expressions of self-autonomy or self-governance are paralleled on more subtle levels by individuals.

Autonomy, meaning self-governance and self-determination, is the ability to control, guide, and steer oneself. All living biological and social organisms require this capability. The butterfly with a torn wing lacks the ability to steer and so dies. The mentally retarded person who lacks self-control needs a caretaker. The society without some form of government disintegrates. Self-governance is particularly crucial in this day and age because of the multiple choices and possibilities resulting from freedom of expression and rapid technological and social change.

The symbols of the Tarot's Major Arcana represent principles of life that apply to all areas of human endeavor. The Major Arcana are in essence a reference book. The principle of self-autonomy is symbolized by the Emperor in the Major Arcana. Autonomy implies, however, much more than the Emperor who represents formal government, the process of making, executing, and adjudicating decisions. A tenet of the Major Arcana "book of life" is that to fulfill any one principle, such as autonomy, requires adherence to the other twenty-one major principles as they apply. In relating the entirety of the Major Arcana to the Emperor, it becomes clear that self-governance is composed of the following qualities:

Sense of Self: Represented by the Magus, Chariot, Star, Priestess, and Strength.

Community: Represented by the Lovers, Sun, Empress, Hanged Man, and Moon.

Government: Represented by the Emperor, Justice, Judgment, Wheel of Fortune, and Devil.

Adaptability: Represented by the World (or Universe), Hierophant, Hermit, Death, Art, Tower, and Fool.

Autonomy applies to collectivities such as nation-states, groups, organizations and businesses, and to individuals. The principle of the Universe or World symbol is that the microcosm (the individual) and the macrocosm (group, society, world, universe) are reflections of each other. The individual embodies all that is manifested in the universe and vice versa. Individuals govern themselves in the manner of groups and societies, and collectivities guide themselves similarly to individuals.

Governance is for the most part conducted with greater awareness amongst collectivities than by individuals. Groups have positions specifically designed for the function of guiding and leading. Individuals unconsciously grope through life, not knowing where they are going or how to get there.

Tarot is often referred to as a map of life or of consciousness, but it can also be viewed as a set of rules for the roadway. The twenty-two concepts of the Major Arcana represent principles of navigation. Adherence to these tenets enables individuals and groups to steer their way more effectively through the course of life. These guidelines suggest, therefore, not only routes and goals but also the principles that must be followed to get there, wherever *there* is. The Tarot itself is a guide, a core of principles upon which to base one's movement anywhere in body, in mind, in heart, and in spirit.

SENSE OF SELF

The first step toward the autonomy common to groups and individuals is the will and desire for self-determination. Motivation comes with an emergent sense of self: self-responsibility, self-identity, self-esteem, self-trust, and self-expression and assertion.

Magus

Governance is taking responsibility for one's self and direction in life. Self-responsibility develops with recognizing the *Magus* within, or that our world is created by ourselves. The principle symbolized by the Magus, communication of logos (the word) is that reality is created by the way we think; that our life is the product of our conceptualizations. Understanding that we possess the magic of The Magus, or the ability to create any reality for ourself through purposive thought, leads inevitably to the conclusion that we can control the events of our life. This knowledge inspires individuals and groups to assume responsibility for themselves and their lives.

Chariot

Responsibility arises with self-identity. There is little motivation to take responsibility for the self if an underdeveloped sense of self exists. Self-identity is symbolized by the *Charioteer*, the armored man in the Crowley-Harris Tarot.[1] His armor is the boundary separating himself from others. Self-governance requires that such boundaries be established. The woman who sees herself primarily as the extension of her husband and the black man who sees himself as the property of another may have very little control over the direction in which their lives (the Chariot) moves.

Governance implies not only boundary but also an understanding of what is behind the borders, who the self or collectivity is; what the consitutuents of the individual or group are that need to be governed. The constituency is that which dwells within the armored shell, the home of the Charioteer, who represents the crab, Cancer. The constitutents of the individual self are the mind, heart, body, and spirit, which are identified by the four animals pulling the Chariot. These animals symbolize the fixed signs of the zodiac and the four suits of the Tarot. The constitutents of groups are its members and their physical needs, mental values and beliefs, emotional feelings, and spiritual destinies.

These constituents represent the home and are inviolable. Inability to protect one's borders compromises autonomy. Self-governance requires the armor of the Charioteer and the claws of the crab to defend and maintain self-identity and integrity.

It is impossible for a group, state, or individual to govern itself if its constituents are subject to outside control. Self-determination among nation-states according to the Charter of the United Nations demands noninterference in domestic affairs by other states. A prominent reason for international instability is that governments are unable to govern because the constituent populace, its minds and hearts, are subject to external influence through communications systems and networks that transcend national boundaries. Among individuals, if one's constituent parts such as beliefs (mind) are unknowingly influenced and conditioned by others, and emotions (heart) are reluctantly captured by another, autonomy is compromised.

Star

Self-esteem is often asserted in demonstrative ways upon first discovery of a sense of identity. New states parade their arsenals. Groups sloganize that "Black Is Beautiful," "Cowboys Do It Best," "Indians Were Here First," "Sisterhood Is Good," "Gay Pride;" and individuals claim that they have "got it," engage in daily self-affirmations, and restyle their lives from hair to occupation.

Priestess

Unlike the often heady and starry expressions of self-esteem, self-guidance also requires sober decision-making. Governance is the process of steering the self by making decisions that come from within, for only the individual or group knows what is right for itself. Appropriate decisions for oneself come from the *Priestess*, one's own predilections and intuitions. The Priestess represents the repository of instinctual knowledge and perception dwelling within the individual or group that is called upon for guidance.

Self-governance means independence. As exemplified by the Priestess, autonomy is the ability to determine our course in life without reliance on others for our decisions. Following our own judgment requires self-trust. Confidence develops with the recognition of our Priestess nature or understanding that our instincts are naturally right for ourselves.

Strength

Once the inner guide, the Priestess, has shown the way, the individual or group must assert itself in that direction. Self-autonomy means acting upon decisions. Self-assertion is symbolized by Leo, *Strength* or *Lust*. The woman riding the lion portrays getting a rein on the lion (our life) and riding on that lion (self-expression).

Self-steerage is charting our own course in life independent of the routes taken by others. Individuality is intrinsic to autonomy. To be oneself requires the leonine courage epitomized in Strength.

The trend towards self-determination in the world has resulted from individuals and groups recognizing that their lack of self-responsibility brings interference and control from others, to their own detriment. Dissatisfied with themselves by their consequent low self-esteem and motivated by the recognition of their capability to govern themselves, they have taken lionesque leaps of revolutionary proportions, movements of liberation, to assert themselves. Transformed into new identities—colonies become nation-states, Indians become Native Americans, homosexuals become gays, Mexicans become Chicanos, girls become women—they become capable of independently determining and governing their own lives.

Similar growth of autonomy has occurred among those working with the symbols of the Tarot. Instead of becoming dependent upon Tarot as a crutch, adherents of Tarot find that the meanings and visual power of its symbolism produce greater independence, expression, and assertion.

COMMUNITY

Governance requires a sense of community, which results from the integration of minds (swords), bodies (pentacles or disks), hearts (cups), and spirits (wands). Community implies on the mental level, a commonality of beliefs, values, and perceptions. Community is also mutual interdependence—living, working, and playing together. These associations instill a feeling of "we-ness," togetherness, an emotional allegiance and sense of common destiny, purpose, and karma.

Without a sense of community, it is difficult, if not impossible, to steer or govern effectively. National governments are powerless under conditions of disintegration; witness Lebanon, a state composed of many states with differing values and allegiances, and dissimilar languages and support systems. Individuals are functionally paralyzed when the mind, emotions, and body do not work together, such as the person who is emotionally pulled towards another but mentally attracted to multitudinous relationships and physically comforted by the isolation of the mountains.

Lovers

Collectivities are governable when there is a meeting of minds, the mental integration represented by the two figures merging in the *Lovers*, the Gemini-mental symbol. Common language, standardized schooling, and mass media produce a commonality of views and perceptions that allow governments to know their constituents and the decisions and directions which are acceptable to them.

The two lovers represent the dualities of the mind. Individuals are capable of self-governance through the integration of these polarities: right-brain creative imagination (Empress) with left-brain rational logic (Emperor), dream and fantasy (Moon) with reality and fact (Justice), memory (Hierophant) with expectations (Star), beliefs (Magus) with absolute knowledge (Priestess), scientific understanding (Sun) with intuitive knowing (Fool). This mental synthesis produces clear and resolute decisions because all of these constituents of the mind are consulted.

A sense of community flourishes under conditions of equality, symbolized by the Lovers, the joining of equals. Self-autonomy requires equality among participants. Inequalities produce internal conflicts, power struggles, and civil wars. The individual whose mind, heart, body, and spirit are equal participants with equal voices in decisions is effectively self-governing. Organizations and states whose varied interest groups are equally represented in the decision-making process are governable.

Sun

Community is also established through interdependence, symbolized by the *Sun*. Dependence upon the sun for food, warmth, energy— life—is characteristic of societies in that people depend upon others for food, housing, work, money, transportation, etc. Similar symbiotic relationships abound within the individual, a single example being how one's physical health is dependent upon one's state of mind.

The sun and earth working together to create life is a synergetic relationship. Individuals working together is synergy. Through such cooperation, all can realize a better life, a place in the sun. Within the individual, allowing and encouraging the body and mind to function harmoniously, for example, produces a synergized and unified self.

Empress

An emotional bond is created from mental integration and synergic association. In states, there arises a love of country, love for the motherland. This emotional allegiance, commonly termed nationalism, is a manifestation of the principle of love symbolized by the *Empress*. As the archetypal mother, the Empress represents the love of the mother for her children. National unity results from this love of country. Self-integration is also produced from love of self.

Hanged Man

Love and allegiance often produces sacrifices, the mother sacrificing herself for her young. Sacrificing for the good of the whole, for the state or society, is symbolized by the *Hanged Man*. Hanging upside down on the cross represents the restraint of the man's own desires and self-expression. The Hanged Man manifests itself in the context of the individual as one who puts aside, sacrifices desires of the mind, for example, to take care of other priorities and responsibilities that the inner voice deems more important. Control of the self requires this ability to make sacrifices so that goals which have priority are attainable.

Moon

Community, which implies mutual love and sacrifice, is particularly evident where there is a sense of karmic or spiritual bond. The *Moon* symbolizes the Piscean sea of the collective unconscious, where one moves in unison with others amidst the tides and currents of life to complete the flow and direction of one's particular destiny. A sense of nation is produced when fellow countrymen—united physically, mentally, and emotionally—feel they have been brought together to fulfill some common purpose, such as that felt among the founding fathers of these United States. An individual experiences unity and wholeness in recognizing that one's body, mind, and emotionality have been placed together for a reason, to fulfill the potentials and directions of one's spirit or higher self.

GOVERNMENT

Once the will of an individual or collectivity to govern itself is manifested and there exists an integrated body politic that can be governed, an agreed-upon, legitimate system of decision-making is required.

Emperor

This formal process of government is symbolized by the *Emperor*, who holds the scepter of authority. Without this authority or legitimate decision-making process—whether it be entrusted in a constitution, unwritten tradition, the monarch, politburo, or the army-states are ungovernable. Similar disorder is experienced within individuals when a non-legitimate way of arriving at a personal decision is made. This circumstance is exemplified by the individual who allows him or herself to be pushed into a decision by another rather than make the choice legitimately from within.

Decision-making is the legislative process and must consider all the interests within the body politic, self or state. The Emperor, as he gazes over his domain, is looking out for all the rights and goals of his constituents. His crown represents bringing into his awareness the variety of claims and ambitions that circumference his domain. By holding the globe, the Emperor introduces the interests of the realm into the actual physical process of becoming law through their representation in the legislature.

As the state must consider the demands of its constituents, so must the individual. The imperatives of the physical body, the desires of the mind, the feelings of the heart, and the pull of the spirit must be represented and consulted in the decision-making process. The art of politics is the ability to bring these interests together and fashion decisions with which all can live and benefit. The Emperor symbolizes this legislative skill as he is the builder, the number 4, representing his ability to fit together opposing and cross-cutting aims and demands into a structure that supports and houses all.

The Emperor symbolizes not only the legislative function of governance but the executive as well in his capacity of executing the laws and decisions. Like the sun, he radiates or promulgates the decisions. He carries out or physically performs the decision, which is symbolized by the scepter (law) he holds in his hand—an expression of physicality. Decisions made by states, groups, or individuals are as effective as their implementation. Good decisions do not constitute good government unless properly executed.

Justice

As conditions change and new situtations arise, what were once legitimate and fair decisions and laws become unjust and inappropriate. In these instances, it becomes necessary to make adjustments, adjudicate the decision, as symbolized by *Justice* or *Adjustment*. As states have judicial systems for adjusting the law, so do individuals. The self has an internal judge that evaluates and judges the appropriateness of a decision. This system of review is a feedback function that allows the individual or collectivity to reevaluate and readjust its course. This adjudicatory function enables the body politic to keep up with changing times and events, and to steer away from directions that become cloudy and obstacle-filled.

Judgment

Effective governance also depends upon virtuous decisions. *Judgment* or *The Aeon* symbolizes the principle of virtue through the law of karma—that our thoughts, words, and actions sow the seeds for the future birth of our lives and circumstances. Lack of virtue creates unfortunate, deleterious effects, while virtuousness brings reward.

Virtuous decisions and actions are those that one knows in his or her heart of hearts is right. The Priestess or conscience dwelling within the individual or within the collective hearts of the nation must be consulted. Lack of virtue creates malaise and weakness within the body politic (witness the effects of Watergate). Virtue produces strength, self-respect, and integration—necessary ingredients for effective autonomy.

Wheel of Fortune

Good governments produce benefits for their constituents. Autonomy is the process of moving oneself around, like the *Wheel of Fortune*, to enhance well-being. Decisions or laws should change situations to bring new rewards. Virtuous decisions are those that distribute rewards equally. The Wheel of Fortune is a 360-degree circumference that represents the whole domain. Thus, as it revolves, touching the entirety, the rewards reach all, whether it be the entire populace of a state, all the employees of a firm, or all the constituents of the individual—mind, body, heart, and spirit. A decision that benefits the mind by placating its ambitions but that does not reward the body and places undue burdens upon the physical self is not virtuous.

Devil

Rewards do not result without work. *The Devil*, as the goat, symbolizes the hard work, "working like the devil," required in climbing the mountain to attain the rewarding grasslands. The Devil, as the pre-Christian concept of Pan, also represents play and merriment. To be alive, to have *lived* (which is the devil spelled backwards) requires an equal distribution of work and play. Virtuous decisions require equal burdens of work and equal opportunities for reward. Unfair divisions of labor amongst citizens, employees, and constituents of the self produce ineffective governance. In states, the "working classes" revolt when they feel their work is not commensurate with their rewards. In the self, the body breaks down by carrying the burden of work in supporting and pleasing the desires and ambitions of the mind.

ADAPTABILITY

Universe

The lesson of *The World* or *Universe* symbol is that we must be aware (turn the Crowley-Harris card sideways, and it becomes an eye) that there is nothing permanent or static within the universe except change. Because of its impermanence, the universe is a continual process of evolution.

Governance is the process of evolution, responding or adapting to changing circumstances. States, organizations, or individuals die if they do not adapt, just like plants and animals that cannot adjust.

All is interrelated within the universe. Although it is necessary to protect one's boundaries and self-integrity, borders are always porous. Any change within the natural or social ecological web of the universe affects individuals and groups, and requires adaptation.

The individual or group is a microcosm, a reproduction in miniature of the macroworld, the universe. Therefore, changes occur spontaneously within the microcosm, as in the universe. These internal developments also require adjustments.

Hierophant

Effective self-autonomy is established through this universe-consciousness, whose features are also depicted in the *Hierophant*. Adaptiveness is the capability to learn, to teach oneself. The Hierophant, as the revealer or teacher, represents openness and receptivity to new information coming from the external and internal universe, and the ability to learn from or adapt to those new inputs. Learning or adapting requires curiosity, the curiosity represented by the child in the heart of the Crowley-Harris Hierophant.

Hermit

It is impossible to adapt and make adjustments unless one is free to change. The *Hermit*, as the solitary and self-sufficient person, is free to move in new directions because he has no one dependent upon him nor is he dependent upon anyone else. Individuals and nation-states that are dependent upon the resources of others are limited in their expression, and thus less viable.

The Hermit is the 9 card (the number of completion) and Virgo (the sign of the completor) symbolizes the ability to achieve goals. Lack of completion prevents one from being fully free to journey into new experience. One is hung-up by the incompleted past, as illustrated by the love relationship that is terminated before it has run its full course and so prevents the individual from involvement in new relationships.

Completion implies having goals, which is central to the process of governance. Without goals there is nowhere to steer, nothing to govern. Life is meaningless. These goals must be reasonably attainable, otherwise one becomes stuck in futility. Realistic goal-setting comes from Hermit-like introspection, of going within and seeing one's own real needs, preferences, and capabilities. Too often goals are determined by others' standards and values.

Death

Once goals have been realized or even cut short of completion by unforeseen circumstances, the adaptive self-governor is able to let go and move on, as represented by *Death*. Hanging on for comfort and security to outmoded perceptions, values, feelings, structures, and circumstances ossifies. This is the antithesis of flexible adaptiveness. Individuals who play out their lives in marriages that exist only in name and bureaucracies that produce regulations and budgets only to maintain their existence are examples of living death. Those who have mastered the art of letting go and terminating are truly alive.

Art

The process of death, of releasing one's hold, creates new life. Death, in the Crowley-Harris Tarot, is followed by *Art*, or creativity. Adaptiveness is the ability to create new goals, direction and purpose. The void left by the letting-go process of death allows new life to emerge.

The Art principle symbolizes the alchemical or creative progression of death bringing life by the breakdown of old structures and *modi operandi*, or the dissolution of elements (death), that are then put together into new forms and behavior.

Tower

Truly adaptive systems regularly induce change, which automatically dissolves rigidity and promotes the death-rebirth process. Political elections exemplify this *Tower*-like, self-caused change. The figures flying out of the Tower symbolize the process of clearing out the old governors, politicians, forcing them to adapt to the changing times or be unseated by those who are representative. Democracy, because of its elections, has the virtue of adaptability.

Many individuals, like most nation-states, lack peaceful and regularized means of change and so suffer its extreme expression, which is revolution, symbolized by the falling Tower. Revolution is a fiery and abrasive form of adaptation made necessary when systems have blocked or resisted change for lengthy periods of time. Built-in processes of mandatory, periodic reevaluation make adaptation a gentle process of letting go and recreating.

It is the rare individual and state that espouses "permanent revolution," like Maoist China, which is continual upheaval and change. The reason is that extreme flexibility results in no continuity and stability. States and organizations, like individuals, need cohesiveness and a sense of self, self-understanding, and self-integrity. Without that base, one is merely reacting to external forces. The self or state is rudderless and flounders this way and that, going nowhere. Adaptiveness is the process of going with the winds, blending in with the environment without losing one's sense of self, direction, and purpose.

The Charioteer's self-identity and the Hermit's search for himself, to know who he is and where he is going, produce this inner core of stability. The Constitution, or one's inner self-constitution—the understood structure of principles and philosophy that guide oneself—is a stable framework upon which a variety of forms, masks, and modes of behavior can take shape. The chameleon changes its colors in adapting to different environments, but its essence remains the same.

Fool

Adaptability is not only the freedom to change but also willingness to adjust. Change is moving from the security of the known to the unknown. Adaptive individuals and organizations must have an element of the *Fool* within them, as the Fool is like the trusting child without fear, stepping off and leaping into unexplored territories.

As the number zero, the Fool is always in a zero-space consciousness, meaning that every moment of life is a new experience, a new situation that requires response and adaptation. Life is a process of always being at zero, of new beginnings from moment to moment. By approaching life as the Fool does, the individual or collectivity is continually reborn. The Fool is the springtime. He represents renewal, the new life that results from taking steps into the unknown.

SUMMARY

Awareness of these guiding tenets in one's life enables us to get in touch with ourselves, with the different constituencies of the self such as mind, body, heart, and spirit. Knowing the self is automatically self-integrating. Awareness is the glue that unites these facets of the self.

The eye of the Universe not only holds it together but guides as well. Awareness of self is the governor, the Emperor. Awareness coalesces the constituents and interests, and translates these claims into decisions, policies, and direction. Self-awareness is intrinsically adaptation. Through awareness, one adjusts to the inputs from the constituencies of the self.

Tarot is essentially a tool for enhancing awareness. That heightened consciousness empowers the individual to direct and achieve his or her destiny.

NOTE

1. The particular symbolism, titles, and zodiacal significance of the Major Arcana principles are taken from the Thoth Deck, authored by Aleister Crowley and illustrated by Lady Frieda Harris.

From Sex and Romance
to Love and Oneness

David Quigley

O■O■O■O■O■O■O■O■O■O■O■O■O

Human sexual desires have long been regarded by traditional Christian teachings as a barrier to the soul's spiritual progress. Much was made of the difference between "profane love" (sex = sin) and "sacred love" in Christian literature. Many of the symbols in conventional Tarot decks reflect this dualistic attitude. In the Devil card for example, the Greek god Pan—patron of sex, wine, and song—becomes the symbol of evil incarnate. The Moon card, for untold centuries the symbol of fertility and sexual love, rules in the medieval Tarot over a nightmare of baying dogs and a lobster crawling from the depths. Usually interpreted to mean "superstition, illusions, and madness (lunacy)," this card again reflects the low regard for human sexuality characteristic of patriarchal Christian teachings.

In 1962, a meditation group in Big Sur, California, received through the mediumship of a Ouija board, a *New Tarot for the Aquarian Age*,[1] a deck which returns to veneration the Mother and her creation. This deck regards sexual love not as a gross perversion of divine love but as a necessary and sacred part of learning what love truly is. It is, in fact, our sexual and familial urges which provide the push toward intimacy and compassion. Without these desires, we would wander aimlessly in our self-centered preoccupation with material goals.

Through the card-symbols of the *New Tarot for the Aquarian Age*, we see how the individual's spiritual development is intimately connected with the transformation of sexual energy into compassionate love. This is not achieved in the Aquarian Age by suppression or control of sexual desires but by deliberately and joyfully embracing our sexual nature, and by experiencing through relationships both temporary fulfillments and frustrations. It is through these efforts at relationship that we gain the experience necessary for an understanding of true love. As we experience the frustration of our romantic attachments, each of us learns eventually to focus the intense energy of romantic feelings on the exploration of our own subconscious minds. Here we discover the Mother, the source of all love who is within every heart and who gives us the foundation for a new kind of love, in which sexual and familial expectations take a comfortable second place to the blissful and all-embracing compassion of "True Love," a love founded upon the unity of male and female within our own individual hearts.

FROM SEX TO LOVE: THE SEVEN STAGES

The twenty-two major symbols of the *New Tarot for the Aquarian Age* are divided into seven stages in this journey from ego-centered separateness to spiritual unity. These stages correspond to the seven "chakras" or energy centers of the human psychic body.

1. Survival: The survival chakra, located at the base of the spine, is the center of the physical body. The desire for material gain, sexual conquest, and gross physical power are located here. The body at this level is seen as an object to be manipulated for pleasure through sex, drugs, and physical activity. The body is adorned and worshipped as a symbol of one's social status and attractiveness. (Tarot cards 1-3 *Royal Maze* through *Seeker*.)

2. Dependency: The second chakra is located just below the navel, and opens our capacity for emotional connectedness to lovers and family. It opens us to the experience of need, humility, and trust. (Tarot cards 4-8, *Deliverer* to *Renewer*.)

3. Power: Located at the solar plexus, the third chakra rules our personal power and the development of a personal identity based on creativity and self-knowledge. (Tarot cards 9-11, *Thinker* to *Hanged Man*.)

4. Compassion: Located at the heart, this chakra opens the person to an experience of pure compassionate love. Depending on the inner self for love and strength leads to a new sense of peace and a new capacity for selfless giving. (Tarot cards 12-16, *Mother* to *Donor*.)

5. The Creative Word: The throat chakra rules our speaking and healing power. The awakening of love brings the capacity for healing the world through speech and action. (Tarot cards 17 and 18, *Speaker* and *Doer*.)

6. **Vision:** Opening the "third eye" (a light-sensitive organ located behind the center of the forehead and labeled the "pineal gland" by modern science) gives one a direct vision of the souls of all beings and the nature of Godhead. (Tarot cards 19 and 20, *Changer* and *Wayshower*.)

7. **Being:** Located at the top of the head, this chakra opens us to a unity with the Higher Self. Represented as the halo over the heads of saints and messiahs, this chakra is our direct connection to the God-essence. (Tarot cards 21 and 22, *Knower* and *Citadel*.)

First Chakra: Survival, Sex, and Ego

In the first chakra, we experience sex as an orgasm-centered pleasure, a mere manipulation of bodies inextricably tied to one's personal pride and desires for conquest or social acceptance. At this stage the soul is neither prepared for nor interested in true intimacy. The moral tenets of society frown on such attitudes toward sex, thus often producing the "idol-prostitute" complex, in which available sex partners are regarded as base or disgusting, while unattainable idols are worshipped with religious zeal. Here, the needs for self-indulgence and self-assertion coexist with fears of intimacy and responsibility.

Royal Maze: This represents pursuit of sexual pleasure, material gain, and social prestige. Drunk on the wine of desire, we sail upon the vast ocean of life, holding aloft our frail egos and seeking an ever-elusive vision of success, security, and peace. The seven chakras are seen as seven wheels. In contrast to the *Citadel* card (the very highest level of human consciousness), here we see the chakras of one who is lying down—spiritually asleep. Our "Wheel of Fortune" (the earlier name of this card) is spun by two lions: *pride* and *anger*.

Nameless One: Alas, the pleasures of casual relationships and lusty self-indulgence do not last long. The Fool falls from the cliff to find disappointment, disease, frustruation, and loneliness at the end of each round of self-indulgent escapism; if we are lucky, we see the uselessness of our selfish behavior. In the face of sorrow and death, we wake up to the uselessness of lives lived only for pleasure. (Beware of the bitterness and self-pity of those who reverse this cards' meaning.)

Some people find it easier to blame "cruel fate" or "evil humanity" for their misfortune than to see the *Nameless One* as a valuable lesson about their own egotism.

Seeker: In reaction to the greed, lust, and egotism of the Royal Maze, our Seeker now pursues the purity and bliss of a transcendental goal, often with a degree of fanaticism which surprises his old drinking buddies. Many paths are open to the Seeker. He may pursue Christianity, Zen meditation, *est*, or a highly romanticized vision of love. If he is of a more practical bent, he may become an activist or revolutionary (Seeker reversed). The path he follows is often valid, but several qualities label this blindfolded Seeker as a raw beginner on the path of spiritual awareness: dogmatic beliefs which exclude the validity of other paths, an attitude of superiority and aloofness to all those who do not share one's particular breed of fanaticism, a zealous evangelism which fails to take account of other people's real spiritual needs, impatience with the gross material plane, and repression of normal emotional needs leading to a pervasive angry tension which may be poorly masked as "concern." The Seeker's rampant egotism is expressed in the dogmatism and pride with which he enters his spiritual path.

Second Chakra: Romance

Now we enter the second chakra of emotional dependency and need, the beginning of the "Romance Cycle":

Deliverer: This spiritual house of cards tumbles and falls when one meets that mysterious other, the stranger across a crowded room who suddenly and unexpectedly turns a key inside of us to a new world . . . the world of Love. Having drunk the cup of passion we find the old answers, the old lusts, delusions, and spiritual pretenses become a heap of rubbish as we fall in love with a real person. Lucky are those of us who fall in love with a spiritual guru or spirit guide, who will take us much farther into consciousness than the earthly lover whom most of us find in that magic moment. (The reversed meaning of this card is all too common. Unrequited love is a product of our own sense of inadequacy and desperation, and not a doom cast upon us by fate. Relax your desperate clinging, and love will surely come your way.)

Victorious One: The glorious payoff of the romance cycle comes when our love is returned by the ideal being whom we love. The world seems so rich and beautiful when our love is returned. Somehow even the most cynical and hard-boiled realist among us is bound to experience the joy of being loved as a kind of giddy excitement which no rationalization can seem to push aside. However often the romance cycle may have failed, with each new beginning, the heavens seem to open with the sound of bells, birds, and sweet, sweet music. I should mention that the Romance cycle which begins at the Deliverer can be played for stakes other than a lover. We may choose a family, a friendship, a creative pursuit, or a career as our Deliverer from loneliness, alienation, or spiritual egotism. The romance cycle begins whenever we place our salvation in the hands of anyone other than our own inner self!

Reverser: In the hot brilliance of the noonday sun, the Reverser turns the waters of love into the fires of disappointment, frustration, anger, and intuitive understanding. All the grandiose illusions of the Victorious One are shattered by the Reverser, as the real differences between the expectations and the reality of a lover or family member are exposed in the course of the relationship. This threatens not only the viability of the relationship but also one's whole sense of self-esteem built on the false hopes of the Romance cycle. Now we discover how close are Love and Hate!

So what is our response to this situation?

The Actor: Most of us, alas, find it too easy to bury the hatchet and make peace without resolving the conflicts brought up by the Reverser. To preserve our identity as the beloved, we play a game of love we no longer really feel. Not that all of these whispered promises are conscious lies. On the contrary, it is quite customary to deceive ourselves as much as we deceive our beloved; to repress the shattered ideal of love completely and play the romance game over and over within a framework of mutual self-deceit. Gradually, however, a raging, dark, nameless hatred builds up in the unconscious mind, slowly but inevitably eclipsing all the joys of romance, until one partner or another is forced to back off in revulsion and terror from the cruelly distorted face of the beloved. Then we ask, those of us who are left behind: "Why did she leave without any explanation, as if she couldn't even stand to be near me? What happened to our love that only yesterday was so beautiful, and why is there not even a friendship remaining?"

Renewer: Thus we enter the gateway of the Renewer, the old card of Death. The card means to abandon one's expectations of a relationship. It does not mean that the relationship must end, though often the experience of the Renewer will shatter a weak relationship. But one must abandon the hopes and expectations of the romance cycle. One must admit, with Jackson Browne:

Looking deep into your eyes
It was no one I had ever known
What an empty surprise
To be so alone.[2]
—Jackson Browne

"To be so alone" . . . to accept one's basic aloneness in this world is the hard, bitter lesson of the Renewer, yet it is a lesson we all must learn. There is no soulmate except the one who is within one's own self. Nor is "true love" ever founded on mutual expectations.

Although the emotional nature (the kneeling woman) weeps at Death's bitter lesson, the rational mind sees within the eyes of the skull the lemniscate, symbol of eternal life. Only as we are freed from the limitations of our romantic attachments do we discover the infinite potential of the free soul.

Beware the common trap. Refusing to accept the experience of the Renewer, many of us seek consolation in another lover or a return to the safety of family and friends. While these retreats are necessary and valid at times, these cycles will all lead back to Death's dark doorway. Why not enter that doorway now, and experience the sorrow, bliss, and true transcendence waiting on the other side?

Third Chakra: Power

Here in the third chakra of personal power begins the "cycle of the dragon's belly," the journey into the self through meditation, solitude, and therapy. This cycle is so named for the hero of a thousand legends who is swallowed by a dragon (or whale), only to be transformed.

Thinker: One's initial attempts to transcend are represented by the Thinker. Seeking to detach himself from his overpowering feelings, he sits in meditation. But his head is chained between two symbols. A couple in embrace represents his persistent yearnings for sexual fulfillment. Yet the bleeding heart on the other side shows the sorrow which he experiences every time he tries to remain detached and contemplative. He bears in physical and psychic tension a world of pain and sorrow held back by the dam of intellectual analysis. His constant thinking sits on top of his repressed feelings, while he reads books, consults friends and therapists, and may even compile lists of appropriate changes in his mode of relationship.

But while this kind of work may be necessary and important, it is no solution to the heart's endless ache.

Feeler: Instead, he must delve into his feelings, exploring within his own unconscious mind the primal pain, ecstasy and sorrow which have been buried so long beneath the cycles of romance. In screams of rage and aching sobs of pain, the unmet needs of childhood are vented, released by the healing embrace of the Feeler from the muscular and psychic armor where they have been trapped for so long. Primal therapy, Gestalt, and bioenergetics are all techniques by which we release the pent-up panorama of feelings which have so long ruled our lives from behind the veils of repression. The Feeler discovers not just a person who needs love but a whole world of "inner personalities"—the tiny baby craving the breast, the old man fearing death, the ecstatic hermit, the suicidal hater of self and life—all combat mercilessly for control of the conscious mind. Fortunately, the guiding light of the Mother (the sign of Cancer behind the Feeler's head) leads us through the agonies and ecstasies of this stage, while the conscious mind is bowled over by the panorama of irrational feelings it can neither dismiss nor explain.

Hanging Man: Having sounded the depths of the Feeler's conflicting passions, the Hanging Man realizes that what the Thinker regards as a problem is in fact a paradox. His dilemma is expressed by the two figures who hang from his arms. The woman on his right seeks to rise above the dark prison of the romance cycle. While the Thinker seeks to figure out a solution for his emotional dilemma, the Hanging Man knows from the experience of his own inner contradictory feelings that there is no solution in human love for his endless frustration. The error is not in his partner or his approach or even in his neuroses, but is a basic condition of human existence. While romance does not exist without mutual dependence, this very dependence dooms our efforts at love to frustration! Thus, he weeps. And in remaining open to this paradox is the Hanging Man's redemption. For the sun that rises behind him will soon show the light of the Mother.

Fourth Chakra: Compassion

Now the heart chakra opens, center of compassionate love.

Mother: Despairing of a solution to his loneliness and sorrow, the soul takes a "leap of faith" into the arms of the Mother, who rocks him on the ocean of her unending love. Trust is the power and love of a greater self is the only escape from the limitations of earthly love. When one trusts, all the gates of paradise open, and fill the suffering soul with all the love one needs.

This card represents a belief in an Inner Deity who has no fixed doctrines, no judgment of nonbelievers, and no moral imperatives other than the one law of Love. This distinguishes the Mother from the Judeo-Christian Father, who punishes or rewards his children according to their beliefs and adherence to his strict laws. The Mother loves all her children in whatever ways they may approach her and by whatever names they may call her.

Reactor:

"I have finally found a place to live
In the presence of the Lord
And I know that I don't have much to give
But I can open any door."
—Blind Faith

The reborn child of the Mother, his heart bursting with joy and gratitude, holds two keys to the seven chakras (trust and surrender). Abandoning all ego-directed activity, he relies completely on the love and protection of the Mother/Moon which, in the background, illuminates his new path to wholeness. He is ready for a new spiritual journey unfettered by the needs and frustrations of his past. He is aware of his weakness and need, but trusts in the Mother to make all things right.

Virgin: Now is the time to return to the world from the dragon's belly to develop the Reactor's newfound love. The Virgin is just learning how to relate to others with a new perspective that is neither romance nor ego-oriented. She seeks to become a pure vehicle for the radiance of divine grace. Through relating to the opposite sex, she now seeks a new wholeness of male and female within her own psyche, so that she may attain the inner peace of Unity.

Unity: Here, the Virgin's goal of hermaphroditic wholeness is achieved as the inner mate (*anima* or *animus*) merge with the conscious ego. The feelings here are similar to those of the Victorious One, but now an inner wholeness (rather than external lover) is the permanent and reliable source of the blissful feeling of completeness which is "true love." It is this urge toward Unity that drives us mortals from one incomplete romantic attachment to another and finally reaches its only true fulfillment in the inner Unity of the Androgyne.

Donor: Now begins the task of manifesting love through action in the world, a task which begins with the Donor. Here the free giving of love is a spontaneous expression of the joy of Unity. But the moral responsibility of the Donor weighs heavily upon her, because in the New Age there is no rule book of virtue; in her own hands she holds the pillars of good and evil. She must learn to trust the greater hands to support her in developing the moral judgment that is of the greatest importance to her in creating the capacity for loving action.

Fifth Chakra: Creative Word

Now the fifth chakra of the throat opens to reveal our latent powers of teaching and healing.

Speaker: Speaking the words of Truth is the Donor's next step, the opening of the fifth chakra. Unlike the Pope or Hierophant of earlier decks, the Speaker wears no robes of traditional doctrinal authority. Instead, he speaks from the glowing heart of his awakened consciousness. He holds the circle of inner Unity and the key to understanding, as if to say: "I have found the circle of wholeness, and with this key you may find it, too!"

Doer: Development of inner discipline and the power of action is the next step for the spiritual aspirant, whose whole life must now become an example of the truth of her teachings. In the light of the Sun, the Doer's actions are an open book in which others may read the lessons they read for their development.

Sixth Chakra: Vision

The "Third Eye" of Inner Vision now opens.

Changer: One level above "doing," the Changer practices "not doing" (*wu-wei*) to heal the earth on which he stands. While appearing to do nothing, he is using his third eye to bring the things he needs into his life and the lives of others. All of us have experienced those peculiar "coincidences" in which it seems that a Higher Power sets up lessons or gave us much-needed help at a moment when we could go no further without it. Prophetic dreams or sudden insights from a total stranger, the random turning of a book's pages or the shuffle of a pack of cards. . . . All of these are examples of the mysterious power of the Changer (formerly the Magician). While all of us experience brief glimpses of the Changer's power, only after climbing above the futile cycles of romantic and egocentric addictions and learning the true nature of love do we gain total control of the creative powers of the Changer. Simply by focusing our intention, all things can be brought to us, to serve the only true purpose for our transformed lives . . . to love.

Way-Shower: The Star of earlier decks comes to life at the dawn of the Aquarian Age. Operating in the night of the subconscious mind, the Way-Shower communicates wisdom from higher planes to Earth without the need for activity or speech. He knows others' needs and can heal them through the powers of telepathy, inspiration, revelation, dreams, and prayer. The cup of many colors reveals the multiplicity of teachers and teachings through which God creates a new covenant—the rainbow—with humanity.

Seventh Chakra: Oneness

Now the seventh chakra, the "crown," opens; and the Adept experiences Oneness with the universal Godhead.

Knower: The Knower stands firmly in both the fires of passion and the waters of love, from which he has distilled the steam of insight. In his hand, he holds an egg, symbol of the New Life sprouting forth. Over his head the glowing sun of God-consciousness illuminates the Knower and the world to which the Knower returns as savior and teacher. In the Piscean Age, Gabriel's horn ends the world in the Judgment card. Now in this Age, each of us ends our own cycle of reincarnation by opening the inner door to God-consciousness.

Citadel: Here are the seven chakras of completed man. The old trump pictured the Tower struck by lightning, showing how God destroyed man's attempts to build an institution of spiritual perfection. Now, in the New Age, each of us builds our own inner temple of seven stories . . . a Citadel that can never be destroyed!

Seven symbols complete the Citadel, a picture of the seven chakras of the psychic body:

The closed book (First Chakra) represents the closed mind of the escapist Royal Maze and the dogmatic Seeker. The Yin-Yang symbol (Second Chakra) shows the male-female polarity of the romance cycle. The lion grabbing its tail (Third Chakra) shows the power of mind turning inward upon itself in the search for truth. The torch (Fourth Chakra) is the light of Love, lit in the heart by the Mother. The embracing couple (Fifth Chakra) shows love in action through communication. The serpent is the *Kundalini* force reaching the third eye (Sixth Chakra) to illuminate the Adept's higher vision. At the Seventh Chakra is the glowing top of the Lighthouse, which guides the Seeker through the snares and pitfalls of the lower chakras to the unchanging One, the Source.

This Lighthouse will be my guide through all the egotisms, the expectations, and the programs which we mortals use to fill the hollow places in us, and which (I will finally discover) only the light of the Goddess can fill. I will live out my fantasies, explore my passions, and embrace my desires, dancing to the rhythm of every passing excitement and every new relationship. Yet this Lighthouse may serve to remind me that only in that last dance with the One who made me will I find my Home.

NOTES

1. John Cooke and Rosalind Sharp, *New Tarot for the Aquarian Age*, Western Star Press, Box 248, Kentfield, CA 1968. This deck should not be confused with the *Aquarian Tarot*, (Palladini, Llewellyn Publishers), an attractive reworking of the traditional symbols.
2. "Late for the Sky"—from the album of the same name. The entire album is a must for the serious student of the Romance cycle.

WHEELS OF CHANGE
Unfoldment Through Tarot

Medieval Astrological Calendar

T arot itself is a "living wheel." As the
leaves of a tree mark the seasonal changes
for the tree, so do the varied symbols of Tarot
mark the seasons of change within one's psyche.
Just as the snake moves to guard, heal, change
and reveal aspects of the tree and itself, so do the
symbols in Tarot reveal the type of movement
and growth within consciousness. Tarot provides a pathway for the four stages of transformation: emanation, fruition, dissolution, and
reemanation. These four stages of transformation comprise the structure for change repeated
symbolically by the four aspects of the tree, the
four seasons, the four universal transformation
snakes, the four elements, and the four suits of
the Tarot.

In summary, Tarot can be used as a tool to
encourage transformation and change that yields
growth. This is evidenced in the application of
Tarot for changing beliefs (Turner), flexing the

body (Cole), pouring out feelings (Bolinger), and transforming and creating qualities of personality and character (Stine); (Gombold). Like the tree, with its deep roots and solid trunk, the Tarot stabilizes growth-transformation through its structuring properties. The Tarot balances movement with stability, flexibility with structure, transformation with maintenance, and integration with expansion.

The Seed

Within all life transitions, the beginning of transformation is initiated internally with existing archetypes emerging at different rates of emphasis to prod the beginning of each new cycle. this is the state of "no season." It is the seed, the source, the period of germination. In the Tarot, it is represented by the Major Arcana, the 'major teachings' or 'archetypes' that are present in the subconscious. It is the threshold.

Anne Stine, in " Archetypes, Tarot, and Self-Transformation," elucidates how the connection between the Tarot and archetypes stimulates awareness of origination. Often it is the Tarot symbol which pictorially reveals the archetype that is prevalent in consciousness. The Tarot, as a visual expression of archetypes, establishes a relationship between the individual psyche and the archetype. This, in turn, generates and transforms energy. In nature, this is the relationship between the earth, as psyche, and the seed, as archetype.

○■○■○■○■○■○■○■○■○■○■○■○

Japanese Heraldic Crests

Archetypes, Tarot, and Self-Transformation

Anne Stine, MA, MFCC

O■O■O■O■O■O■O■O■O■O■O■O■O

As a result of working with Tarot symbolism in my own life and in consultation with individuals, couples and groups, I found myself noticing that something very significant and powerful occurred—namely, specifically heightened sensitivity to one's internal and external life; a willingness to see this life differently; an increased participation in choices and decision-making, and a stronger health profile - mentally, emotionally and physically. This all amounted to "change"—a change in which relationships became smoother; working and living conditions moved more in alignment with what individuals wanted; and, most significantly, a feeling of self-love and self-esteem grew and could be more fully shared with others. I began to wonder: "How does the Tarot work so uniquely with each individual?" and "Why do I know I am looking at myself and at a wider aspect of human experience as well when relating to the symbols on any particular card?"

The study of these questions led me to explore the significance of the archetypal images in the Tarot and their role in the transformation of individual and collective consciousness. After a brief look at the nature or patterns of the archetypal symbolism in the Tarot, particularly in the framework of Jungian psychology, a lengthier discussion of "how" the process of transformation can occur within an individual through recognition of the meaning of these archetypes will follow in this article. Tarot will then be described as an important visual tool which gives meaning to this symbolic process through the relationship it triggers between the individual psyche and the archetypes. The article concludes with the presentation of an individual case study to illustrate this process of transformation.

ARCHETYPES AS ENERGY

Jung refers to the elusive and difficult task of describing the archetypes when he says that "the only thing consistent with their nature is their manifold meaning, their almost limitless wealth of reference which makes any unilateral formulation impossible."[1] A full appreciation and amplification of any archetype is an inexhaustible undertaking. Archetypes are essentially paradoxical and ambiguous and cannot be contained within a single meaning or interpretation. However, their meaning is revealed through common patterns of human experience and in universal images evident in culture from time immemorial.

Jung found evidence or indicators of the core of the archetypes through his in-depth cross-cultural study of dreams, visions, myths and fairytales. He observes that certain archetypal themes and images exist in the collective unconscious[2] influencing and shaping individual thoughts and actions and can be seen universally as patterns governing human consciousness. "From the unconscious there emanate determining influences which, independently of tradition, guarantee every single individual a similarity and even a sameness of experience."[3] The archetypes are the energy (or vibration) which forms the images within the collective unconcious. Their content only fills out with meaning as they become conscious within the individual through experience. In other words, the archetype is a constellation of energy which gives unique meaning to individual and collective consciousness through experience and a recognition of its presence.

The meaning of the archetypal images cannot be grasped by the linear mind but only through symbol and myth, or the symbolic experience. Thus, the "basic or original unit of mental functioning is the image."[4] From these basic images the linear mind creates "safety islands" of concepts in order to function in the world. Continual and direct experience with the collective unconscious could be overwhelming—as if one were submerged in a vast, limitless ocean with no boundaries or containment (madness is just such an experience). Yet, it is the direct contact with the symbols arising from this oceanic experience that can reconnect an individual with the wholeness or totality of being, creating meaning in their life and providing access to healing for a fragmented psyche and civilization. Symbols and myths then become the doorways which lead us back to and even precede direct experience of ourselves. It is important to understand here that it is our relationship to these archetypal images which creates and allows for the flow of energy through conscious experience.

INTEGRATING THE ENERGY OF ARCHETYPES

Recognition of archetypal images and themes and integration of their energy into the individual psyche is the key to wholeness in a growth process Jung called "individuation." Because the archetypes are understood as the original structural forms of potential energy in the collective unconscious, they have an autonomy of their own. If they are not made conscious, i.e. if they are repressed, consciousness projects them outward and the energy of the images and themes then hides behind ideas and figures which may become problematic, or blown out of proportion. At this point the conscious psyche of the individual may feel possessed or overshadowed by the autonomous archetype. It seems that when the unity of the psyche is split off into parts, the nature of the conscious mind is to resist the archetype, thus creating the experience of being controlled or possessed by their energy. This is seen very dramatically in intimate relationships when both parties become infatuated with their own positive or negative qualities by projecting them onto the other person. They both feel a "need" to be with the other because s/he has something the other one does not recognize within her/himself.

Jung used the term "individuation" to denote the process by which a person becomes a psychological "in-dividual"—that is, a separate, indivisible unity or "whole."[5] The process occurs naturally within each individual if the dialogue between the conscious and unconscious is not "suppressed or injured"[6] in some way. A meaningful dialogue between the conscious psyche and the archetypal world is essential to growth and creativity. The ego is neither fully defended against the contents of the unconscious, nor is the latter ruling the individual life through chaos and irrationality. Rather, there is "open conflict and open collaboration at once"[7] which leads ultimately to the fully individuated creative person.

Individuation can occur once the autonomous patterns of the archetypal images are recognized. The resolution of the conflict of separation or denial of the energy is then possible, and one can come to terms with it by owning and integrating the potential energy held within the symbol. This usually happens when one is faced with a particularly difficult problem and feels stuck. The goal then is "higher consciousness by means of which the initial situation is overcome on a higher level."[8] In other words, the goal of the symbolic process is to make the symbol conscious. This requires insight, recognition and meaningful application of the new energy released. The energy that had been repressed now becomes available for some form of creative expression.

This process of transformation, then involves the establishment of a meaningful relationship between the individual ego and archetypal images and themes. Edward Edinger has outlined three possible "patterns" for this relationship. The first two, total identification with the archetypes and total alienation from the archetypes, do not give the psyche any access to the energy at their core. In the first relationship, the individual runs the risk of being overwhelmed by the force of the archetypes through hallucinations, paranoia, superstitions or even madness in which they may actually feel that the inner symbols are external reality. The second relationship denies the power of the symbols as pointing to any real meaning beyond what is already known. In other words, life loses its vitality and mystery.

In the third possibility the ego remains "open and receptive to the effects of symbolic imagery" without denying or identifying with the archetype(s). "The symbol is then able to perform its proper function as releaser and transformer of psychic energy with full participation of conscious understanding."[9] In this experience, the archetypal image is seen as a symbol or "picture of meaning."[10] The integration of the symbol into one's life involves a "conscious realization of the underlying drive as a powerful impulse towards meaningful activity or experience."[11]

It thus becomes clear that understanding and relating in a meaningful way to the core energy contained in archetypal images and themes is essential to change. Times of crises are particularly powerful opportunities for encountering the potential of what may previously have been unconscious energies. Powerful emotional experiences of loss, separation, fear, joy, love, faith and exaltation provide opportunities for confronting unrealized parts of the psyche and thus give one the choice of either expanding consciousness or denying the meaning in their experience. Depending on the individual response in these difficult and intensely creative times, one is motivated to further accept and actualize the self or immobilize the energy which arises within.

Becoming aware of the symbolic dimension gives meaning and value to the difficulties and joys of life and allows one to live and grow more fully through both. We can either experience life as a series of painful events or as a "succession of meaningful symptoms, or encounters between the ego and Transpersonal (archetypal) psyche."[12]

USING TAROT TO TAP INTO THE ENERGY OF ARCHETYPES

The Tarot is a powerful and effective tool that aids in this symbolic process of releasing potential energy and establishing a meaningful relationship with the core of archetypal imagery. Edward Whitmont could be describing this ancient initiatory process when he says:

> *The universe manifests in individualized forms—a given personality seems 'called' to incarnate highly specialized facets of the total range of human archetypes. He will live these forms whether he knows about them or not, but their more constructive aspects can be contacted if he does know and can understand them*[13]

The Tarot (meaning "royal road" or map) originated in the Egyptian initiatory tradition when "primitive pictograph writing" on the walls of initiation chambers "conveyed the most important things the ancient wise ones found out about the human soul."[14]

The cards today present us with an archetypal symbolic arrangement of human consciousness, outlining distinctly the various gifts, tests, and opportunities an individual can experience in the process of individuation. The Tarot symbolizes a road along which we pass again and again, (re)learning and (re)experiencing the same lessons, at greater depth and breadth, much like a spiral that leads us back to the same place but from a different perspective.

The Tarot's approach to consciousness is not that of seeking out what is "wrong" or needs to be fixed. Rather, the Tarot focuses on what our gifts are, what we have come here to experience, where we are blocking ourselves, and how we can recognize projected parts of ourselves and move into high-frequency creative states. The assumption here is that our natural state of consciousness is highly creative and abundant and that "negative" or low-frequency states offer lessons or doorways to "knowing" more of who we truly are.

In the process of self-transformation, it is not only the individual with whom we are concerned, but, as Dane Rudhyar has put it, "the relationship of the lesser whole to the greater whole."[15] This implies that we are whole already; our responsibility is to remember that. The individual is viewed as a perfect miniature of the Divine whole. The relationship is like that of the cell to the organism: essential and individual. Tarot emphasizes that the individual's responsibility is to fulfill what s/he is, in terms of the larger whole, and thereby contribute to the transformation of the whole. Tarot offers an initial evaluation of the individual's gifts and blocks to full creative expression at any given time, including birth. The archetypes make their appearance through the symbols on the cards, and offer the opportunity to dialogue with them (as Jung did in active imagination) and establish a meaningful relationship with all of life.

Working with the Tarot, whether it be in consultation with another individual or alone, produces an accurate "outpicturing" of one's consciousness at that moment. The value here is that the symbols, which are the language of the "archetypal psyche,"[16] are drawn to the ego's attention. During difficult times in one's life, this conscious recognition of living symbolic imagery, which the Tarot represents, can release blocked energy (i.e., help one recognize [own] projected parts of the psyche) and offer meaning and understanding of what is occurring. Even more importantly, the power to change and recreate one's internal and external reality is returned to its source within the individual.

The Tarot is most frequently used during periods of change and/or crisis. Through the cards, one meets the archetypal images behind the often-painful symptoms of change. The symbolic imagery of the Tarot establishes this dialogue (à la Edinger) between the transpersonal ego and the unrecognized or painful parts of the self. Suddenly, there is a relationship that signals the connection between the parts of the individual and the experience is transformed. "It may be just as painful, but now it has meaning."[17] Blocked energy is released, and there is a heightened sense of wholeness and relationship to other humans through common experience. In addition, one is given a visual tool that provides access to the core of potential creative energy (the archetypes).

As Edinger writes, "The symbol leads us to the missing part of the whole man. It relates to our original totality. It heals our split, our alienation from life. And since the whole man is a great deal more than the ego, it relates us to the suprapersonal forces which are the source of our being and our meaning. This is the reason for honoring subjectivity and cultivating the symbolic life."[18]

A CASE STUDY OF SELF-TRANSFORMATION

The case presented here is a study of an individual's learning to know himself. It is an example of how work with the Tarot symbols and contact with the archetypes can awaken latent potential within a psyche. "To open up this store in one's own psyche, to awaken it to new life and integrate it with consciousness, means nothing less than to save the individual from his isolation and gather him into the eternal cosmic process."[19]

The purpose here is to highlight certain Tarot cards as they appeared in three consultations over a two-year period. Through contact with the archetypal symbolism, the client was able to begin to touch the source of his experience in the archetypes and to direct his life with meaning and choice. The interpretations ascribed to the symbolism on the cards come from studies with Angeles Arrien as well as this author's own personal experience.

In general, the Minor Arcana (the Ace through 10 in each of the four suits) are seen as aspects of the archetypes at work. The Major Arcana or trumps symbolize the actual archetype at work, the primordial experience they represent. The Royalty Cards—the Knight, Queen, Prince, and Princess of each suit—symbolize mastery (at the time of the consultation) of a particular aspect (or suit) of a life experience.

The case presented here thus becomes an example of the map of Tarot at work, pinpointing what the client is (un)aware of in certain areas of his life and where he can choose to focus his energy to actualize himself more fully. Although all the cards in each spread are addressed equally during the consultation, only a few are presented here as examples of archetypal energy at work in this case.

The Case: Marc

Marc was in his early thirties, and a business writer in the corporate world, when he had his initial Tarot consultation. He felt significant internal changes and new perspectives about himself. What he wanted in his work and relationships was surfacing, but he was not yet ready to act on his decision. He was seeking guidance and meaning in his life.

The "Whole Person Spread," with its probability line (ladder) into the future, was used to give an overall evaluation of his internal experience and how this was being externalized in various aspects of his daily life. In addition, his personal lifetime card, the Hierophant, and his current growth pattern (then symbolized by the Hermit) were discussed. The lifetime and current-growth cards are determined by a numerological system based on the birthdate (day, month, and year) of the individual. (The system was devised by Angeles Arrien.) The lifetime card represents the basic archetypal energy with which an individual works during a lifetime. The growth card symbolizes the current pattern of energy at work.

Marc's initial response to the Tarot was one of attraction mixed with fear and mistrust. He was particularly affected by the strength of the Hierophant, specifically as it symbolized the archetype of the spiritual teacher within each individual. He felt no personal relationship to the inner wisdom of this card, nor could he see it operating in any way in his daily life. He felt nervous and uncomfortable with his growth card, which was the Hermit, the symbol of completion, perfection, and introspection. He saw the inner search of the Hermit as a withdrawal from life and contact with others, and was afraid of what he might find if he turned within to know himself. The natural gift of the Hermit is to be true to oneself through deep inner exploration.

His initial reading was strong and balanced. However, Marc was very hard on himself, with the Nine of Swords indicating that he was putting himself down very dynamically and needed to make a decision to complete some unfinished business. This card is an aspect of the Hermit (both are 9 on the cards) and indicated he was turning away from his true nature. The High Priestess in the subconscious position indicated that he mistrusted his emotional/intuitive nature which, together with the Nine of Swords, caused him to fear the changes he wanted to make in his life.

Marc felt very disturbed after his first consultation. He was very drawn to what he had seen in the symbols, yet he felt little inner connection with the energy they held for him both internally and in his daily life. He felt somehow controlled by the Tarot, as though the symbols reflected who he was without his having anything to do with it directly. He liked what he saw of himself in the cards, but this outpicturing of himself had little to do with how he was experiencing himself at the time.

Between the first and second consultations (a period of about one year), Marc bought his own Tarot deck, listened to the tape recording of the first reading several times, and began to work with the symbols in his daily life. Gradually, he began to integrate some of the meaning of the symbols and, instead of putting himself down as with the Nine of Swords, he also began to find his self-confidence surfacing, at first internally and then in his outer life. He began to see the Tarot as a reading of his inner self which he could use to actually expand and deepen his self-awareness and give meaning to his experience. With the belief that his whole life mirrored his inner reality, Marc discovered that the symbols did not control him but that he could choose to give them meaning. His relationship with the Tarot began to develop, and the contents of the first consultation were no longer just outside himself, beyond his control. The Six of Disks in the position of his conscious awareness was indicating that he was reaping the rewards for his internal work and that his life had expanded as a result. He was beginning to "know" that he could generate his own success in the world, and he felt comfortable with it. As the first consultation became more alive for him, Marc began to experience the clarity of his own nature as well as his awakening commitment to what was true for him, which was symbolized by the Ace of Wands. It was also becoming clearer to him that he wanted to begin something new in his work, which was symbolized by the Princess of Wands in the position of his creativity. These last two cards indicated that he was coming closer to freeing himself from his work situation but that he was also very frightened and not yet willing to trust his awakening intuition to guide him.

The Prince of Swords (in the relationship position) represents moving through the self-imposed limitations and restrictions that arise when one wants to begin something new. Marc felt determined not to limit his self-expression in his close relationships. He was particularly sensitive to the energy of the Two of Cups (the last card in the first consultation), which symbolized his desire for more depth, meaning and expression of feelings with others. He was becoming aware that close relationships and family solidity were very important to him.

By the time Marc returned for his second consultation, he had decided to give the Tarot "credibility," to give the symbols his own meaning which had developed over the months as he experienced them deepening his awareness of his inner life and place in the world.

This was apparent when he pulled the Star card (XVII Major Arcana) to replace the Nine of Swords in his decision-making position. The Star card symbolizes self-acceptance, and a deep recognition of one's true nature that simultaneously brings about an expansion of creativity in oneself and in one's life. The Nine of Swords appeared again, in the second consultation—this time, in his future work position, indicating his low self-esteem in this area and his reluctance to take action to change it. His concern for the future was also indicated by the Ten of Swords, which expressed his fear of financial ruin. If he followed his inner guidance and left the security of his work situation, would he fail financially? Marc had taken a new but unsatisfactory job. He had been motivated more by financial need than by a feeling that the job was "right" for him. He was not feeling good about himself in his work, and the consultation confirmed for him (with the Nine and Ten of Swords) that he would have the opportunity of coming to terms with his work in the coming year.

The appearance of the Lovers card (VI Major Arcana) in his conscious-mind position revealed that Marc's personal relationships were more fulfilling and that he was aware of this. This card also indicated that he was more in harmony with himself and was therefore relating more creatively with others. He could now experience the balance within himself and how it was reflected in his intimate relationships.

Between the second and third consultations (again a year's time), Marc deepened his relationship with the symbols; and instead of reaching outside himself for meaning in his life, he used the cards daily to reflect this inner search. He found himself taking note of the symbols in his life, so that when he redecorated his home, he chose the colors for the meaning they held for him. He began to discover that this new meaning enabled him to make the changes he wanted in his work and relationships. He was feeling that the Tarot was effectively helping him stay on his "path" and enriching his life.

At the third consultation, the Knight of Swords appeared in his decision-making position, symbolizing his determination to risk the changes he had been leading up to for two years. The Death card (XIII Major Arcanum) revealed symbolically to Marc that he was ready to cut through the limitations and restrictions of an old identity of how he "should" be. He experienced excitement and fear as he felt himself letting go of the old images and beliefs that had been familiar in his life. The Hierophant (his lifetime energy symbolically) was now a real force in his life, and he expressed his commitment to follow the directives of his inner guidance and to make decisions based on that awakening energy within him.

Several weeks after the third (and most recent) consultation, Marc left his job. He described this decision as a clear "inner knowing," which he now feels is his responsibility to follow. His current "job" is to allow the process of healing to occur within him as he makes the transition from what he describes as the "should-be Marc" back to himself, to the child within (which can be seen on the Hierophant card in the Thoth deck) and the emergence of his true being. He feels excited about the uncertainty of his future and is learning to trust the outcome of the choices he has made for his life.

This example holds particular interest because it occurred when Marc was making the transition between the two phases of individuation Jung described.[20] He was struggling to let go of the developments of the first phase—his strong ego and ability to meet the demands of the external world—while wanting to follow the pull to turn inwards, know himself more deeply, and explore his unconscious. In a sense, he was ending one period of his life and initiating a new one simultaneously.

The use of Tarot symbolism at this time drew further attention to and activated the contents of his unconscious, and enabled him to establish a meaningful dialogue between the conscious and unconscious life. In addition, his passage into a new life and transformation of self were eased. His choices were clarified, and he found meaning in his internal conflicts and other events in his life that had seemed beyond his control to handle. The Tarot provided the "sign posts and milestone in such an individuation process . . . [by way of] certain archetypal symbols whose form and manifestation vary with each individual."[21]

NOTES

1. Carl Gustav Jung, *The Archetypes and the Collective Unconscious.* Bollingen Series II, Vol. 9, Part I. p. 38.

2. "...contents resulting from the inherited possibility of psychical functioning in general" within which the archetypes constitute specific universal human patterns. Jolande Jacobi, *The Psychology of C.G. Jung.* New Haven and London: Yale University Press, 1973 Edition. p. 8.

3. Jung, p. 38.

4. Edward Whitmont, *The Symbolic Quest.* New Jersey: Princeton University Press, 1973. p. 28

5. Jung, p. 275

6. *Ibid.,* p. 288.

7. *Ibid.,* p. 288.

8. *Ibid.,* p. 39.

9. Edward Edinger, *Ego and Archetype.* Penguin Books, 1983.

10. Whitmont, p. 80.

11. *Ibid.,* p. 80.

12. Edinger. p. 117.

13. Whitmont. p. 113.

14. Doris Chase Doane and King Keyes, *How to Read Tarot Cards.* New York: Funk & Wagnalls, 1968. p. 19.

15. Dane Rudhyar, *Transpersonal Living.* Cassette tape by Cognetics, Inc. 1976.

16. Edinger. p. 116.

17. *Ibid.,* p. 116.

18. *Ibid.,* p. 130.

19. Jacobi. p. 49.

20. *Ibid.,* p. 108.

21. *Ibid.,* p. 109.

Ouroborus

Roots:
Discovery/Identification

O nce an individual begins the process of growth, there is a period of discovery, extension, and exploration. In this stage, the seed creates its initial root system. It moves from the state of origination and "no season" to the state of discovery and stabilization. This is the period of identifying and labeling the new topography that is being explored. In the psyche, this topographical state is where one initiates the beginning of formulated beliefs and attitudes about the new experience.

This is the season of winter for the tree. A period of unseen exploration and growth. It is the state of mind where ideas are stabilized, explored, and rooted. In Tarot, mental beliefs are symbolized by swords, which represent the variety of attitudes and beliefs in pictorial form. Karen Turner in "Transformational Beliefs and Tarot," shows us the power of belief systems and their function in shaping one's reality. For her, the sword is a tool for cutting through self-limiting beliefs.

How ideas, attitudes and beliefs are constantly changing is represented by the *uroboros*. This snake, in the shape of a ring, looks like a seed, but a seed in motion. By its example of eating its own tail, the uroboros illustrates that change is the only constant and that everything, including ideas and beliefs, are in constant motion, dissolution, and creation.

O■O■O■O■O■O●O■O■O■O■O■O■O

Transformational Beliefs
and Tarot

Karen Turner, MA

O■O■O■O■O■O■O■O■O■O■O■O■O

"A person is neither a thing nor a process but an opening or a clearing through which the Absolute can manifest." So wrote the great philosopher Martin Heidegger. He saw us as "creative workmen" who have the potential for greatness. If we spend a few minutes contemplating this quote as an aphorism (a contemplative statement of truth), we can experience ourselves as that opening, sensing the Absolute flowing through us. Heidegger has poetically written a statement which, when contemplated, actually moves energy. The challenge is to make that opening the purest possible.

Two hypotheses form the basis of this brief article. The first is: the beliefs and images we hold structure the nature of the opening Heidegger talked about. Because of this, we can either facilitate or hinder the flow of consciousness through the way we use beliefs.

The second hypothesis is: the Tarot deck, when used as a symbolic language of transformation, can greatly facilitate connection with and evocation of higher states of consciousness through the aforementioned opening. We will explore these in order.

Whatever the individual or group is attached to by way of images and attitudes will dictate whether the channel to Spirit will be rigid and closed, or flexible and open. Given this, the most valuable and skillful beliefs we can hold are those that lead beyond themselves continuously to higher and deeper levels of consciousness, eventually to the "isness" of the Absolute, the Godhead.

Intention backs up the intuitive choice of which beliefs and images we choose to hold. If a person intends to let go of the limited images she holds of herself, then she will choose beliefs which reinforce this intention.

When dealing with beliefs and images effectively, it is vital to be willing to let them go when they have served their purpose. The most alive and viable way of "holding" any attitude seems to be to hold it lightly and flexibly and to be willing to re-examine it at any time. For example, when our present *experience* tells us that a belief we are holding is no longer accurate, then we can expand awareness, letting go of the old and formulating a new attitude that will carry us into new levels of consciousness.

Assuming that we intend to use the Tarot cards to best advantage, we will look at some beliefs that will help us skillfully use the deck, after first exploring what the cards actually represent.

Viewing Tarot as a symbolic language of transformation, we see that the cards represent various archetypes (patterns of energy in consciousness) and states of consciousness. A person's ability to perceive or experience these states is controlled by the individual's own "filters" and level of evolution. Research shows us that the cards act as doorways through which the state of consciousness represented on the card connects with the corresponding state within the individual's psyche, thus evoking the actual experience of that state. Now, this can happen *regardless of whether* the person *believes* it can. Holding beliefs that attest to the wonder and beauty of this process will greatly facilitate its occurrence, while beliefs stating that this phenomenon is impossible will inhibit and slow down the process—but such beliefs will not stop it altogether.

As an example of how symbols evoke experience, think for a moment of your favorite food. Make it a *vivid* image and memory, and note your experience. Now do the same with perhaps an internal picture of a Nazi swastika (or other symbol that evokes a strong negative reaction inside), and now a star or a Christian cross (or other symbol that evokes for you the highest, most loving state you have ever been in). Symbols are undeniably very powerful evokers of experience.

To carry this experience a little deeper, imagine that you believe that it is very healthy and wonderful to contemplate joyous symbols of Divine Union. How would this belief affect your contemplation of the star, or the cross? Now imagine you believe that it is evil and very wrong even to think about symbols of such union. This belief would also most certainly affect your experience. However, holding such an attitude will not stop the evocation of experience when you see such a symbol. It will merely affect the type of experience, which is your choice. Apply this ritual to one of the Tarot cards, and observe your experience.

TRANSFORMATIONAL BELIEFS

We now come to two examples of beliefs that skillfully help a person use Tarot to facilitate his/her growth. The attitudes aid us in using Tarot as a tool that evokes experiences of higher states within individuals and thus transforms consciousness.

According to the first belief, there does not have to be an "external" reader for the cards to function and be understood. The best interpreter of the cards and their symbolic meanings is the individual using them. This belief, most obviously, puts the individual in charge of his/her own growth and helps increase confidence in one's own ability to be the *best* interpreter possible. It removes the need to look outside of oneself for answers and "expertise." This belief also places the cards at the disposal of everyone, anytime, to be used daily if desired.

The second belief is that working with the various states of consciousness represented by the Tarot cards will lead us to a place of shared experience among all people and a common purpose in life. This is an essential belief for us in our present world situation. Holding such an attitude while working with the cards opens us to internal states that correspond with everyone, which helps us break down barriers that separate us from our deep inner spiritual nature and cause us to judge one another. The more we come to realize our connections and similarities (while honoring our uniqueness), the closer we come to experiencing the reality that we are one people on one planet, basically all striving for the same goals. Working with the Tarot cards, backed with the intention to become whole, leads us to these experiences of common humanity over and over again, and to the knowledge that the ability to experience all states of consciousness lies within each individual.

These are rather brief examples of the types of beliefs that can dramatically aid the Tarot user in facilitating growth. It is worthwhile for you, the reader, to examine the beliefs you hold about the cards and their use. If you find beliefs that are not helping you get the maximum benefit from the cards, explore the source and the intentions behind such beliefs. Perhaps they no longer serve you, and you can let go of them. Affirm those that you find useful plus those you now *want* to believe, and do so each day, allowing them to grow in strength and conviction within your awareness. In other words, place yourself in control of your own attitudes.

In conclusion, *we* do not have the choice whether Absolute Reality exists or what it consists of. It simply is. We can, however, decide whether we wish to perceive and experience Reality. We can wisely, skillfully, and artfully choose our own beliefs and images to be used for personal and global growth. Tarot, as a symbolic language, can be a beautiful, practical, and powerful tool when used to evoke the experiences of transformation within our psyches. Thus, human beings can become clearer instruments through which Spirit can manifest.

ARCHETYPAL EVOCATION

Employing skillful beliefs while using the cards as growth tools is a powerful and often astonishing, effective method of transformation. I conclude this article with a ritual to be used with any Major Arcana card, as an example of how an "evocation of an archetypal experience" may be put into practice:

1. Strongly affirm your skillful beliefs to yourself.

2. Choose the card you will work with (we'll use the Hierophant here).

3. Hold the card as you contemplate its meaning for you. Simply allow yourself to experience. Allow fifteen minutes for this, so that you can truly notice your experience.

4. Think about what a Hierophant, a Spiritual Teacher, means to you. Imagine this archetype, making it as vivid as possible. What would it feel like to be a spiritual teacher, what would it physically be like? What would the world look like? How would a spiritual teacher feel towards people, him/herself?

5. Using the card as a doorway, step through it and imagine *yourself* as a Hierophant. How do you feel? About others? About yourself? Literally become a spiritual teacher and experience what happens. Make this as real as possible. Even position yourself physically as a spiritual teacher would. What would you think about? What values do you hold? Again, how do you feel towards the world, towards yourself?

6. Be aware of what you are experiencing and *how you accomplished evoking this experience.*

7. Record your experiences for future reference.

8. Remember that you can repeat this exercise anytime you need or want to be in contact with this state.

Faust in His Study by Rembrandt van Rijn

Trunk:
Breakthrough/Realization

*T*he second stage of transformation is realization or breakthrough. For the plant, it is the state of emergence—breaking ground. It is associated with the regeneration or vitalization of spring and the announcement of new growth. This stage is symbolized by the snake in the Garden of Eden, the snake that brings realization into conscious awareness. In psychological terms, this is the peak experience, the ecstatic experience, the "aha" experience, the "flash," the "hunch," or "insight."

In Tarot, the aspect of awakening is symbolized by wands. Cross-culturally, the wand is the symbol of transformation and awakening. The fairy godmother in Cinderella transforms Cinderella from cinder garments into elegant clothing with a wand. In consciousness, a similar experience of awakening is seeing new patterns or making connections that have not been made before. This stage of transformation or breakthrough is exemplified by Dori Gombold's article, "The Psychodynamic Effects of Tarot Symbols." Gombold has found that visualization of the Tarot symbols stirs consciousness-to breakthrough by experiencing the vibratory rate of the various colors, lines, and forms of designs, the numbers, and the sound mantras associated with the images. Gombold describes for us the inherent ability of symbols and their power in dreams or meditation to produce a state of realization.

The breakthrough stage is symbolized by the active motions and contortions of a snake shedding its skin. Breakthrough or realization requires the letting go of something no longer usable and the embracing of something new. This creativity is symbolized by the winged serpent of Aztec and Mayan mythologies, Quetzalcoatl. It is the winged serpent within that motivates each individual to bring ideas into new form.

The Psychodynamic Effects of Tarot Symbolism

Dori Gombold

O◼O◼O◼O◼O◼O◼O◼O◼O◼O◼O◼O◼O

In the beginning was the Symbol. Primitive man used symbolism in his first attempt to communicate an idea, to express a concept, or to record a breakthrough in his struggle to comprehend the cosmos. As the art of writing developed, symbols became the basis for calligraphy. And it was from this rich and potent source that the Tarot evolved. One of the most widely accepted theories is that the Major Arcana were compiled around 1200 A.D. by sages from all parts of the world who met in Fez, Morocco, the scientific and literary capital of the world at the time. Since differences, not only in language but in philosophical terminology as well, made communication difficult, Tarot symbolism was the result of their attempts to embody the most vital teachings into symbolic form that could be universally comprehended.

The actual origin, development, and dissemination of Tarot is difficult to trace. There are many allusions, but few hard facts. Documented references to the use of Tarot cards in Europe date from the fourteenth century and refer to them as playing cards, which indicates that, at least on the exoteric level, their original intent and significance was obscured or distorted. By the fifteenth century, large numbers of gypsies had arrived in the West, and their adaptation of Tarot cards for divination (or fortune-telling) created an aura of mystery, superstition, and even fear that still exists today. This attitude is exemplified in T.S. Eliot's symbol-laden poem, *The Wasteland*. In one stanza that contains references to the Tarot, he introduces: "Madam Sosostris, famous clairvoyante... known to be the wisest woman in Europe, with a wicked pack of cards."[1] Now, after centuries of relative oblivion (except to students of the occult), the time has come to reintroduce the fundamental purpose of this symbolic expression of Ancient Wisdom and to use its enormous power as a tool for personal integration and transformation.

THE TRANSFORMATIVE POWER OF SYMBOLS

One of the most valuable aspects of Tarot is that it speaks directly to the subconscious mind through symbols and archetypes. Through the vibratory rate of the various colors, lines, and forms of the designs, meditation on the Major Arcana stirs the consciousness. While reacting to the symbolic patterns, one is able to harmonize with and awaken deeper and more expansive fields of knowledge in the subconscious. On the conscious level, it is necessary only to decide to move into a higher state of consciousness and then direct or focus attention on one of the Major Arcana, each of which symbolizes some aspect of evolution. The symbols are ancient and universal, and using the language of positive suggestion, they can reach into the subconscious. The subconscious mind, which can be either our most powerful ally or our worst enemy, is amenable to control by suggestion, particularly pictorial symbols that evoke emotional responses. These suggestions then set in motion changes, which may be so subtle and gradual that one may not be aware that anything is taking place; or they may be sudden, dramatic, and unmistakable.

These psychodymanic effects result from the essence of the symbol itself, which is described by the Italian psychiatrist Roberto Assagioli in his book *Psychosynthesis*.[2] First of all, a symbol is capable of attracting psychological energy. It then acts as a "storehouse" for that energy. The cross, for instance, which for nearly 2,000 years has symbolized Christianity, is actually far more ancient and universal. Its use in prehistoric times and appearance in other religions in all parts of the world only enhances its psychic potency for healing, protection, and strength. Finally, the dynamic aspect of the symbol results from its ability to transform psychic energy so that it may then be used in a variety of ways. In other words, symbols like the cross or those pictured on the Tarot cards act as an "energy bank." Deposits are made by focusing on the symbol with faith, love, or reverence. Transformed energy (energy plus interest) can then be withdrawn and put into productive action, the most vital being the initiation of changes within the human psyche: personal transmutation, sublimation, or integration.

As New Age thinking influences both physical and mental healing, the power of symbolism is becoming more widely recognized. Through dream analysis, Sigmund Freud helped reintroduce modern man to symbols. But it was his student Carl Gustav Jung who opened the door to a deeper understanding of the workings of the mind. He introduced the concept of a collective unconscious and explored the importance of archetypal symbols. He expressed the belief that the symbol is the psychological machinery that transmutes energy—that actually sets it in motion. The change-producing crises that seem to appear so suddenly and produce such traumatic effects are, according to Jung, a direct result of the activation of an archetype, which then works with astounding efficiency through the subconscious to arrange the necessary crisis.

For the most part, this activation of archetypes is done on an unconscious level, making the resulting crises appear "accidental," or out of context with the "normal" routine of life, and leading to pain, often both mental and physical. An athlete, for example, who has dedicated most of his life to perfecting his body and physical skills, may suddenly find himself stricken with a debilitating disease or a crippling accident, forcing him to change the focus of his life. There have been several television dramatizations of the inspiring results of these deep and painful inner struggles that have had transforming effects not only on the person directly affected but also on all those privileged to share in the experience.

Transmutation, however, can be just as effective and often much less painful when it results from a firm decision to make integration and personality change a *conscious* process. Jung referred to this as the process of individuation. What must be integrated are the three aspects of consciousness: (1) subconscious, (2) conscious, and (3) superconscious. Working with and meditating on positive archetypal counterparts of these states of consciousness (so effectively represented in the Major Arcana) makes conscious initiation and direct transmutation within one's self possible.

The effectiveness of symbolism as a psychological tool was described by the French psychotherapist R. Desoille in a 1945 publication entitled *The Waking Dream in Psychotherapy - An Essay on the Regulatory Function of the Collective Unconscious.*[3] The waking dream involves, first, guiding the person into an altered state of consciousness, and then suggesting that various symbols be visualized and actively experienced. Desoille considered archetypal figures to be particularly effective, especially when these figures lead the person to basic cosmic laws of existence, or are instrumental in his making a decision of vital importance to his growth. This involves delving into the collective unconscious, in which he is able to see his individual problems and conflicts as having an impersonal and collective background. He also learns to recognize and control negative archetypes and thus loses his fear of them.

Remembering that there are negative as well as positive archetypes is essential. Hidden in the depths of the subconscious are those archetypal patterns that surface in the sleep state as nightmares and in the waking state as nameless fears and anxieties, negative responses, or uncontrollable urges. A classic example is the *anima* and the *animus*, described by Jung as the archetypes of sexual polarity. Negative aspects of the anima, or feminine archetype, could be expressed as the destructive, smothering "mother" or as a seductive temptress. The negative aspect of the animus, or masculine archetype, sometimes appears as a cold, inexorable "father" figure, or an inescapable monster or ravager.

The Tarot, however, personifies the positive aspects of these important polarity symbols. In the Empress (card III in the Major Arcana) is seen the Cosmic Mother, who represents loving, nurturing creativity and fecundity, just as its number (3) suggests multiplication and growth. The Emperor, as the Cosmic Father, represents the security and order implicit in its number (4); and also the power of reason and wisdom over physical force. Thus, negative aspects can be controlled and eliminated by focusing emotional as well as mental energy on positive archetypal images.

Symbols play a prominent part in the technique known as psychosynthesis, originated by Robert Assagioli. Both he and Jung came under the influence of the Freudian school, but both expanded their theories far beyond the limitations of Freudian analysis. Assagioli believed that the conscious and unconscious drives that produce so much pain and conflict, both individually and socially could, if properly channeled, have inestimable human and spiritual value. Since symbols attract power on both the conscious and subconscious level, they are particularly suited to initiate and promote this process of transmutation. In his book *Psychosynthesis*, he lists seven types of symbols that are particularly effective:

1. **Nature symbols**—mountains, water, (Sun, Moon, Star in the Tarot).

2. **Animal symbols**—lion, snake, eagle, etc. (Hierophant, Chariot, Universe, Wheel of Fortune).

3. **Human figures**—father, mother, wise old man, magician, etc. (Emperor, Empress, Hermit, Magus).

4. Man-made symbols—castle, path, sword, etc. (Pentacle, Wand, Sword).

5. Religious and mythological symbols—temple, priest, angels, Venus, etc. (Tower, Priestess, Lovers).

6. Abstract symbols—numbers, geometrical forms (cross, circle, cube, etc.) (78 Cards, Wheel of Fortune, Hanged Man).

7. Individual or spontaneous symbols—the result of dreams, meditations, and therapy sessions.

He also suggests three methods for using these seven groups of symbols:

1. The therapist selects a definite symbol from the first six categories and presents it to the person.

2. The therapist takes advantage of the symbols that arise spontaneously during the session.

3. The therapist may suggest a symbol such as descending (i.e., into an underground cave) or ascending (climbing a mountain) and then allowing the person free rein to develop his own symbols.

The visualization of these symbols sets unconscious psychological processes into motion; and the conscious use of symbols encourages integration between the conscious or logical mind and the unconscious or nonlogical mind.

This renewed interest in the importance of symbols and their use in the search for personal wholeness and integration should lead more New Age healers and therapists to the powerful, esoteric symbolism of the Tarot. Edwin Steinbrecher in his book *The Guide Meditation* [4] combines Tarot, astrology, alchemy, and analytical psychology in what he calls a "gestalt" in which the lost archetypal guides return to teach and lead us in our personal spiritual quest. Perhaps others will follow, and eventually Tarot symbolism will be more widely recognized for its true worth as the dynamic instrument of growth and evolution.

THE PRACTICAL APPLICATION OF TAROT SYMBOLISM: B.O.T.A.

One of the most dynamically effective approaches to applied Tarot symbolism is that undertaken by Builders of the Adytum (B.O.T.A.). This international organization (headquartered in Los Angeles) was founded by Paul Foster Case, author, lecturer, teacher, and former Praemonstrator General of the Order of the Golden Dawn for the United States and Canada. The material that follows is a very brief description of courses covered over a period of seven years. It outlines the various methods in which Tarot symbols can be applied and also the subtle and cumulative effects of the B.O.T.A. approach upon the student.

The course outline that follows is not necessarily in the same order that current courses are being presented. References are to the Rider Waite deck.

INTRODUCTION TO TAROT

In the first course, "An Introduction to Tarot," the student works with two Keys (cards) each week, learning the names, the numbers, the Hebrew letters, the Hebrew nouns (or letter names), and the numbers associates with the Hebrew letters. For example, The Fool is Key 0; the Hebrew letter is Aleph (A), which also means "oxen" and the numeral one. By meditating on the uncolored Keys,[5] the student familiarizes himself with the various forms, figures, and symbols, relating the pictorial symbols with the more abstract numerical and alphabetical symbols. This calls into play the powers of Concentration (represented by the Magician, Key 1) and Memory (the High Priestess, Key 2). The student is encouraged to assimilate this information through association rather than memorization by rote. Each lesson gives short dissertations explaining the symbolism, the purpose, and the meaning of each Key. In this way, over a period of eleven weeks, a definite, tangible bond has been established with the Tarot archetypes.

TAROT FUNDAMENTALS

This course is followed by "Tarot Fundamentals," which expands the material on each Key to two full lessons. During this period, the student begins to color the Keys. The act of coloring becomes a form of meditation, as he concentrates on the particular colors to be used and on the symbols and archetypes being colored. By the end of the course, which lasts forty-seven weeks, the Keys have begun even more noticeably to activate the subconscious mind. There is a heightened state of awareness resulting in an increase of synchronistic experience.

On the conscious level, a feeling of warmth and friendship develops for what had once been impersonal pieces of cardboard. Magically, they begin to seem very much alive and real. There may also be a strong attraction to certain Keys, as well as negative reactions to others. Both responses should be carefully studied, especially the negative feelings, as these could indicate an area that needs adjustment or attention. One student had an aversion for the Emperor Key, which stemmed from her very negative feelings for her father. After working with the concept of the Emperor as her Cosmic Father, her dreams began to include symbols from this Key. Eventually, she was able to dream about her own father with less and less hostility. This led to noticeable changes in her ability to relate to men in general.

TAROT INTERPRETATION

In "Tarot Interpretation," thirty-two weeks are devoted to a study of the Keys as they relate to each other, beginning with the Tarot Tableau, which is set up as follows:

```
              0
    1   2   3   4   5   6   7
    8   9  10  11  12  13  14
   15  16  17  18  19  20  21
```

Keys 1 through 7 symbolize mental states or principles; Keys 8 through 14 represent these mental states or principles as they are expressed as activities or Cosmic Laws; and Keys 15 through 21 symbolize conditions or stages of unfoldment resulting from the expression of the principle through the application of the Law. The student begins by meditating on the interaction of these three groups of seven keys :

Key 1—the Magician = The principle of Concentration (focused attention).

Key 8—Strength = Concentration expresses itself through the Law of Suggestion.

Key 15—the Devil = The stage of unfoldment is the recognition that bondage is the result of illusion and ignorance.

Examples

1. The student who wishes to release himself from a negative relationship would begin by concentrating his attention on all as-

pects of the situation, being aware of his reactions and feelings, and then projecting a firm belief that the situation will end in the best way possible. This seed-thought is then consciously planted in the subconscious mind (the garden of the Magician).

2. In Key 8, this garden is symbolized by a wreath of flowers around the head of a woman. The figure 8 above her head signifies that the power of the Magician (conscious mind) has been transferred to the subconscious. The subconscious, which is amenable to suggestions, will carry them out with total efficiency. In this case, it will set up the perfect situation through which the student will be able to recognize what is holding him in bondage.

3. Key 15 pictures two figures chained to a block upon which the Devil sits. But the chains can be easily removed—indicating that bondage is the result of ignorance of the true situation. Once the student clearly sees what his bondage is (fears of being alone, fears of rejection, lack of self-esteem—whatever it is), he then has the power to remove the chains.

In this way the three aspects of the Tableau are consolidated, setting up another frame of reference for the practical application of Tarot principles.

This segment is followed by a study of Tableaus based on a certain mathematical principle, so that every arrangement of nine-key squares expresses a certain numerical order designed to stimulate a transforming change of consciousness. Since the possibilities of Tarot combinations are inexhaustible, through dedicated meditation morning and evening the student will eventually discover that Tarot does not *put* something into his mind—it *evokes* what is already there.

If the student wishes to find an answer for a specific problem, he chooses a key that symbolizes his problem and then selects one of the nine-key squares in which his Key is the central unit. He then forms a definite intention of evoking the perfect solution from inner consciousness. He must relax and not try to force an answer, or not be discouraged if the answer does not emerge immediately. Often it will present itself quite unexpectedly. For a better understanding of his own individuality, for example, this same procedure may be followed using the Key that represents his Sun sign as the central unit. In the case of Taurus, Key 5 (the Hierophant) occupies the center of a square in which the horizontal and diagonal keys add up to 6 (derived from 15), numerical symbol of harmony, reciprocation, and equilibrium:

```
1  2  3
4  5  6
7  8  9
```

The Hierophant acts as the central agency or connecting link to the Keys around it. Between 1 and 9, for example, which suggests that intuition (5, or the Inner Teacher), connects conscious mind (1, the Magician) and the superconscious (9, the Hermit). By examining each of the combinations in this way, the student can acquire a great deal of insight into his own make-up.

THE MASTER PATTERN: TREE OF LIFE
(THE THIRTY-TWO PATHS OF WISDOM)

The three courses which follow "The Master Pattern," "The Tree of Life," and "The Thirty-Two Paths of Wisdom," represent approximately a year-and-a-half study, revolving primarily around the Qabalistic concept of the Tree of Life. The emphasis now moves from the pictorial symbols of the Keys to an exploration of the subtle abstract symbolism of numbers, and the magical language of Gematria, a form of cryptic writing which was used to preserve and transmit the occult secrets of Ageless Wisdom. It combines Hebrew, Greek, and Latin, since the letters of these three alphabets also serve as numbers. Consequently, each word, phrase, or sentence has a numerical equivalent that is the sum of the values of the letters. There is usually a paradox as well as a correlation, however subtle, between words of similar values. For instance, the Hebrew words for "love" (*ahabeh*) and "unity" (*achad*) both have a value of 13. However, the words for "desolate, void" (*bahu*) and "anxiety, care, grief" (*dageh*) also have a value of 13.

Jacob Boehme, the German mystic, wrote: "The second alphabet is the Hebrew, which reveals the mystery of the language of nature, and names the tree with the branches and twigs." Obviously, he was referring to the Tree of Life, to the ten Sephiroth, and the twenty-two paths that connect them, each of which is associated with a number, with a Hebrew letter, and with a Tarot Key. In this way, the student is introduced to the power of the Word or Mantra.

SOUND AND COLOR

The course on "Sound and Color" expands upon this introduction to the vibratory power of words and numbers. The important basic concept is that in the order of the Life-power's expression, sound precedes light (color). In other words, sound has an infinitely lower vibratory rate than light. St. John wrote: "In the beginning was the Word, and the Word was with God, and the Word was God." The divinity of sound is also found in the ancient Sanskrit writing, where it is referred to as the root-potency of all manifestation: "Through sound the world stands." The Mantra is actually a method of control over natural forces by sound vibration, whether articulated or in the form of thought. Although the vibratory rate of sound and color differs so radically, there is a definite correlation between sound and light as it manifests as color. For example, 256 vibrations per second are perceived by the sound center in the brain as middle C on the musical scale. By doubling 256 a sufficient number of times, the exact number of vibrations is reached to produce the sensation of "red."

Since the whole concept of transmutation is based on establishing control, first over our own physical being (body, personality, thoughts, and emotions) and then over our environment, becoming familiar with the vital forces with which the student must work is essential. By relating a tone and color to each Key, he adds another dimension of control to the symbolism of that Key.

Introductions to the vital concepts of physical healing and insights into the very essence of the physical world are condensed into this eleven-week course. Several effective meditations—all of which utilize the Tarot Keys, color cards, and vocalized mantras—are included in the section on Healing.

The preparatory meditation, which should be used daily, is designed to harmonize the seven vital centers (chakras), and uses the keys assigned: Saturn (the World), Mars (the Tower), the Sun (the Sun), Jupiter (Wheel of Fortune), Venus (the Empress), the Moon (the High Priestess), and Mercury (The Magician). The student thus draws on vital planetary influences and integrates himself in a personal way with cosmic energy. There are also more specific healing meditations that utilize the Keys connected with the zodiacal signs and the body parts governed by each sign.

The use of Tarot Keys, color, and sound for healing has a scientific basis in the fact that normal body cells constantly emit radiations of varying wavelengths, corresponding to the spectrum of sunlight. Therefore, the characteristic wavelength of every cell and of every organ has its definite color and tone, and each of the twelve areas of the body has a tableau selected to establish the balanced functioning of those parts of the body.

Since the word "Adytum" means temple, Builders of the Adytum actually refers to the concept that the body is the temple of the spirit, and in the process of not only building and maintaining, but also *perfecting* the temple, the student is actually effecting changes in his body chemistry and the cellular structure of his body, particularly the brain, to be receptive to ever higher rates of vibration.

THE GREAT WORK: ART OF ALCHEMY

One of the ultimate disciplines for mastery, not only of the physical body but also of the natural environment, is the art of alchemy. The misconceptions associated with alchemy are similar to those surrounding the use of the Tarot. Webster's dictionary provides one of the most commonly accepted definitions: "The medieval chemical science, whose great objects were the transmutation of the base metals into gold, and the discovery of the universal cure for diseases and means of indefinitely prolonging life." Although an alchemist may have it within his power to produce such "miracles," these are not the ultimate goals. To a true adept, alchemy is a process of moving from the imperfect physical condition into which man is born, to the transcendent spiritual state of total union with the One that *is* the ultimate goal of all human beings. This process is instigated, guided, and completed by the archetypes of superconsciousness, but it requires conscious consent and cooperation to succeed.

In the course entitled "The Great Work," the Qabalistic approach to practical alchemy is developed in twelve stages, each stage related to a sign of the zodiac. In this way, the Tarot Keys are employed to symbolize the sign, as well as the planets that rule or are exalted in each sign.

The process of transmutation through symbolism is particularly exemplified in the discipline of alchemy. Stage One, for example, is Calcination, which is defined exoterically as the expulsion of the volatile substance from a matter by the action of heat. The sign is Aries (Emperor), which is a fire sign in which two fiery bodies are dominant: Mars (Tower) rules, and the sun (Sun) is exalted. In this first stage then, the element is fire and the radiant energy is that which originates in the Mars Center and Sun Center of the body (centers that have been activated through the "chakra" meditations of the preceding course).

Meditating on these Keys without any further knowledge of this stage of alchemy could still activate powerful archetypal patterns. The Emperor, divine masculine principle, is a Key that symbolizes reason, order, dominion, taking command. The Tower, the disintegrating power of Mars, is used here for the expulsion of the "volatile substance," i.e., habit patterns, responses, emotions, prejudices and opinions, which, because of their negativity, restrict the flow of the Life Force: positive love energy. The Sun, a symbol of the Higher Ego, may then take its rightful place of exaltation. It can be said that the Great Work is truly the "operation of the Sun," not least because the length of the course is fifty-two weeks—the length of time it takes the sun to move through the twelve signs of the zodiac. The student is therefore given a perfect opportunity to more closely align himself with the cosmos and participate in the universal flow.

DEVELOPMENT OF SUPERSENSORY POWERS

The expansion of consciousness effected by the alchemical practices of "The Great Work" prepares the student for an intensive year-long exploration of each Tarot Key on an even higher level through a course entitled "Esoteric Extension of Tarot to Develop Supersensory Powers." Now, symbols are used to open up the channels represented by the various Keys. Since each Key of the Major Arcana is a focal point for a specialized state of consciousness, the meditations included in this section encourage the student to work with the mental and emotional principles of the Key for the transmutation of his personality, as well as using the symbolism to stimulate supersensory perception. This is accomplished through very potent visualizations which activate the Keys and also utilize the powerful influence of color.

The student projects himself into the Keys, imaging three-dimensional, life-size figures in vibrant color. Using his heightened powers of creative imagery, symbolized by the Empress, he is able to set the symbols in motion: the water flows, the lightning strikes, and the archetypes come to life on a higher and more intense level. Each Key has its own particular psychic influence, and the cumulative effect is dynamic in a very personal way. Since each individual is unique in his level of approach, the results, too, will vary. However, no one could persist in these exercises for a year and not experience positive inner changes.

ESOTERIC ASTROLOGY

The opening of channels to supersensory influences leads to a greater understanding of cosmic consciousness and its influence on the physical plane. Man's destiny is the development of mastery over his fate, and, since each lifetime is structured by the patterns found in his astrological natal chart, it is essential to learn as much as possible about this unique and personal connection to the cosmos. The material included in the next course, "Esoteric Astrology," helps the student relate the microcosm of his finite physical being to the vast macrocosm of the universe, revealing to him his true cosmic being. Through Tarot symbols, he is taught to recognize the patterns that hold him in bondage to astrological forces and, by using these symbols effectively, to become master of the stars by transmuting his responses to these forces which affect his life so powerfully from the day of his birth until he leaves his body.

The course extends over fifty-two weeks. During this time the student becomes familiar with astrological symbolism, relating the Tarot Keys specifically to the planets, luminaries, and the signs of the zodiac. Each of the sections devoted to the planets contains a meditation that uses the Key, the color, and the tone-mantra associated with that planet, and is designed to open the consciousness to the influence of the planetary vibration. The connection between the planets and their corresponding chakras (which has been established in previous meditations) is now increased and intensified.

The planet Saturn (the World), which is usually viewed with apprehension as the source of limitation, obstruction, and restriction, is seen from a different perspective in a meditation that includes Uranus (the Fool), planet of revolution. As these two Keys are visualized and activated, the student experiences the universal flow of the Life Force, the inhalation and exhalation, limitation followed by liberation, restriction then release. Key 21 itself, picturing the androgynous Dancer within the green ovoid wreath, does not suggest harsh, unjust punishment. The postive aspects of the Key encourage a warm acceptance of Saturn's influence as the discipline, or focusing of energy, needed to prepare the student for the inevitable changes that are promised by Uranus. Saturn then becomes our teacher, guide, and mentor.

Each sign of the zodiac is then explored from various aspects: the influence of the ruling or exalted planets, its positive and negative characteristics, the application of Tarot symbolism, and so forth. Each sign also has a very effective meditation based on a Tarot Tableau containing Keys that represent the sign, the ruling planet, the ruling planets of the two signs sharing the same element (i.e., fire, water, earth, and air), and the planet of exaltation. Aries, a fire sign, would have the following tableau:

1. **Zodiacal Sign: Aries**—Key 4, the Emperor (Red—middle C)
2. **Ruling Planet: Mars**—Key 16, the Tower (Red—middle C)
3. **Exalted Planet: also ruler of Leo: Sun**—Key 19, the Sun
   (Orange—D natural)
4. **Ruler of Sagittarius: Jupiter**—Key 10, Wheel of Fortune
   (Violet—A sharp)

After visualizing the color while sounding the tone mantra, the student meditates on the positive qualities of the sign and the planets, affirming the perfection of these qualities in his own life. As a result, the student begins to see himself as a part of the entire zodiac, not just an expression of his sun sign or ascendant. In truth, each person reflects the characteristics of all the signs, and responds to the vibrations of all the planets. What makes each individual a unique expression of the cosmos is the placement of the signs and the location of the planets in his natal chart. These life patterns are the framework within which he will work out this life experience. By accepting this concept for himself, the student eventually is able to apply this acceptance and tolerance to others.

Finally, the student is taught to create his own personal tableau based on his sun sign and ascendant. It contains the Keys for his individuality, personality, life problem, the solution, the means for solution, and an integration Key. The possibilities of this tableau are inexhaustible, since as the student grows, he is able to gain deeper and deeper insights into the meanings of this pattern of Keys.

SEXUAL POLARITY

Upon completion of this course, which has provided a basis for establishing cosmic wholeness, the student is presented with the challenge of recognizing and destroying the most formidable blocks to personal fulfillment and spiritual growth. The course entitled "Qabalistic Doctrines on Sexual Polarity" offers an in-depth exploration of the creative Life Force as it expresses through the Divine Feminine and Masculine archetypes.

The student delves into his own attitudes toward himself, toward the opposite sex, toward the use of sexual energy, and toward love and union. Again, transmutation is effected through particularly powerful meditations on Tarot Keys connected with the planetary centers (chakras), designed to break down erroneous habit patterns that set up negative relationships or in some way thwart the flow of love energy. New, consciously selected, positive patterns can then be established.

Learning to achieve a proper balance in his own sexual polarity allows the student to correct any problems he may be having in relating to the opposite sex or to his own sex. As he rids himself of old attitudes of guilt or shame connected with sex, he can begin to see it as a method of achieving spiritual union. Sexual energy transmuted becomes creative energy ... love energy ... and the student sees himself as a creative center of expression for the universal love in the world.

A very effective meditation features the Empress and the Emperor, archetypes of the Divine Feminine and Masculine aspects of Life Force. If the student is a male, he will visualize himself as the Emperor, tuning into the reality that his physical body is a channel for the creative "yang" force. The Empress then becomes his complement as well as his polar opposite. She may symbolize his wife, womankind as a whole, or his own feminine polarity. As he visualizes Key 3, he is also visualizing the perfect essence of the creative "yin" force. He sends her his strength, love, protection, and respect. He receives from her love, tenderness, warmth, and inspiration.

When the Empress and the Emperor are placed side by side, the stream from the waterfall in Key 3 can be joined with the river in Key 4. The power of the meditation can be greatly enhanced by mentally directing the flow of that "spiritual water" from one archetype to the other. The result will be a greater balance in the student's inner polarity, and a noticeable increase in his rapport with the opposite sex.

SUMMARY

The B.O.T.A. studies may be continued as long as there is the need or desire to do so. The inherent, often unconscious drive toward perfection will unerringly guide each human being toward the tools that will aid him in his growth and spiritual evolution. The Tarot is just one of many such tools, but is is one of the most direct and powerful. Its power rests in the fact that it uses dynamic symbolism to create a link between the aspirant and his archetypes. This enables him to become a conscious participant in his own return to the Source. George Bernard Shaw aptly described this transition in *Man and Superman* when he said: "To be in heaven is to steer; to be in hell is to drift."

NOTES

1. T.S. Eliot, *Collected Poems, 1909-1962*, New York: Harcourt Brace Jovanovich, 1936. p.70.

2. Roberto Assagioli, *Psychosynthesis*, New York: Viking Press, 1971. p. 177.

3. R. Desoille, *The Waking Dream in Psychotherapy—An Essay on the Regulatory Function of the Collective Unconscious*, Pacific Grove, CA, Brooks/Cole, 1978.

4. Edwin Steinbrecher, *The Guide Meditation*, York Beach, Maine, 1987.

5. These Keys can be found in *The Tarot* by Paul Foster Case. Richmond, VA, Macoy Publishing, 1978.

Branches:
Unfoldment/Emanation

*A*fter breakthrough and realization comes the period of demonstration, emanation, and unfoldment of what has been realized. To the tree, this is the season of fullness and greenery—summer. It is the healthy tree, or the state of well-being. It is the physical branch of the tree, which is represented by the suit of disks or pentacles in Tarot. Like the protective branches and medicinal essences of the tree, Tarot is a healer. Just as we can climb to the top of the tree and get a broad perspective, we can, through the symbols in Tarot, diagnose problems and potential. As the tree is majestic and inspiring, so is the Tarot motivating and uplifting.

The serpentine guardian of the summer tree is the caduceus—the two merging winged serpents, which symbolize the need for union, balance, and integration in any healing or transformative process. As a snake moves to maintain its own state of well-being, so must all living creatures. Susan Cole, in "Tarot and Dance Therapy," shows the healing power of movement combined with visual symbols. She illustrates the use of Tarot as a tool for identifying physical blocks and for teaching rhythmic movements that can release blocked energy. Cole shows how dance can be used as a moving meditation that can maintain health much like the oriental body art of *Tai Chi*.

Siva Dancing the Tandava

Dance and Tarot:

Personal Symbols Set to Movement

Susan K. Cole

O◼O◼O◼O◼O◼O◼O◼O◼O◼O◼O◼O

Long before dance became a performing art it was ritualistic therapy in primitive cultures, a turning point for the expression of joy, ecstasy, love, and the hope of abundance, or for the casting out of dark shadows that had leapt into the bodies, minds, and souls of ancient peoples.

In today's culture, dance, movement, and many of the arts are being used on a different stage as growth-oriented therapy. Just as movement is the lifeline that connects a series of poses in a dance, movement therapy is a link between emotions and the physical body. It is an active experience of ourselves as we create transitions toward understanding, integrating, and moving as a whole and balanced person.

Dance therapy employs movement as a medium for communication and expression, a means for self-actualization and realization of potential. It is a process for moving through and transforming personal obstacles.

Tarot cards, along with their symbolic interpretation, are a means of identifying these obstacles and the level of awareness where they may exist. A block or obstacle can manifest within the perceptual, mental, emotional, or physical levels of consciousness. If a perception or an intuition is not allowed to come completely into conscious awareness from its subconscious source, a perceptual block is created. Mentally, a block may be a fixed attitude or idea. Emotional blocks may be feelings that need expression or fears that require transformation. When we are not nourished by our environment or when our physical body is in pain or discomfort, this problem can create a block on the physical level. A physical block often results from an obstacle that has not been dealt with on another level.

In any counseling session, progress depends on two things: identifying the blocks to growth and then dealing with those blocks. By using movement, dance, music, drama, and visualizations, a process takes place for moving through and changing those blocks or obstacles into energy that can then be channeled into creativity. Tarot becomes the tool for identifying an obstacle, and the creative arts are used for the process of transforming them.

The focus of this study is how to combine Tarot and body movement to change blocks in consciousness. While the Tarot is helpful in identifying an obstacle or block, the point in using movement is to go beyond the verbal. Verbalization can be an aid in clarifying issues as they exist, but it is often not enough. The use of movement enhances transformation while leaving words behind. When a person is in a negative or depressed state, they can literally transform that obstacle, feeling, or image by moving their body. This can be done through improvisational movement with or without music; it can be through running, swimming, riding a bicycle, making love—using the body as a vehicle to move through that negative space in time and to motivate us toward a realization of positive potential, energy, and emotion.

MOVEMENT THERAPY

In a movement therapy session, too much information can overwhelm a client and be limiting in itself. Optimum results are achieved in a series of sessions. For example, a first session could focus on a person's lifetime cards. Pictorially, these cards hold a set of personal symbols, or archetypes, that represent a person's lifetime gifts, abilities, tests, and obstructions. As such, they become a rich symbolic resource and a catalyst for movement.

Let's take the example of a client whose personal lifetime symbol is the Hermit (IX in the Major Arcana of the Thoth Deck). The Hermit symbolizes completion, introspection, and perfection. The Hermit is also know as the "Hander" because he is gifted with his hands and has an innate ability to lead. In a therapy session, this person works toward completion through creative movement that begins by initiating a movement with only the hands. Gradually, as the hands lead, each part of the body follows into the movement sequence. The pattern continues until completion, when the whole body is following and every part of the body is moving in this Hermit's dance. For the Hermit person, total acknowledgement of creativity is initiated with the hands and brought to completion by moving the entire body. This is the Hermit's fluid knowingness of his inner strength and energy. He realizes, through his own patterns, that he can create with his hands, lead, and work toward completion by introspecting and perfecting. He listens to his potential through his body's vocabulary of movements.

The actual movements will always be different. One Hermit may begin by rhythmically clapping the hands and allowing the body to join in a rhythmic move-stop-move pattern. Another Hermit may flutter the fingers of one hand, then the other, and bring one side of the body into a pattern first, then the other side. The symbolic meanings are universal, and as each of us is different, so will our interpretations of the symbols come out in varying patterns of movement.

Another movement therapy session involves the "Flying Arrow Spread." This consists of pulling three cards from the deck: one to represent the Body, one for the Mind, and one for the direction that the Spirit, or inner energy, is moving the person.

First, any negative cards that appear are dealt with. For example, if the Eight of Cups, Indolence, is in the body position, the client is giving out too much emotionally, and thereby harming the physical body. The client works with movements that are overstimulating, exhausting, as in moving with great speed from a prone position into jumps and back down again, or improvisational movements to music such as Ravel's *Bolero*. Both the music and the movements will build in speed and intensity. This is conscious acknowledgement of the exhaustion one feels from overgiving and overdoing. The body movements and music allow the levels of awareness to adjust and balance.

If there are no negative cards, the first one considered is the Spirit card. As the motion element in this spread, it represents movement at some level that is vital to the client's growth and awareness. Let's look at the following "Flying Arrow Spread" and the resources it holds for movement therapy:

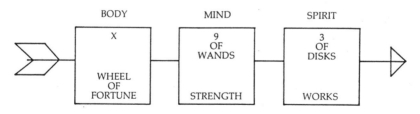

Here, the symbols of the Body and Mind will reinforce the movement in the Spirit card. This person is going into a period of dynamic application symbolized by the Three of Disks. The Body is supporting that movement with an abundance of creative energy, the Wheel of

Fortune. This woman is ready to apply flexibility, objectivity, and creativity (symbolized by the monkey, sphinx, and crocodile, respectively). It's interesting to note that Yoga was suggested as a long-term activity to help her gain and retain flexibility in the body; and the Wheel of Fortune was used as a meditation card while she practiced Yoga. Strength, the Nine of Wands, symbolized the importance of staying mentally focused on the task and the ability to do so.

With the Three of Disks as the focus, the work was application of a detailed movement sequence to memory. This client was given three sets of choreographed movement sequences. Then she created two sequences as transitions through the original three. Her mental strength served to keep her focused as she applied herself to the task of learning, creating, and performing. (The latter being the final application on the physical level.) For her, this is a movement meditation she does daily, often enlarging and adding new patterns of her own.

In follow-up sessions, the "Flying Arrow Spread" can be used again, or the client can choose just one card from the deck as a focal point. Often the session is augmented by having the client draw a visualization on a large piece of paper with crayons, paint, or oil-base pastels. This is helpful, again, for going beyond the verbal. It becomes a visible score of hidden resources. Visualizations, Tarot, and movement enhance a therapy session by actively involving every aspect of the client's awareness. These tools are especially useful in working with a group.

In one group session a woman was concerned with her inability to trust her perceptions, her world, and other people. As a result of selecting the Aeon (XX in the Major Arcana), she brought into awareness her fear of being negatively judged by others. The Aeon card holds a complex set of symbols that focus, in part, on the qualities of communications, creative judgment, and critical perception, and on handling these factors in a balanced way. The Aeon also symbolized her ability to communicate, with balance, from a deep inner source. Next, she drew an abstract visualization of differing geometric forms over and around a small, pastel-orange circle of fire that wound into itself. In her movement sequence, the group members portrayed the geometric figures by creating various primitive-like sharp and jagged movements around her. The pattern built in intensity as she, with soft, round movements began to turn more and more into a small space she had designated for herself on the floor. Through this sequence, she was herself as a child being criticized by family and friends. At the end of this sequence, she drew another card from the Tarot deck, the Queen of Cups, known as the "Reflector." With this image in consciousness, she again used the group to reflect and mirror her movements, ranging from breathing with a gentle lifting and lowering of the arms, head, and torso, to turning and swirling her entire body through different levels of space. The group supported her by continually receiving her movements, following and giving back a variation of her movements. Through this sequence, she became aware of her ability to communicate, to be seen and listened to, and, in turn, to receive her communications back in a different and supporting form.

CARDS ASSOCIATED WITH MOVEMENT PATTERNS

All of the cards hold various elements that catalyze movement. However, here the focus will be on specific cards from the Major Arcana of the Thoth deck.

Lovers

One example is the Lovers card, VI. This is a card of relationship. When it appears as a focus, one is dealing first with the relationship that one has with oneself. If one wants a friendship or a romantic relationship and does not have one, an inner balancing process needs to take place. The Lovers card indicates that there is work to do in balancing out one's magnetic and dynamic aspects. The magnetic is the receptive or feminine side of the self, and the dynamic is the active or masculine side of the self.

The Lovers card is associated with Gemini, astrologically an air sign, and the primary work is focusing on the breath. The breath becomes an example of how a person loves himself on the inner, and how he nourishes himself there. Lying flat on the floor, the client breathes naturally, just noticing the way the breath comes in and goes out. Next, he begins taking the breath into a deeper place, focusing on how breathing is really a way to massage the inner, a way to love the self on the inner. The breath becomes a base from which to initiate balance inside.

In a group setting, people can use the symbolism of the Lovers to inspire balance-work in pairs. Here the emphasis is on noticing how receptive (magnetic) or how active (dynamic) a person is, and then learning how to blend energies, again with breath as the primary focus.

The two people lie flat. Person A has his back to Person B's front. Person A breathes normally. Person B becomes the receptive breather by joining his breath pattern to A's, who is the active breather. Then, they switch. It's a subtle movement (one feels it in the torso and in the chest). Then they begin to blend their patterns. From the receptive/active state, they blend; the two patterns work simultaneously. It's the balance of the receptive/active, the balance of blending in a relationship symbolized by the Lovers card.

The next movement sequence begins in dyads on the floor—the receptive/active/blending—and is extended to a sitting position, with the movements using the head, torso, and arms. It's not so much a mirroring, but rather an opportunity to flow with one another. The objective is neither to lead nor follow but to blend movements, to create a relationship of movements that flow from one to the other. This same process is continued while standing still and then while moving across the floor. The standing and moving sequences experiment with actual balance or standing on one foot—playing with the concept of balancing weight at different levels. The exercise also involves learning how to have someone else support you, learning how to be supported at the appropriate time, and then, when you have that balance, letting go and moving from the balanced place, letting your partner receive your weight and giving your weight. This again is the active/receptive blending, the balancing of the magnetic and the dynamic.

By using the Lovers symbolism as a catalyst for this form of movement sequence, the breath becomes a base. The receiver is receiving in relationship to what the giver is giving. It's not being passive, it's actively choosing to receive, assertively manifesting your magnetic nature in a relationship. This assists in becoming quiet and feeling the inner breath that moves through the body and in feeling the inner energy of the other person. Music, such as Johann Pachelbel's *Canon in D*, can greatly enhance this sequence—a simple theme woven into a dance of two people moving through and enlarging their relationship.

Fool/Emperor

Another card associated with movement is the Fool, 0 in the Major Arcana. In a Tarot consultation, the Fool is often associated with an inverted energy, the place where a person holds himself back. Within our lives, there will always be fears connected to creativity and relationships. The Fool symbolizes breaking through fear, and this energy assists us in establishing a new relationship with our fear. Performing artists are continually using and working with their fear in a context of creativity. The old expression "stage fright" refers to the performer's adrenaline motivating him to go center stage with his work. We can learn to use fear in a new and different way. We can use it as a catalyst, much as our bodies utilize adrenaline at various times.

The classic forms of movement associated with the Fool are leaps and jumps—movements that use a large amount of space. These movements need a strong foundation, an energy symbolized by the Emperor, IV. When we move in relation to our fear, the Emperor, or "four" energy, involves pioneering and building a strong base from which to move. In combination, the Fool/Emperor energy is a catalyst for jumps—taking a "leap" into and through fear from a strong base of support.

When jumping, a concrete foundation for take-off and landing is important. Jumps, and also running, require contact with the earth. The body becomes the base as well as the launch pad and the rocket. A movement sequence using the Fool/Emperor involves beginning in a standing position, with the feet about one foot apart, establishing the base. Then the knees bend and the body's weight sinks into the earth. Next, the bending continues with the addition of a propelled energy to lift the body off the floor and, as the body reconnects with the earth, the feet completely touch the floor and the knees bend with each landing. This is reconnecting with the earth base for support in each succeeding jump—building a foundation for going through fear. The sequence is continued by moving across a floor in small runs that eventually proceed into jumps and leaps.

These are the dynamic and powerful movements that reflect the strength and dynamics of the Emperor. His, truly, is an energy that reenergizes and vitalizes. The movements will reflect this through the strength of the foundation, the power of the movements, and the balanced, fearless vision that propels the Emperor ahead.

Empress

While the Emperor's movements are dynamic and powerful, his complementary counterpart, the Empress (III), symbolizes fluidity and receptivity in movements. Her dance exudes a magnetic choreography of gentle turns, movements initiated with the spine, and soft impressions into space. Through her symbology of movements, she encompasses and nourishes, always conscious of the delicate dance she does to unify her heart and mind. This unification of the emotional and mental levels is apparent in the deep love the Empress will feel as she moves through her dance. This is love for herself, for her creativity, and love for the Universe she moves in.

Universe

This brings us to the Universe card, XXI. The symbolism relates to the creative center of the body, the pelvic bowl. This card is often associated with creative energy that wants to be moved from that center. People who have a sexual block often have difficulty in moving the pelvic area, and this card is a good one to initiate and complete a movement sequence with, or to use as a meditation card.

By moving the pelvic area, a sexual block will transform and the energy that has been stopped in that area will begin to expand and move. The completion aspect of this card is helpful in locating, moving, and completing a movement sequence that is correlated to a sexual block.

The Universe card holds a woman who, symbolically, has taken her limitations and restrictions and woven them into a shimmering web of light. She then dances upon and through this web in a completion dance that transforms her limitations and restrictions. Behind her circle of light is a structure resembling the pelvic bowl area of the body. When this card surfaces in a spread it can represent a sexual block that is ready to be transformed. It is an opportunity to move the pelvic area. In a therapy session this card, and all it symbolizes, gives a client permission to move the pelvic area which is to deal with sexuality, to be sexual and sensuous, often given a negative connotation in our culture and often seen and interpreted in a restricting way. By moving the pelvic area, a client has the opportunity to unlock creative sexual expression. Belly dancing is one form of movement that corresponds to the Universe energy. When the Universe appears in a therapy session, the client begins moving from the belly, or pelvic area, first. Eventually, the body follows and enters into the Universe dance—a dance that travels through all the levels of space, the earth, the air, and the middle level that the physical body uses in daily living. This dance uses a universe of movements, all there possibly is.

The Universe card is a beautiful symbol for the combination of movement and Tarot because the woman is dancing through the heavens in her limitless quest for completion. She symbolizes the harvest dances, reflecting the completion of a season, a cycle of work, a major project. Her movements easily represent the final session in a series of dance therapy—the celebration of a block being broken through, a fear overcome, and a goal realized. She inspires a dance of joy and gratitude to the spirit for help in completing the work. She dances the circle of life in the shining arch of heaven. She dances the final dance, the finale. Then she rests, and begins anew . . . .

Empress Tarot Card from **Voyager Deck**

Fruit:
Actualization/Harvest

*E*very process of transition or change yields harvest or the fruits. This is the season of autumn—the capacity to harvest what one has cultivated or brought to fullness. It is the cornucopia, autumn's cup. The cup is also the womb that protects and nurtures its fruit. As a structure, the cup contains the life-creating waters of the womb and life-bearing fruits of the cornucopia.

In her article "From the Universe to the Empress: Pregnancy and Transformation," Judith Bolinger shows us the power of the natural cup, the womb, and the stages of transformation that the womb goes through to bear its fruit, the water child.[1] Through poetic expression, Bolinger brings understanding to the creative process of birthing and mothering by structuring the process of birth through the contemplation of relevant symbols such as the Empress (Mother) to the Universe (Child).

Through Bolinger's dynamic poetry, we witness the process of bearing fruit and the feelings and emotions generated in that process. In Tarot, the suit of cups represents the emotional aspects of growth. It is the symbol that reveals the responses and reactions of the heart, or the state of one's emotional fullness/harvest or barrenness/no harvest. As a structure, the cup contains

---

[1]Judith Boilinger and Jane English, *Water Child*, Hunter Press, 1980

the waters that nurture, comfort, support, and sustain growth.

All harvests represent a rite of passage as we see in the article by Richard Hyde on the Fool's mythic journey described in T. S. Eliot's "The Wasteland." The birth canal becomes in itself a symbol of the first rite of passage: the simultaneous process of detachment/ attachment. To the tree, autumn is the season of bearing fruit and of shedding leaves. The guardian snakes of the autumn tree are represented by Buto and Mertseger, the Egyptian serpents of death/ rebirth who stay coiled at the portals or gates to guard and protect those making the ultimate passages of birth and death. It is the final stage of transformation, the stage of bringing something into form—to bear fruit.

From the Universe to the Empress:

Pregnancy and Transformation

Judith Bolinger

O◼O◼O◼O◼O◼O◼O◼O◼O◼O◼O◼O◼O

As a writer, I became interested in the Tarot by using it as a tool to deepen my experience in the symbolic world. Late in 1973, I began to keep a dream journal. Out of these experiences poems began to emerge, and I began to realize that my writing had a life of its own, that my dream/ fantasy experiences moved through me and surfaced as words almost of their own. I was compelled to write, and found it sometimes emotionally painful and sometimes a joyful light experience, but always with a sense of nourishment once I had expressed myself on the page. It was like being introduced to a part of myself for the first time. Initially, my writing material arose from a dream or memory as an extension of myself in the form of a persona that appeared at first larger than I was, and slowly became myriad personalities that I learned to recognize and dialogue with.

The process of moving dream or fantasy to word was largely visual. I was attracted to the Tarot as a tool for adding dimension to this process. Much of my writing on the Tarot originates from a workshop I participated in, led by Diane di Prima, from October 1978 to March 1979. The techniques used to elicit writing centered on guided imagery. Diane would suggest that we create a landscape that we could enter as our place of power. Here we would meet a guide of our own choosing and make visual forays into the unknown. The Major Arcana became characters in my inner drama. I could introduce them to existing guides and teachers. I could have the different characters dialogue with one another, and the detail, the texture of the worlds in which these characters moved, would ultimately become a part of me. The Tarot essentially became for me a method for trying on new ways of being. The characters I created were unfamiliar parts of myself.

In November 1978, just a few months before my second pregnancy, I began exploring with this process, discovering new and deeper identities. There is throughout this writing the feeling of uncertainty, of being on the edge of something new and fragile and not quite known.

EXPLORING THE ADJUSTMENT CARD THROUGH POETRY

We started the workshop by choosing a card from the Major Arcana for meditation. Using the Crowley deck, as I would throughout my writing on the Tarot, I was immediately attracted to the Adjustment card. From this meeting came the poem "Adjustment."

Adjustment

Of the spine, or foundation
splintered light of
memory

She of the blue robe

cells manifest/come apart
in her hands

something Nordic about her
and rueful
and terrible

Her number is four
balance at the apex of a
spinning ball

howling wolves

and her whip cracks the ice
gather'd round my spine

the ice melts
and the eye w/ it

thru the clearing
the fir trees dip their branches
to the cold clear river

and she offers me her gift
low in the body
the balance
is lightning-in-the-belly

the balance is memory

to adjust the eye to it
to harness
to reap

10-30-78

EXPLORING THE UNIVERSE CARD THROUGH POETRY

In "The Universe," a landscape is constructed for my work in the poetic through the Tarot. It is a visual mapping that establishes for me a place to work from. It is the place of power. In the "Prologue," the external symbols on the card become a way into the dialogue with Earth as Mother. "The Dream" is an attempt to make connection with the Mother, with myself as both Mother and Daughter, and as the energy that connects these two. It begins with an instruction:

Sometimes it is essential to open up the dream space and have the voices
come all at once.

It reflects my own birth and the birth of my second daughter, Rebekah. Within the dream there is the journey out, the birth as separation when the body is viewed as separate from the Earth Daughter; and finally, the return to beginning with the work on myself as spiritual energy and my body as receptor.

The Universe

1. Prologue

serpent spiral
sickle & globe
steps thru thousands of windows

stardust we cd see with
like so many eyes

her head a conch shell
w/ eyes of a sea
creature floating on
air

beneath her a temple
her triple layered
Father-Mother-Daughter

at its pinnacle the blue light

where the foot rests on the serpent's head

where the ship's horn sounds its way
among the animals

where the breath pulsates
against the wall
Jonestown, Vietnam
or some other natural
catastrophe

where she flickers between light & dark
at the command of that
distant eye

& the four beast guard
her coming & going
that which is & that which will be

where we sing praises
Holy Holy Holy
is her Name

2. The Dream

About the Universe she said:

I am falling and

falling and

falling

and cup i hold becomes
the dome i am falling into

And she told this to her mother, tearfully
feeling the edges come in on her, and the
mud she said was oozing over her skin &
covering her up. She said that she was the
Empress experiencing the Universe, and did
her mother believe it.

And then she fell some more and turned
around and saw her mother standing next to
her looking very disgusted as if she cdn't
believe she had birthed such an obscenity.

And she said to her mother,
Look, this is the Daughter of both of us—
all that is and all that will be

descent into what we have named the Dark,
that which we call the Other

this is what we long to free ourselves
to, Mother

menstrual blood on the wall
Mother, the horror in yr
twelve-yr-old eyes when you saw
Persephone in the mirror

and i stood there
behind you some distance from the edge
of yr abyss i cd have been
that bit of root you kicked

over the edge
and i fell

and fell

and fell

and it was okay there
inside you
i knew the cup was mine

* * *

How strange the journey out
brings us to this commonground
that we stand a-part
like two islands
wearing thinner & thinner

is it for love
that we defend this place of rest
even from each other

that our mothering becomes
the point of retreat

and the Daughter screams for release
presses in on us
offers topaz

asks for exact measurement
or what the price of peace

EXPLORING THE ACES THROUGH POETRY

Immediately following "The Universe" came the poems on the Aces, the sense of oneness, of beginning in each of the elements. The one I loved the most was Disks, a symbol for the groundwork I'd begun to lay.

Ace of Disks

fern, or feather wings
curling in on each other
layers and layers
of ovals

amber at the center
of a pentacle

the first direction is earth
the second, water
the third, air
the fourth, fire

the fifth direction, pivotal
thrusting from the center
the balancing point

place of emergence
light burst forth
illuminescent shape of letter
or
the particular skin i wear

amber beam
from the navel

the shoulders,
hundreds of folded wings

the seed asleep
except for the light

*but the fifth beam
unused*

*and the light
or what we thought was*

*time as dimension
wearing thinner*

12-14-78

EXPLORING THE TREE OF LIFE: A PRACTICE READING

By this time in the Tarot Workshop we had begun to do practice readings. This Tree of Life Spread was inspired by Diane di Prima.

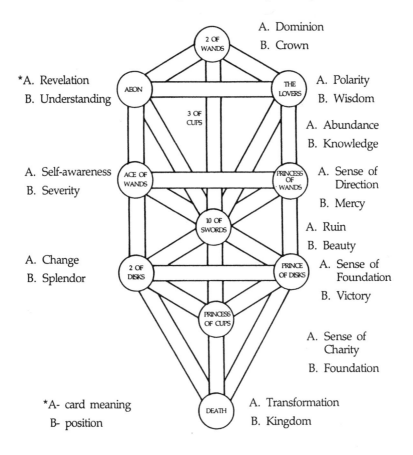

In the reading, we talked about bringing the fire energy from the upper part of the Tree down into the physical body and about the apparent closing down of those fiery energies (represented by the Wands) at the place of Victory (Prince of Disks). It was suggested that I try to make a liaison with the Prince of Disks; and so came the poem "Queen Of Cups to Prince Of Disks"; also, that to effect a smooth change I might try a daily friendly contact with Hermes as trickster and magician. He comes up in the following meditation as the Magus, who traditionally represents communication.

Meditation On The Tree Of Life Spread 5-11-79

Ascending the steps to an oval-shaped room with thick carpeted floor, I sink my feet into the rich colors. The light all around me is blinding blue-white as if the room is suspended under water, and I see the water through windows on two sides. To my left is a wall hanging, a blue netted veil that moves with soft, undulating movements, in and out. I am drawn toward it magnetically, as if I could step through it into another world, and as I approach, the movements, very hypnotic, extend further into the veil and inside emerges the figure of a child reaching out toward me with its hands, as if it has something to give me, and now I'm trembling, feeling both love and fear for this persistent, gentle child whose power overwhelms me. I want to reach the child, but the leap from the floor where I stand—from the known walls and things and objects of home—is too frightening. Instead, I go just to the edge, and extend my hand to the child. He places his hand flat against mine, and when I pull my hand away there is the impression of the Magus, a small blue figure that does several twirls in my hand, then disappears and re-emerges from beneath the surface of my hand. "These are your instruments of magic," he says, flying off the end of a finger and swooping down to the center of my palm. "Use them frivolously; use them for your own pleasure." And, I find my hand is getting so large, the weight of it becomes extremely painful. I set it down on the rug, and through it see the myriad colors of the past which the rug represents—strong, earthy reds and browns, and a purple which represents a European strain. "This is just the framework," says the child, and I see the colors flatten as I look through a small square of rug as through a skeleton that in some ways obstructs the view beyond and in some ways quickens it. "This is the alchemy of it," he says, "that you must learn to bring these two faces together. You are a child of the Aeon. Your gaze is a question. You cannot know that you know—that is the skeleton to get rid of." And again, the

Magus disappears with raucous laughter into the blue veil, which I recognize now as the robe which the Princess of Cups wears. (She appears on the Tree of Life spread at the place of emotional foundation and she represents unconditional love.) And, I see my hand getting smaller— shriveling like an old riverbed.

CONTACTING THE AEON THROUGH POETRY

After the Tree-of-Life meditation, it seemed appropriate to make contact with the Aeon. She was beginning to appear as a faint outline of a moving spirit within me, one not yet manifested physically. I had seen her during the Tree meditation as a pink cloudlike shape. She seems to exist as color, as a question I had not yet formed within myself and as a symbol for writing as physical transformation. It was suggested that a daily contact with nature would be important to facilitate this process; also, that the Child Aeon in the place of Understanding on the tree could be compared to the quality of silence as innocence and could be a way of uncovering the inner Will.

The poem that follows, "Queen Of Cups to Prince Of Disks," is a dialogue between the Queen, who represents receptiveness, and the Prince, who represents my inner foundation. In the dialogue, I consider the consciousness of Silence as a way of making contact with the Prince of Disks, and the child (Aeon) within me becomes a symbol for that experience. It is as if the Aeon, as that questioning mind of the child, becomes the meeting ground between the Prince and the Queen.

Queen of Cups to Prince of Disks

Light
from the belly
becomes

the thought-creating-body

Let your yellow light shine through me
I am vessel of the dream you have not dreamt

Peace is the cleansing
Silence the clearest vision

the pure tones that resonat through the skin
after the word is spoken

or the in-betwen time when I sweep the floor
the mirror takes on a life of its own

and the blue line that separates
light and body

the thought before the word
is fragile as the bone before it calcifies
and steadfast as a cancer moon

male and female
you are the marriage of my body

you are snake and porpoise
dancing in my blood and belly

child of my coming and going

the silence between breaths
is the blank page we share

5-12-79

The Aeon

You offer me a part of myself
that longs for opening

pueris: light child
         shadow child

the long night recedes into silence
searching for form

you are handle or spout
of a vessel just beyond reach

hand on hand i weave my way
my fingers tremble with messages
a glyph for every dream emerging
from the blue veil

your palms impress the veins of my face
i rip away the lifeless skin,
cocoon i wore of known walls
resonate with laughter from a childhood dream

you emerge once again
spiralling from my palm
small blue figure that spreads my fingers
then returns to seed in my palm

my hand grows larger, heavier
and painful—i set it down
on the rug among the reds and browns
the strong European purple

the flattened colors are the universe
through a square that limits and quickens
the stilted 'figures' elongated dance
of death 'round the fire

Is this the warning
of death 'round the fire?

Child of my Aeon
your birth is my death

we see ourselves both ways
through this double flame

we measure by nerve and sinew
the fire where the chalice spills
its blood

the night multiplies

we are the sum of it

waiting for

the next note

a gathering

crescendo

when the foundation splits

we are part

and a-part

naked vertebrae

the wind informs our bones

5-26-79

Here I speak directly to this Child, The Aeon. It marks for me a beginning to incorporate this energy into my body through the element fire:

we measure by nerve and sinew
the fire where the chalice spills
its blood

And what seems to exist as an exoteric change actually is a mirror of its source within me:

when the foundation splits

we are part

and a-part

I fluctuated from a sense of security to a sense of fear, feeling that this invisible genetic coding process determined who I was and who the child I was pregnant with would be. Somewhere within this process there is a merging of our bodies, physically and spiritually. So the experience of this poem is the experience of how we are constantly affecting each other's identities, and the joy of Motherhood comes in complementing this process by constantly discovering relationship with our own children.

The Empress Experiencing the Universe
So now it is your spirit that infuses my body, my tears are a cleansing, that we meet in this empty place where the mind is cast to sea. This is the Daughter of both of us—all that is and all that will be the Empress experiencing the Universe:

Root and flower child
your arms are a circle of light
crescent moons intertwined

the lotus roots in your belly
you are blood on the wall
before the ascent

and the marriage, Chokmah to Binah

You are Venus opening the door
at high noon
we are the light
there is nothing more to see

disrobed and facing the throne of God
the darkness we had loved
is behind us

unclench the jaw
open your eyes

Lie down in green pastures

12-15-79

T. S. Eliot and Tarot:

The Quest for Wholeness

Richard Hyde

O■O■O■O■O■O■O■O■O■O■O■O■O■O

Perhaps the most famous occurrence of the Tarot in all of literature is found in "The Waste Land" by T.S. Eliot. Not only is there an actual Tarot reading in the poem, but images directly from the Tarot deck and images strongly suggestive of it appear throughout.

Anyone who has made the Tarot a part of their life can easily discover that the protagonist of the poem is on a mythic journey much like that of the Fool through the Tarot. While the Tarot depicts the growth of the soul from individual incarnation through an enormous variety of situations leading to death and transformation, the journey of the poet, while also varied, is necessarily more specific. Even so, the poet wears many masks, male and female, ancient and modern, as he tells his tale. A friend of mine once told me how thrilled he was as a young man to hear T.S. Eliot read "The Waste Land" at Columbia University. The poet spoke in dozens of voices, varying the pitch, intonation, timbre and dynamics, actually singing some of the parts: "O O O O that Shakespearian rag." His famous recording of the poem, on the other hand, is a boring monotone because he needed an audience in order to perform.

As Eliot says in the first set of footnotes ever provided for a poem, "the plan and a good deal of the incidental symbolism of the poem were suggested by Miss Jessie L. Weston's book on the Grail legend. " A brief exposition of the Grail legend is therefore in order before we enter "The Waste Land."

A young knight, Percival, Parzival, or various other names, is raised by his mother in the woods. She wants to keep him away from human society so he will not become a knight and get killed in battle, like his father or brothers before him (note the parallel to Achilles). Nonetheless, he grows up and one day meets some knights wandering through the forest and runs away with them. Since he has grown up in the woods, his civilized companions regard him as quite a young fool (hmmm). Yet he is very strong and bests some of the finest knights in jousts, so he is knighted and given his first suit of armor, which he puts on right over the tattered old cloak that his mother made for him, symbolizing the abruptness of his transition from youth to adulthood, and from rustic to civilized life.

Then he goes off in search of the Grail, not knowing quite clearly what it is. (The authors of the legends did not know, either. Some depicted the Grail as a cup, if not the very cup of Jesus at the Last Supper. Wolfram von Eschenbach, the most mature of the writers, depicted it as a stone. Scholars connect the Grail and the structure of stories surrounding it to the cauldron of Celtic mythology and various Celtic fertility myths.) He meets a damsel on the way. As he never has met one before, he does not know what to do and, uh—the stories aren't quite clear—well, er, uh, ravishes her. Then he leaves her as quickly as he found her. He meets a man fishing in a boat in the river, who invites him to his castle to spend the night. Once there, he takes his place at the King's table. In the middle of the meal, a strange procession crosses the room: a chalice on a tray carried by a blonde-haired maiden, followed by attendants carrying, among other things, a sword and spear. They proceed into a room where the man he saw in the boat lies in bed, disabled.

Young Percival thinks to inquire about these strange goings-on, but remembering the advice of his mother ("Don't ask too many questions so as not to be thought a fool"), he says nothing. Eventually dinner and conversation draw to a close and he is led to his room for the night. The next morning he awakes in the middle of a field. The castle has vanished. Shortly, he meets another maiden to whom he relates his remarkable adventure. Horrified, she informs him that he was in the castle of the Grail King, because of whose wound the land lies infertile and desolate. All he had to do was ask about the Grail and whom it served and he would have cured the King and the land. She execrates him for being so foolish.

Percival's adventures go on from there in a variety of forms, but the story thus far provides the mythic background of "The Waste Land," a poem full of loveless sexual encounters, a hero who cannot speak, and a spiritual quest that ultimately fails.

Most scholars agree that the old Celtic stories behind the Grail legends are about a dying and rising god, who dies in the fall and rises again in the spring. These stories parallel those of Osiris, Adonis, and Tammuz of Mediterranean mythology, Lemminkainen of Finnish mythology, and, of course, Jesus of Christian mythology. Thus, dying and rising gods and, perhaps, goddesses, form another part of the background to "The Waste Land."

So let us thus, you and I, go through the poem, using the images of the Tarot as an aid to understanding. Eliot states in his own footnotes, "I am not familiar with the exact constitution of the Tarot pack," but as usual it is difficult to discern exactly what he means. Is he being truthful, evasive or simply overly modest? What deck was he talking about? Most scholars agree that he must have looked at the Rider-Waite deck, for it was popular in the early 20's when he wrote the poem. There were not many other decks in circulation at the time. The correspondence between the cards he specifially mentions and the Waite deck are too close to be a coincidence. The Waite number cards especially have a stark, haunting quality to them that matches the atmosphere of the poem. There are also some interesting correspondences between the images and characters in the poem and those in both the Rider-Waite and Harris-Crowley Tarot decks. I have provided a comprehensive chart at the end of this article, but I will mention as we proceed only those that are particularly interesting.

The poem opens with a quotation in Latin and Greek—Eliot was so literate—from the Satyricon of Petronius: "I saw the Sibyl at Cumae, one said, with mine own eyes. She hung in a cage, and read her runes to all the passers-by. Said the boys, 'Sibyl, what do you want?' She answered, 'I want to die.'"

Part I of the poem is entitled "The Burial of the Dead." The first six lines are spoken by someone — the poet, Tiberius, the Grail king — who likewise prefers death to life. April stirs his memories, which he would rather forget. Nietzsche described this state of mind, this life in death, as "that tired worn-out little want that does not want to want any more." Then the consciousness shifts—there is one consciousness in the poem, uniting all the characters, male and female, ancient and modern, and the reader, but it speaks with many voices — to the happy recollections of Marie, followed by some biblical ruminations, then the archetypal situation for the entire poem. Two people come back from the hyacinth garden and one of them—presumably the man—fails to speak. This is parallel to Perceval in the Grail Castle asking nothing and is the central unredeemed failure. This is why the consciousness prefers unconsciousness. The Crowley card for this situation is the Five of Swords, failure. The old saying: the brave die once, the cowardly die a thousand times.

Now comes the explicit reference (lines 42-59) to the Tarot and a bit of comic relief, which is very serious. The name "Sosostris" comes from a passage in *Chrome Yellow* by Aldous Huxley, where "the crocodilian Mr. Scogan, for a Bank Holiday charity fair, dresses up as a gypsy woman to tell fortunes and advertises himself as 'Sesostris, the Sorceress of Ecbatana'".

T.S. Eliot was born on September 26, 1888. Thus he is a 15/6. His constellation is the Art and Craft of Relationship. His true cards, the Devil and the Lovers, are the perfect cards for a man who took a rather sardonic view of love.

Using the method of divination provided in the Waite deck, the Madam gives the following reading to the man/woman of the poem: the drowned Pheonician Sailor (a card that Eliot invented) is the significator, placed faced down. The next card covers him. "This is the person's environment at the time, the influence with which he is actuated all through" : Belladonna, the Lady of the Rocks, the Queen of Cups, whose throne rests upon a pile of stones, a queen of water with cherubic mer-people on her throne, the master of emotional integrity; which certainly is the issue here. When reversed, Waite tells us that she is one not to be trusted, which reminds us that Eliot's women flip-flop from being Aryan-pure Grail maidens to horrible neurotics, just as the men as either ditherers or creeps.

The second card is the obstacles. If the card is favorable, Waite says, it will not help in this situation: the Three of Staves, a young man in Biblical attire gazing at a sea with three sailing ships. "Those are his ships, bearing his merchandise," says Waite. A good card, but no help. "I associate this card quite arbitrarily with the Fischer King himself," says Eliot.

Next comes the third card. This crowns him, says Waite. It represents the best he can arrive at, but it is not his own at present: the Wheel, good fortune; but not yet.

Now the fourth card. This is beneath him. It is his own — that which he has to work with and can use: the Six of Pentacles, a very good card, a one-eyed merchant, richly clad, holding the scales of justice and distributing alms to the poor.

Thus far I can say from the first card that the madame's client is under the strong influence of a very powerful woman who is not to be trusted. The next three cards all point to the world of business, trade, finance, and fortune, a comfort on the worldly level, but no help for the wounded heart. When Eliot wrote "The Waste Land" in 1921, he was taking a rest-cure in Lausanne, Switzerland, on Lac Leman, after several years of a terrible marriage with a woman who ultimately went mad. He worked at a bank during this time, specifically on foreign transactions. These four cards present a remarkably accurate picture of Eliot's world. Did he actually deal himself these cards at random when he wrote the poem, as did Jung when he threw the *I Ching* for the introduction to the Wilhelm translation? Or did he consciously choose them? Whatever the case, they certainly fit.

Next comes card number five, or, rather, it doesn't come. "This card, which is blank, is something he carries on his back, which I am forbidden to see." "This is behind him. It is the current from which he is passing away," says Waite. The Madame cannot see what the client is escaping from, trying desperately to escape from.

"Carries on his back." Hmm. "He has a monkey on his back" is a expression for drug addiction. I do not know if Eliot had a drug problem, but these lines can certainly refer to a big, heavy, nameless burden being carried. This burden is well symbolized by the Five of Swords, Defeat, or the Three of Swords, Sorrow; and was well named by James Joyce about the same time as "the agonbite of inwit." The Waite Three of Swords shows a heart pierced by three swords, a graphic depiction of heartbreak. The situation is that of Western civilization ca. 1921, a civilization with a monkey on its back, burdened by the sorrow and defeat of World War I, full of addictions and lack of love. Things have not changed much since.

There is no sixth card, unless "fear death by water" is understood as advice, in which case, a card depicting death by water could represent what is to come. There is no drowning depicted in the Tarot, but the Waite Ten of Swords depicts a very literal death *beside* water. So the Madame could be saying: Beware of death by water, which would be total ruin. Remember civilization once perished by a flood (Gen 7:11); it could do so again. On a personal level, Mr. Eliot, do not drown yourself while you weep by the waters of Leman. "By the waters of Leman I sat down and wept." Or as the old song says:

Sometimes I live in the country,
Sometimes I live in the town.
Sometimes I get a great notion
To jump in the river and drown.

She could continue by advising him not to be overwhelmed by the feminine. One of Eliot's poetic contemporaries, Hart Cane, drowned himself one night by jumping off a ship into the ocean. I am positive that

T.S. Eliot himself is the consciousness of the poem. I mean in a literal sense. The figures and emotions are personal fictions or inventions that are very real aspects of his own personality. If, then, Madame Sosostris is giving the poet a reading, it is a remarkably accurate reading for a man wrestling with a bad marriage and a difficult relationship to the feminine, yet who eventually would achieve fortune, and eventual surcease for his broken heart through his second wife and the comfort of religion. The key is working through his sorrow, the card we do not see, which he accomplished through his poetry and plays.

Grover Smith, in his book *The Waste Land*, suggests that the one-eyed merchant is the Fool and the man with three staves, the Hierophant. I do not think his case is very strong. This gaily-dressed young flop is a very odd-looking merchant and the three bars on the Hierophant's staff hardly qualify as staves. Nonetheless, if you place these two cards in the Madame's reading, you still obtain a very accurate picture of the consciousness in the poem and the life of T.S. Eliot. If the Hierophant is in the second place, it means religious comfort not now, but later, which in fact developed. Eliot converted to Anglo-Catholicism in 1927. If the Fool is in the 4th place, then that is what Eliot owns and has to work with (*Cf.* the love song of J. Alfred Prufrock):

> *At times, indeed, almost ridiculous —*
> *Almost, at times, the Fool.*

Madame Sosostris does not see the Hanged Man. This is the key to the poem. She does not see the one who changes his perspective, who turns himself upside-down and sets upon the path of transformation. The consciousness in this poem fails to do this. It fails to release its burden of failure. The Christ-figure is not there. Therefore, all the human figures play out roles in the drama without insight and without love. The women are unreachable, too easily reached or downright demonic. The men are sleaze-bags or dissemblers. All live a life in death.

William Butler Yeats said of Eliot, "He wrote the poetry of people who get out of bed and into it with indifference. For all his erudition and control of language, he is nonetheless basically a satirist. Consequently, his work falls short of true poetic utterance." This he said in the mid-30's before the Four Quartets appeared. Elsewhere, Yeats wrote:

> *The best lack all enthusiasm,*
> *The worst are full of passionate intensity.*

"The Waste Land" renders into words a European consciousness torn loose from its center, a world without a heart, without love; a waste land.

Let us continue on our journey through this loveless world. Here are the people the Madame saw walking around in a ring, flowing over London Bridge on the way to work, like the legions of the damned in Dante's Infero. There she/he sees one he knows, asks him if the corpse he planted has begun to sprout, and cries:

> *O keep the Dog for hence, that's friend to men,*
> *Or with his nails he'll dig it up again!*

Lines reminiscent of the burden he carries, a hatchet finally buried, but may surface again, expecially if consciousness keeps hounding it.

Part II, entitled "A Game of Chess," falls into two sections. Both "games" end inconclusively. The first stalemates; the second adjourns. The cards for this section are the Queen of Cups on her throne with the dolphin inscribed; the Devil holding two lovers in chains; and, of course, the Fool. "You are a proper fool." The Waite Queen of Cups holds an elaborate gold chalice with black angels—devils?—on either side. Cupid-like merpeople are carved on her throne. She could easily be Scylla or Charybdis, the lady of the rocks.

All of Part II deals with loveless sex within marriage. The luxurious woman in the chair is an epiphany of the demonic feminine, the negative aspect of the women in the Tarot. Then they converse, or, rather, she attacks and he parries. She presses him for response and we hear his internal monologue. A dreary scene. Then we move on to a bar where two women gossip about another's marriage, which is on the rocks. Another dreary scene, which culminates in the serving of a roast ham, the main course of this demotic Grail Feast.

Part III, "The Fire Sermon," deals with loveless sex outside of marriage. The river is empty, the nymphs departed. "By the waters of Leman I sat down and wept." he writes, echoing the Psalmist, captive in Babylon (Ps. 137). He is the poet, Tiresias, the Quester Knight, the Fisher King, fishing in the Thames, fishing for salvation. Fish = Iesus Christus Theou Uios Soter = Jesus Christ, Son of God, Savior. He catches nothing except the sound of Sweeney coming to Mrs. Porter, like Actaeon to Diana in the spring. In the Tarot deck, this is the Fool coming to the Moon. Indeed, in the Moon card in the Waite deck, one can see two fools in their canine nature snarling at the moon.

> "So rudely forc'd."

A sleazy merchant then propositions the poet, followed by one of Eliot's most brilliant satires: the joyless seduction of a typist in relentless rhyme. (Remember Yeats' remarks.) The gramophone music leads us onward, past the church of the fishermen (Magnus Martyr, a modern Grail chapel) back to the river and three more loveless seductions. The card for this entire section is the Seven of Cups, Debauch.

"To Carthage then I came." After a life of debauchery, St. Augustine converted to Christianity (O Lord Thou pluckest me out), and came to Carthage, a city like all cities then, and now, of decadence and debauchery. St. Augustine's ascetic religion closed off the ancient world. The spirit went inside, into monastaries for several hundred years while anarchy in the form of Goths, Huns and Vikings was loosed upon the world. The spirit came back out when European man stirred Celtic fable in with Moorish music, dance and story-telling, combined these with a fresh wind from the Crusades and the rediscovered art of courtly love. Thus came the Grail Legends, the beginning of European literature. Eliot, coming at the end of this tradition, refers to St. Augustine and the Buddha (who gave the original fire sermon) as the two great renunciates. When the path of transformation through physical love fails, there remains asceticism. The card for these lines is obviously the Hermit.

Part IV, "Death by Water," is the death by drowning foreshadowed earlier. So there is a death in the poem, but no transformation.

In Part V, "What the Thunder said," we see the quest renewed, an ascetic quest this time—no more sex, licit or illicit, just landscapes of desolation. The chapel perilous is empty. Hope enters the poem in the form of thunder, giving the three teachings of Buddhism: *Datta, Dayadhvam, Damyata.* Give, sympathize, control. Then the poet confesses how he failed to do these things. He blundered instead of gave; instead of sympathizing he remained locked up in himself; instead of controlling, he gave in. What he did or failed to do, we do not know. But the transformation does not happen. It does not rain. Defeat remains the card for the poem. Stephen Spender writes that the poem is a succession of visions in the desert of the world without God, dominated by the absence of Christ. At the very least, it is a succession of visions in the desert of the world without love.

We could take much more time to walk through the poem and poke into many other corners, but our brief journey suffices to show that "The Waste Land" touches on the bardo cards of the lesser arcana and some of the archetypal cards of the major arcana. We did not find any blessing cards or transformation cards. I pointed out earlier that the Hanged Man is noted by its absence. Likewise there is no Sun, Universe, Strength or Adjustment. There is plenty of Judgment and Lust, but all negative. There is Death, but no transformation.

Eliot's poem, therefore, is a relatively brief segment of one life's journey, a segment during which he himself experienced his gravest crisis. The resolution he sought in his life did not occur and find full expression until "The Four Quartets," written during and after World War II.

TABLE 1

Person or Situation	Waite	Crowley
I.		
Sybil	High Priestess, 2S, 8S, Queen of Wands Tower, 5W	Priestess Waste Land Tower, 10s
Burial of the Dead	Tower, Death	Tower, Death 10S, 4S
Marie & friend in Hofgarten and with cousin on sled	10P, 6C	9C, 2C
Heap of broken images	5S, 10s	
Fear in a handful of dust		Princess of Swords
Hyacinth girl & friend	6C, Fool	Fool, Queen & Princess of Cups, 5S, 7D
Oed' und Leer das Meer (wasted and empty the sea)	2S	
Madame Sosostris	Priestess, Queen of Wands , 2S	Priestess, Princess & Queen of Wands
Belladonna	Queen of Cups Pope, 3W	Man 2/ 3 staves
Wheel	Wheel	Wheel
One-eyed merchant	6P	
Hanged man	Hanged Man	Hanged Man

TABLE 1 *(continued)*

Person or Situation	Waite	Crowley
Mrs. Equitone	Temperance	Temperance
Unreal City	Tower, Chariot, 4P	Tower
London Bridge	5C	
St. Mary Woolnoth (Grail Castle)	5C	Ace of Swords
Stetson	Fool	Fool
Dog	Fool	Fool
II.		
Woman on burnished throne w/dolphin	Queen of Cups	Queen of Cups
The "lovers" 111-138	Lovers	Lovers, 8C, 7S
People in bar "You are a proper fool"	Fool	Fool, 7S
III.		
River Thames	6S	
Sweeney	6P	
Mrs. Porter	The Moon & Temperance	The Moon & Art
Mr. Eugenides	6P	
Clerk and typist	Lovers & Devil Fool, Star, 7C	Lovers
Taxi	Chariot	Chariot
Elizabeth & Leicester	Lovers & Devil	7C, Lovers
Thames Maidens	3S	

TABLE 1 *(continued)*

Person or Situation	Waite	Crowley
IV.		
Phlebas the Phoenician	10S, Death	Death
V.		
Hooded Figure	6	
Falling Towers	Tower	Tower
Empty Chapel	5 C	
Lightning	Tower	Tower
A moment's surrender	9S	7C, 7D
Blood shaking my heart	3S	5C
Key turn in the door	Pope Tower	Prison Tower
Boat responding gaily	2W	
Fishing on the shore	3W	
London Bridge	Tower	Tower, 4D, 10S

BIBLIOGRAPHY

Moody, A.D. *T.S. Eliot: Poet.* Cambridge: Cambridge University Press, 1979.

Nichols, Sallie. *Jung and Tarot.* York Beach, Maine: Samuel Weiser, 1980.

Shephard, John.*The Tarot Trumps.* Wellingborough, Northhampshire: The Aquarian Press, 1985.

Smith, Grover. *T.S.Eliot's Poetry and Plays.* Chicago: The University of Chicago Press, 1956.

Smith, Grover. *The Waste Land.* London: George Allen 7 Unwin, 1983.

Spender, Stephen. *T.S. Eliot.* New York: The Viking Press, 1975.

Weston, Jessie L. *From Ritual to Romance.* New York: Scribners.

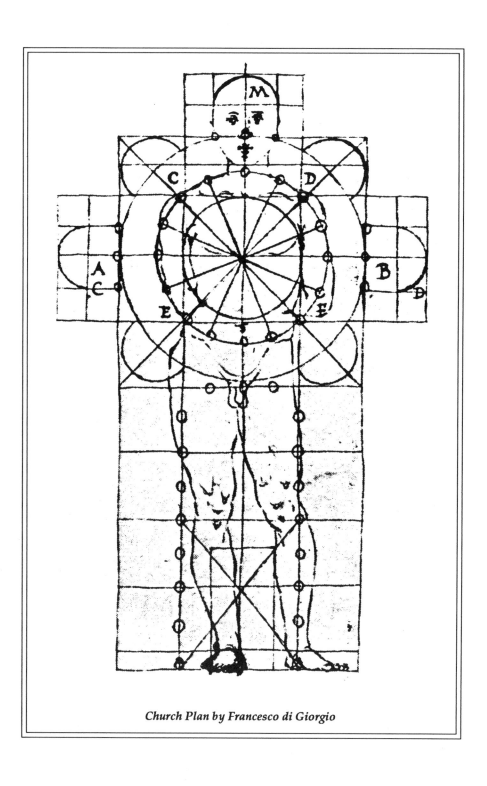

Church Plan by Francesco di Giorgio

MEDICINE WHEEL
The Helping Hand of Tarot

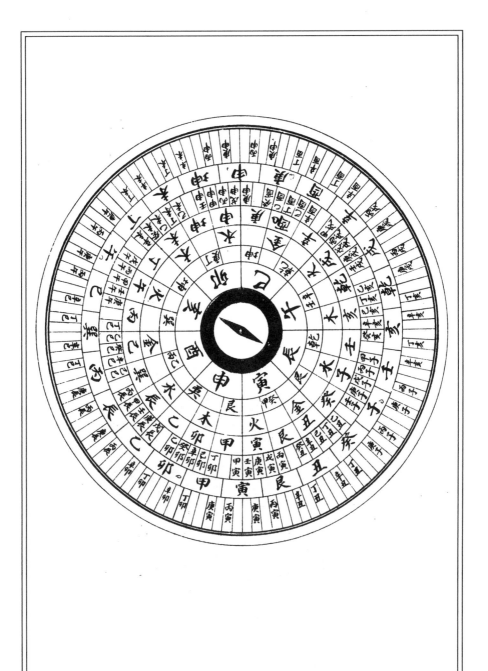

Chinese Geomancer's Compass

*C*ycle III examines the way in which Tarot—
once the exclusive province of the stereotypi-
cal "reader" or "fortune-teller"—has, in recent
times, become a consulting tool for professionals in
a wide range of occupations. Functioning as an
intuitive guide within rational fields, Tarot is the
helping hand to those professionals—business
consultants, psychotherapists, and others—whose
life work it is to help others.

A pioneering use of Tarot in business consulting is detailed by Sharon Lehrer in her article
"Organizational Management through Tarot
Symbolism." A business consultant herself, Lehrer
uses the helping of Tarot in a variety of ways. As
a medium for joining hands, she applies Tarot to
identify how the personality types and potentials
of individuals within an organization can best be
harmonized synergistically. As a healing hand,
Tarot facilitates the resolution of inter-staff conflicts. Tarot enables an organization to "get things

to "get things in hand" by assisting in the management of financial planning. In lending the creative hand of Tarot, Jeffrey is able to stimulate the growth of a business or organization.

Tarot, of course, readily lends itself to the field of personal counseling. Charloe Wittine, a professional mental-health therapist, shows the application of Tarot in psychotherapy through case studies in her article "Tarot in the Psychotherapeutic Process." Wittine uses readings to "gestalt," or "get a handle on," a client's psychological environment and to guide her own approach to a client. As Stine, Gombold, and Turner have already illustrated in Cycle II, psychologists can apply Tarot symbolism in conjunction with Jungian analysis, gestalt, psychosynthesis, and transpersonal psychology.

Clearly, Tarot is a diagnostic instrument. It can reveal unresolved issues of past experience submerged in the subconscious (Culberson). Tarot can uncover reasons for interpersonal conflict (Lehrer), personal disintegration (Wittine and

Stine), *physical tension (Cole), and self-limitation (Turner).*

By the same token, Tarot is a holistic healing art. No problem is diagnosed without consultation of its mental, emotional, physical, worldly, and spiritual aspects. A unique feature of its holism is that the diagnostic process is also often the therapy or remedy. As Charloe Wittine states, "[B]locked energy is released through its exploration." Recognition of the problem through symbols is itself healing.

Visualizing symbols of Tarot in meditation exercises can be powerful therapy (Gombold, Wittine, Bolinger, and Turner). Envisioning negative symbols induces purification through catharsis and release. Positive symbols are energizing and fortifying.

Yet Tarot is more than a curative. It is also preventative medicine. Tarot establishes a set of principles to live by. Adherence to this philosophy of life results in good health on all levels.

Angeles Arrien and James Wanless in "The

Tarot Clientele: Who, When, Why" show why healthy individuals who are not disposed to psychiatric counseling are attracted to a traditional "reading" form of counseling. According to this study, the Tarot reader is most frequently consulted during periods of significant life transition. A reading supports, guides, and structures personal changes.

Tarot is a loving hand that teaches us to embrace and celebrate what is. But, as a finger that points the way, Tarot directs us toward new directions and realities. Like a fist, Tarot empowers us to break through blocks and achieve our destiny.

Organizational Management Through Tarot Symbolism

Sharon Lehrer

○■○■○■○■○■○■○■○■○■○■○■○

The group sat together, focused their energy on the business, and shuffled the cards. One by one, each person picked a card and placed it in the pattern. Everyone's eyes were glued to the cards as they were turned over. There was awe and then agreement with each card as I described its meaning...

One of the most important factors in organizational success is clear purpose and vision. While this sounds obvious, it is often difficult to achieve. Different assumptions, values, or needs among leaders and employees may be present but unrecognized. As a company evolves, external and internal forces may shift the organization imperceptibly until it is heavily invested in process or projects that are unrelated to its original purpose.

Almost as important as organizational purpose itself is the degree to which the individual values and purposes of leaders, managers, and employees are aligned, both with the organization's overall purpose and with the purposes of their own functions within it. Organizations lacking alignment of purpose, values or goals at best suffer from underperformance. At worst, they fall prey to unproductive, time-consuming conflict. Yet relatively few individuals are fully aware of their life purpose or personal development process, especially as it relates to work. Many have taken their jobs based on economic need, remnants of parental "should's," personal relationships, or simply because an opportunity presented itself at what seemed like the right time. Gaining access to an individual's whole nature and developmental process requires digging beneath the surface of consciousness. Unfortunately, the exclusively rational, task-based environments of most workplaces tend to keep these deeper levels of being suppressed—perhaps even to make them more difficult to access.

While many organization problems that manifest as communication or performance difficulties result from a lack of clear purpose or alignment, others may result from interpersonal issues that have arisen through incomplete or unsatisfactory interaction. If not attended to, these issues tend to link with early relationship patterns that lie deep within the unconscious experience of the individuals involved and, as a result, become extremely difficult to uncover and change.

I am consultant trained in rational approaches to problem solving. I am also a woman concerned with our intuitive and emotional capacities. The challenge of my career has been to combine the intuitive and objective in ways that support organization development and fulfillment of purpose.

Providing organization development in this way to address these fundamental success factors requires reaching into the unconscious, then integrating the information gleaned with rational approaches. Because intuitive and visual experience provide a means of reaching the unconscious mind without the conscious filtering that logical language requires, symbols are an indispensable tool in the development process.

Among possible symbolic systems, I have found the Tarot to be particularly effective for organizational application, both because it provides access to a range of archetypal wisdom that is large and rich enough to reflect the complexity and uniqueness of organizational situations, and because its visual impact is extremely powerful.[1]

BACKGROUND ON THE TAROT

The Tarot is an old system of knowing the divine. No one is sure of its origin. Some say it came from ancient Egypt, others think China, Korea, or India.[2] With the establishment of institutional religion, which punished other forms of worship and forbade individuals to connect with the sacred except through its own rituals and official authorities, the Tarot as a tool for spiritual development went underground. Like a plant with deep roots, sometime in the Middle Ages it resurfaced shorn of its spiritual meaning in the form of the playing card deck we know today. Still carrying the stigma of forbidden worship, it was picked up by some for telling fortunes and their sometimes marginal status and association with black magic have given the Tarot a bad reputation. Recently, in this period of rapid change, when people are searching for meaning and purpose in their lives, the Tarot has begun to reclaim its power as a tool for gaining access to higher knowledge for growth and development.

While there are many variants on the Tarot deck, they all have the same basic structure: 78 cards, twenty-two (22) major arcana or principals, sixteen (16) royalty, and forty (40) minor arcana or principals The major arcana symbols represent archetypal energies. Archetypal means the original mold or energy pattern. Interestingly, Carl Jung recognized that these archetypal energies are found cross-culturally and reside in the unconscious. Joseph Campbell's extensive research into the mythologies of the East and West further demonstrated the archetypes' universality. The names of a few of the cards may differ slightly from deck to deck, but the core concepts are universal, with the only significant differences being the visual depictions.

The flavor of the major arcana can be developed from a few examples:

• The Emperor is a compassionate leader pioneering new directions, a visionary, a peacemaker and an adventurer. The Emperor is a strong, sensitive being who empowers others,

• The Lovers are gifted in the "art and craft"[3] of relationships. They are the diplomats and inspire people to work toward common goals. The Lovers, embodying the union of male and female, are great synthesizers of oppositions and polarities. They understand that it is through relationships that they learn about themselves— the mirror of self in others.

• The Star represents innovation, finding new solutions to seemingly unsolvable problems. They exude self-esteem and confidence and are recognized for contributions to humanity. They are highly intuitive and emotional.

The remaining 56 cards are the similar to those in a regular playing card deck, comprising four suits which include the ace through 10 plus four, rather than three, royalty cards, which substitute knight for king and prince for jack, and added princess. The four suits of the Tarot correspond to the four elements, which in turn correlate with four levels of consciousness; Disks (earth/physical), Cups (water/emotional), Swords (air/mental or intellectual), and Wands (fire/spiritual).

The royalty symbols represent mastery of specific skills, for example, the Knight of Wands—vision, Prince of Disks—prosperity, Queen of Cups—emotional integrity, and Princess of Swords—practical thinking.

The ace through 10 of the four suits are numerically linked to the major archetypes and represent minor aspects of them. For example, the 3's of each of the suits—representing Abundance, Virtue, Works, and

Sorrow are aspects of and lessons and opportunities linked to the Empress (major arcana III).

USING THE TAROT TO HELP BUSINESSES DEVELOP

This system, which sequentially orders the development of human growth and self awareness, satisfies the need of the rational mind for linear thinking. Its power to support growth and development, however, resides in its ability to tap the unconscious through the use of symbols: the forms that speak to the imaginative and holistic mind. Marketing professionals have always known that in communicating the value of products or services to customers, visual symbols are more powerful than words alone. Recently, more leaders and managers are beginning to recognize the need to satisfy and integrate both the rational and intuitive minds in communication, decision-making, planning, product development, visioning and problem solving as well. The tarot is an effective tool for leaders and managers who have reached this awareness.

The meaning of Tarot symbols is readily accessible and provides the context for understanding the greater meaning of the whole range of our everyday experience—health, finances, relationships, creativity, and work, whether that experience is personal or organizational. Effective organizational work generally involves integrating both the personal and organizational dimensions.

Cards are linked with individuals or the organization through a variety of interactive processes. Life purpose symbols are established through a calculation based on birthday[4] or day of organizational founding. Recent, current, and future trends and opportunities are established through identifying a card for a year (by substituting that year for the birth year in the same calculation), and/or by shuffling and selecting cards to be placed in the pattern of a "spread," in which the position defines the aspect of experience to which the card refers.

Time and again, clients "recognize" the cards identified or selected, and experience them as providing confirmation of something they have been on the verge of knowing about themselves. The cards may also clarify a challenge they must meet, along with identifying strategic choices and decisions and clarifying direction, goals and actions.

Individual Owner Assessment

For example, a woman who had spent many years in academic study decided she wanted to work as an organization and training consultant.

After several years mastering these skills in the corporate world, she started her own consulting practice. Since being on her own, however, she was receiving mostly training as opposed to consulting contracts. She felt she had to take the training assignments for financial reasons. Not only wasn't this what she wanted to be doing, but she felt she wasn't being appreciated or paid enough for her work. Thinking she couldn't really change this situations given current economic situations, she felt emotionally drained and stuck.

She was stunned when her life purpose symbol turned out to be Adjustment (XIII): a highly creative energy that draws ideas from within, is concerned with implementing them, is gifted at synthesis and perpetually involved in issues of balance and justice. This symbol accurately reflected her deepest nature, desires and talents.

Her current growth energy, however, was the Hanged Man (XII), representing both resistance and commitment to breaking out of restrictive patterns. She was initially taken aback by this, but quickly realized that it corroborated her sense of being stuck.

When a detailed spread for current and future possibilities was completed, it revealed 8 very positive cards that affirmed the success of her recent self-development efforts and indicated both financial reward and emotional fulfillment as likely outcomes. Two cards, however, were problematic: 7 of Swords, Futility, describing her mental block, and 8 of Cups, Indolence, describing her emotional block. In the course of the reading she realized that thinking she couldn't change her situation and over giving to the point of emotional depletion were interrelated, and in fact represented the essence of the resistance depicted by the Hanged Man. Other elements of the spread enabled her to see that she needed to take the initiative in formulating what she really wanted to do and in actively marketing it. Once she understood this she was able to come to terms with the current situation and develop strategies and actions to help her move in the direction of her choice.

Company Assesment

In another example, a $4 million medical instruments training and technical support service brokerage company was facing two difficult challenges. The first was that its East Coast office hadn't been profitable and its costs had been absorbed by the headquarters on the West Coast. However, the firm was avoiding the decision to close the Eastern office partly because they kept holding out hope that a newer, better marketing strategy would generate a profit and partly because close personal relationships made purely business-based decisions difficult.

The second challenge this company had to face was an IRS audit questioning whether the independent training contractors they brokered were "technically" employees of the organization. In fact, much of their success to date could be attributed to the full independence of the trainers whose services the company brokered. Despite the company's confidence in their position, the audit was turning into a long, costly, and psychologically draining process.

The Tarot closely reflected and illuminated these challenges. The life purpose symbol of the company was the Chariot (VII)— a fast moving, well-balanced vehicle that sets new and creative ideas into motion through conscious choice. The company's growth year symbol, on the other hand, was the Hermit (IX), who represents discovering one's true nature through contemplation and being true to that nature by both completing the past and re-envisioning the future. This card suggested that it was essential for the company to review and finish any old business so that it could clearly establish future direction and move into it unencumbered.

The Hermit also appeared as the owner's growth year energy. Additionally one of the executive team members received the Hermit. In these three powerful positions, the Hermit sent a clear message: this is the year to resolve and complete these issues. During the year this company made the difficult decision to close the East Coast office and to re-envision how to preserve the essence of its trainers' autonomy even if the IRS required them to become employees. This whole process was so helpful that the company has built tarot consultation into their annual planning process in each succeeding year.

TAROT CONSULTATION METHODOLOGY

The methodology for using the tarot with businesses varies according to the particular situation. Basically, it involves a group—of owners, managers, or departmental staff. The extent of consulting is determined by the needs and interests of this group. It can vary from a one-day needs-and-strengths assessment to an ongoing consulting and training program. To support these processes, I have designed several spreads and ways of constructing them with groups and individuals to assess the business.

Figure 1 shows a spread for assessing key organizational issues.

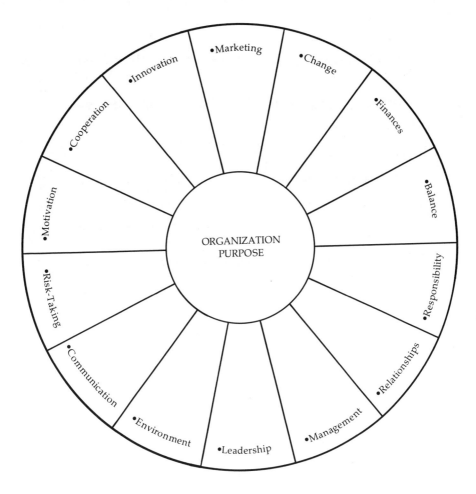

FIGURE 1

Organization Assessment

Figure 2 shows a completed analysis of a business using an organizational adaptation of Angeles Arrien's "Whole Person" spread.[5] I'd like now to turn to this particular business as an in-depth case, to demonstrate more fully the steps that may be involved in a Tarot-based organization development intervention.

CASE STUDY

One of the most challenging Tarot-based interventions I've conducted involved an educational service organization. This case demonstrates the Tarot as an effective tool for:

1. Identifying the organization's purpose and individual staff's life purpose,

2. Assessing the organization's strengths and factors blocking succes,

3. Developing a plan for consulting and training,

4. Identifying strategic choices and decisions,

5. Clarifying direction, vision, goals and actions,

6. Motivating staff for poitive and constructive change.

In my first meeting with them, frustration, depression, and anxiety were masked by much casual joking and playing around with one another. I knew that the Tarot would be an excellent tool for uncovering the emotional issues underlying the tensions, as well as for identifying the beliefs that were influencing the major financial and management problems they were having. The information revealed in the Tarot-based assessment provided me ample data for designing an effective consulting program using traditional organization development approaches. The process I used with this organization included several steps and involved the key decision-makers both in groups and individually.

Step One: Identifying Organization Purpose

The first step is to ascertain the purpose of the organization as represented symbolically in the tarot. The number of the major arcana is determined by adding the month, day, and year of the date of the organization's founding, then adding the digits of the resulting number, and finally, adding the digits of that smaller number. For example:

December 24, 1940 (or 12+24+1940 = 1976; 1+9+7+6 = 23; 2+3=5)

The number and corresponding Tarot symbol for this organization was five, the Hierophant. I showed this card to the staff. They were amazed at the accuracy of its meaning for their organization. The Hierophant is a spiritual teacher who teaches the meaning of life through practical methods. The purpose of this organization was to teach people in business and educational institutions how to work together cooperatively. Their method was to design and produce creative games which would give their customers the opportunity to play together in innovative, non-competitive ways. The Hierophant learns what he teaches by personally experiencing it. In the same way, the staff was learning about their own aggressive, competitive natures so that they could more effectively teach trust and cooperation to others. The Hierophant archetype gave the staff a picture of their purpose and inspired them to learn about themselves so that they would be more effective as an organization.

Step Two: Individual Life Purpose and Assessment

In the second step of the process, each member of the executive team had a private session. In this session, everyone was shown his or her purpose symbol and received a comprehensive assessment of personal work-related strengths and weaknesses, based on the ten-card Whole Person spread. The symbols illustrated areas of immediate strength and identified the issues blocking the person's full expression. With the resulting clarity, individuals were able to evaluate their performance and determine specifically how to actualize their creative purpose within their current job. In addition, individuals can choose to take responsibility for their personal issues and their impact on the organization.

Three of the six staff members had the same life purpose symbol, the combination of the Empress (III) and the Universe (XXI). Since this represented an unusually high percentage of the same-symbol energy in one group, I knew that the themes from these symbols would play a significant role in the makeup of this organization.

The Empress is the earth mother, who brings forth the qualities of love, receptivity, nurturance, and creativity. Her concern is to bring beauty and harmony into the lives of those around her, especially at the physical and emotional levels. She is gifted intellectually and blends this with her rich emotional nature. The people in this organization had a strong desire to structure the business environment to support creativity and to cooperate with one another. Internally, they strove to balance their emotional and intellectual natures.

The Universe energy symbolizes involvement in the world, in this case, the desire to have a significant impact on social and business institutions with the organization's innovative programs. The Empress and Universe archetypes not only represented the purpose of three individuals, but also reflected basic motivations of the organization's staff as a whole.

The fourth person's symbols were the Chariot (VII) and the Tower (XVI). The Chariot, as noted above, is a fast moving, well-balanced vehicle that represents highly conscious choice of direction and the ability to set new and creative ideas into motion. The Tower energy is a cleansing force, as represented by the fire on the card. It burns out old habits and ideas that prevent one's best qualities from being expressed. This person helped drive the organization to actualize its programs, as well as to evaluate and improve itself.

The fifth person's symbol was Adjustment (VIII). This card pictures many blue and green balloons above and below the head of the central figure holding a scale. The balloons above represent a creative mind, while those below represent the actualization of the ideas. The scale represents the ability to balance the needs and complete all of the steps required to implement the ideas. He was the key figure in the creative development and design of the games and brought excellent management skills to the group.

The sixth person's symbols were the Sun (XIX), Wheel of Fortune (X), and the Magus (I). The constellation of these three energies represents the art of communicating meaningful messages to all kinds of people, inspiring people to express their creativity, breaking through any limitation and generating resources. This woman was one of the best trainers and marketers in the company.

The most significant problematic energy identified in the individual readings was the 3 of Swords, which surfaced for three people. The Sorrow energy is an inversion of the Empress, since both are number three. It is a result of their inability to create the Empress qualities of a cooperative, supportive and creative staff environment. Sorrow represented the predominant problem in the organization. These individuals were depressed by their separation from their own creativity and from the other members of the group.

Step Three: Sharing the Group Profile

The third step in the process involves sharing with the group the information from the individual readings. When I placed the purpose symbols of the staff on a chart for them all to see, all were inspired by the qualities and talents of their fellow staff members. As they talked about their combined talents, they also realized how the specific purpose and talents of each member correlated with the organization's purpose.

I then summarized the key personal development issues. This information provided the context for reviewing job descriptions and exploring how to create an effective team. We also discussed the value of individuals knowing their unique talents and their particular opportunities and challenges for personal growth. By knowing this, individuals can choose to take responsibility for creating change and for not putting "their stuff" onto others.

Step Four: Organization Assessment

The last step of this process was a Tarot-based assessment of the total organization. A 10-card spread parallel to the individual Whole Person spread was used, except cards were chosen from the deck and placed in the pattern by members of the group. The spread that resulted from the group process, and descriptions of the spread positions appear in Figure 2 on the next page.

The cards accurately reflected the tremendous upheaval going on in the organization. The group was in the midst of a major crisis, indicated by the following cards: the Hermit, the Tower, Death, 3 and 10 of Swords—Sorrow and Ruin, and Knight of Wands. Basic assumptions and behavior patterns were being fundamentally and profoundly challenged. The truth was that as much as they wanted to be cooperative with one another, they were really being competitive, jealous, and non-trusting.

The Death-Rebirth and the Tower cards validated the need for change—to let go of old patterns inconsistent with its core purpose and future direction. The Knight of Wands, gallantly dressed in bright reds and yellows, pointed to their sincere desire to face and positively resolve these issues. The Hermit showed their deep desire to complete this unfinished business so they could move into the future unencombered.

Sorrow symbolized the source of disappointment, anger, and hurt. An example of this sorrow centered around one staff member who, because of serious personal problems, was unable to work productively. The staff wanted to respond to her in a human way, yet they also were angry and resentful because she was not doing her job and it was affecting the business. They didn't know how to express their feelings, how to help her, or how to develop a constructive and responsible solution.

The 10 of Swords, Ruin reflected the financial situation. The organization was facing a deficit and they were fearful of financial ruine. This symbol pinpointed an underlying belief around money—that it is not okay to make money by doing what you love. This belief was influencing their capacity to organize and implement a successful marketing and sales program.

As I helped the group understand the problematic cards, I explained

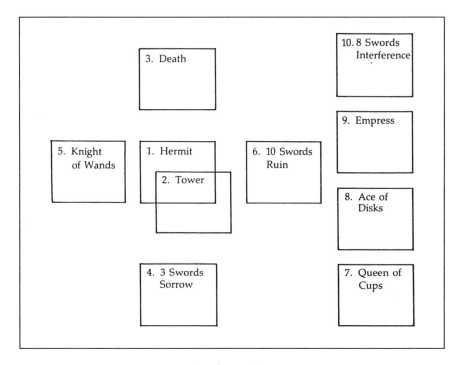

FIGURE 2

Present State of Consciousness
1. The heart of the organization in the past.
2. The heart of the organization in the present.
3. What the organization or decision-makers are thinking about; conscious mind.
4. The underlying issues in the organization; subconscious mind.
5. The organization's creativity. The capacity to structure and complete goals, and to draw opportunities and situation toward the business, e.g., customers, resources, good will.
6. The organization's ability to make decisions and to set in motion its purpose, goals and action plan.

Probable Future
7. Possibilities for innovation and creative breakthroughs.
8. Staff relationships.
9. How the organization handles the differences or polarities within.
10. The business' natural express or what it wants to release.

that acknowledging these dynamics was the first step toward change. After the initial discomfort, they were relieved to know what was blocking their success. It was now out in the open and could be dealt with objectively.

They appreciated, as portrayed in the symbols, their strengths and the ideas for resolving issues and generating organizational success. The cards in the outcome position were positive. The Queen of Cups, the master of emotional integrity, indicated that the organization would learn how to be in emotional integrity with each other and their customers. The Ace of Disks, appearing in the outcome position for staff relationships, indicated that they'd achieved the qualities of trust, openness, and cooperation that they so deeply desired. Both were important values for the group.

The only potential future problem was indicated by the 8 of Swords, Interference. They'd need to continually watch their tendency to be pulled in many directions at the same time. By establishing goals and setting priorities, they could gain control of the divergent forces. Teaching them organization planning gave them tools to deal with the confusion.

Following our session together, the executive team re-aligned themselves around their common purpose, focused on their vision, developed a strategic plan, refurbished and reorganized the office, and within a short period were on course generating clients and income. The woman with the personal problems left the company, realizing that it was not the best place for her right now. It was a comfortable separation because of the understanding and insights she and the others received from the Tarot.

CONCLUSION

Combining ancient Tarot symbols with an analytical approach to business organization and management is a dynamic tool for significantly increasing the power of a group to create success on all levels. However, an organization must be open to using and integrating intuitive faculties with the rational mind in order to make successful use of a Tarot-based intervention. I assess this readiness prior to even suggesting this methodology. If this readiness is present, however, effective applications may range from organizational or individual assessment, to strategic planning, team building, conflict resolution, discovering and exploring purpose and meaning in work, and professional development.

The situations in which the Tarot may be most powerful are where emotional or subconscious issues are blocking organizational growth. People quickly grasp hidden and difficult information and gain insight with efficiency that saves both time and money. The Tarot's positive orientation empowers people to see beyond their limited beliefs, attitudes, and behavior to the potential for change and growth. And the colorful pictures, like an effective organizational vision, inspire and motivate people to perform at their maximum, in turn increasing self-esteem, personal power, and creativity. This benefits the business, for when people are functioning from their own personal power and using their creativity collectively, the power to innovate and solve problems grows exponentially.

Notes

1. It is with deep appreciation and respect that I acknowledge the contribution of Angeles Arrien who has encouraged me to apply Tarot in the business world.

2. Angeles Arrien. The Tarot Handbook, Practical Applications of Ancient Visual Symbols. Sonoma: Arcus Publishing Company, 1987, p.16.

3. *Ibid.*, p. 45.

4. *Ibid.*, p.231.

5. *Ibid.*, p.267.

6. My gratitude to Susan Harris whose creativity and editorial experience enriched this article.

Tarot in the
Psychotherapeutic Process

Charloe Wittine

O■O■O■O■O■O■O■O■O■O■O■O■O

The Tarot, when used by an experienced therapist, can energize the intuition and creative imagination so that inner states can be more directly experienced. The psychic impact of this well constructed set of primary symbols creates an opening to the inner world of the individual.

In my work as a helping professional, I use Tarot in a variety of ways. First, the symbols serve as guides to help me focus on how to proceed in my work with clients. I can examine issues such as what to emphasize, what to let be, what approach I should use. Second, the Tarot serves as an assessment tool which, like the Rorschach, T.A.T. (Thematic Apperception Test), and other projective tests, can present a gestalt of the client's psychological environment. As such, the Tarot triggers dialogue with the deeper self. Third, when Tarot images are visualized and used as starting points for creative imagery or meditation, they act as catalysts in the development and integration of qualities which may be vital to the client's well-being.

Paul Foster Case says of the Tarot, "These are universal signs, and their fundamental significance is the same the world over, in all periods of history, in all forms of religion, in all varieties of philosophy. They are, in fact, drawn from that stock of images, common to all men everywhere. . ."[1] The following are a few examples of how I use Tarot in my counseling practice.

USE OF TAROT SYMBOLS AS A GUIDE FOR THE THERAPIST

I have found that doing a simple throw before a client arrives for a session can assist me in paying attention more clearly to certain aspects of the session. A pre-session throw has helped me to avoid assumptions about a client's well-being or lack of it, or to avoid charging into a technique or approach that may not be appropriate. I have even been able to note that a client would cancel at the last minute and how to respond to this.

I often do a three-card throw before a client arrives to tune my intuitive processes. I choose a central card for an overview of the session, a second card to signify what to be aware of in the session, and a third card to signify what not to be concerned about or emphasize. During the session, these Tarot images serve as internal guides.

Before giving more examples of my work with Tarot, I would like to clarify how to create a throw. First, the issue to be explored should be defined as clearly as possible. Then, a convention appropriate to the situation is set up with meanings assigned to the various positions of the cards representing different parts of the issue. As you relate to the cards during the reading, the agreement of the convention as you have set it up is kept. Respond to the cards within the context that you have established and the positions you have assigned to them. Intuition and creative imagination will do the rest.

Aside from the innate symbolism of the individual cards, the particular situation sparks the intuitions apropos to that situation. When reading, for yourself or with a client in a session, you should never just attempt to read the cards as though remembering a text. The images must be triggers for the very energy of that situation and relationship at that time. Otherwise, the amount of coherent meaning will be akin to a well-trained parrot's recital of some ditty its trainer has programmed into it.

When I do a reading, I usually use two or more decks. Different decks carry different energy or emphasis. The drawings of each deck reflect the interpretations of its author and artist. When the same card represented in different decks appears in various parts of a reading, it assists me in tracing recurring patterns quite clearly. I can see in what areas of the life situation specific patterns appear and the various phases they go through. I most frequently use a combination of the Arthur Waite deck and Aleister Crowley's Thoth deck, although I've been known to use up to four decks in a reading. My suggestion is to use the deck or decks with which you most easily resonate.

The Tarot has assisted me in exploring and clarifying intuitive insights or emerging feelings that I have had about my work with a client. An example that comes to mind involves a woman whom I had been seeing for two years.

Jan (not her real name) had been seeing me weekly during this period. Our work had gone well and, in fact, she seemed to be coming into a very healthy and balanced grasp of herself and her inner patterns. I was feeling that it was time to complete therapy. My main concerns were whether I was correct in assuming this and how best to broach the issue so as not to give her the feeling of being pushed out of our therapeutic relationship. I decided to consult the Tarot to help clarify my feelings.

The reading verified her readiness to complete therapy. The Major Arcana card Strength was a central image for her and reflected her ability to stand on her own and deal with her problems with courage and clarity. The reading also showed that confronting her directly with ending therapy would be abrupt and shocking, possibly disruptive to her newly emerging sense of well-being. The card for this was the Seven of Wands, which I saw as representing the taking of a defensive stance to protect one's position.

I selected some cards to show how I should approach the issue. The sequence indicated that I should remain in a receptive mode. She would bring up the subject herself. The Four of Swords signified a quiet waiting; the Queen of Cups and Two of Cups signified calm receptivity and waiting for a context of mutual trust and spontaneous agreement to arise.

Two months later, Jan announced that she would be out of the state for ten weeks. She said that she was feeling strong, able to cope, and that she felt as if something had shifted within her. I was then able to suggest that we consider this a completion regardless of whether we chose to continue our work when she returned. This would enable her to affirm for herself her ability to "go it alone" without our weekly sessions.

I recently received a card from Jan. She said that all was well. She was feeling quite peaceful and balanced in her life. I may well have come to the same conclusions without using the Tarot, but it helped tune me in on the fine points of how to proceed in my work.

I have found Tarot to be especially useful for determining how to proceed when I feel that a client is blocking—that is, when our work has developed into a pattern of relating that I want to shift and I am unclear about what the obstruction is, how to bring about change, and whether to be receptive or directive. The following is a more detailed example of a throw set up to clarify my process with a client.

I set up an eleven-card reading to work with, consisting of the following positions:

1. Overview.

2. My point of clarity.

3. The client's point of clarity.

4. The transference.

5. The counter-transference.

6. The way in which the client is blocking.

7. How I am buying into the client's resistance.

8. The energy needed to break through the established pattern.

9. Point of right action.

10. The client's reaction to this action.

11. The result of this shift.

Here is a capsule form of the reading that sparked me on how to proceed. You may wish to lay out the cards and see if you notice any of the connections I saw. You may see something entirely different. As I mentioned earlier, the situation itself is the trigger for particular meaning, and the intuitions sparked are apropos to the energy of the situation. Trust in your own intuitive processes is essential. In this reading, I used both the Crowley and Waite decks.

1. Overview: Aeon (Crowley). Interpretation: We are dealing on many levels, in depth and in the abstract; the client's patterns are deeply imbedded; archetypal energies are highly activated; some infantile and regressive behaviors are also present; one of the main goals in the work now is how to pin this all down into a workable process.

2. Counselor's Point of Clarity: Ace of Cups (Crowley). Interpretation: I am open, have a strong feeling response; am fully empathetic; my intuitions are right-on; I understand what is going on at the feeling level; there is a strong maternal energy emanating from me; I am aware of the strength and largeness of the client's emotional energy.

3. Client's Point of Clarity: Star (Crowley). Interpretation: Client is definitely awakened to the transpersonal levels of being; he can understand larger frameworks; is developing increased confidence and self-esteem; is beginning to objectify; at some level he recognizes and is willing to contend with the issues.

4. The Transference: Nine of Wands (Waite). Interpretation: Client sees me as another potential batterer; feels he has to do battle with me to hold his own; has strong defenses; sees me as a force he must fight.

5. Counter-transference: Two of Swords (Waite). Interpretation: I want to show myself as harmless; hold back my perceptions; non-action; internalize my insights.

6. Client's Way of Blocking Therapy: Five of Wands (Crowley). Interpretation: Strong counter-will; seeks either consciously or unconsciously to enthrall me with philosophical and abstract concepts; solid resistance and display of knowledge are masking more concrete issues; note planet Saturn on card and sign Leo, Leo will make a big show, build strong ego defenses with Saturn going solid in resistance.

7. Buying into Resistance: Page of Wands (Waite). Interpretation: I curb my will and fall into coex^2 of my own upbringing, "the appreciative audience and polite listener"; I become the student of his philosophical knowledge.

8. Energy Needed to Break Through Pattern: Two of Pentacles (Crowley). Interpretation: There needs to be a change in the crystallized ways that are beginning to develop in our mode of relating; I must be a catalyst for this change; notice planet Jupiter and sign Capricorn on card; must combine optimism and expansiveness (Jupiter) with practicality and grounding (Capricorn); client also has to be willing for change to occur.

9. Point of Right Action: Empress (Waite). Interpretation: I should begin using processes of active imagination more fully; offer what I have to give fully and with much less reserve; be actively creative in the counseling relationship; need to be more strongly productive; emphasis on birth rather than on death.

10. Client's Reaction: Eight of Cups (Waite). Interpretation: He will be forced into new avenues of emotional expression; moving away from unconscious patterns; will begin honestly searching for missing links in memories and associations; must begin seeking new emotional responses; stronger exploration of the unconscious; client could leave therapy.

11. Result: Nine of Swords (Crowley). Interpretation: Strong attack on mental patterns as emphasized by planet Mars (action, aggression) and sign Gemini (mind, duality); need to actively unify various parts; there will be a deeper facing of the pain and cruelty suffered as a child; the recurring mental nightmare will be pierced; going through the coex, a difficult but necessary next step will be taken.

Having worked out my problem with the assistance of my powerful visual aide, I proceeded to pay attention during the next client session. As my client began moving closer to a very painful and blocked memory, I worked with creative visualization, was direct in allowing my intuitions full and active play. I continued to be dynamically involved as we kept pressing into the issue. As a result he was able to push more intensely and fully on this knot of emotionally charged memories than he had ever done before. He admitted his fears around intense exploration and was unsuccessful with his usual decoying devices. The result was a powerful breakthrough and reassessment of the issue. The time had been right, the energy and relationship ripe, to take this new step. We had entered into a new phase of our work together.

USE OF TAROT SYMBOLS WITHIN A CLIENT SESSION

When it seems appropriate and when a client is open to it, I have used the Tarot in a session. We have used it at crisis points, when energy is blocked, at crossroads in the person's life, and at completion points.

As we work with the Tarot, a dialogue may begin between the client and the images. The issues become clarified, perception expands, attitudes shift, vague feelings become more focused, and ambivalent attitudes resolve as blocked energy is released through exploration. The client may be encouraged to "gestalt" a particularly strong Tarot image. They may be led on a guided imagery exercise with one of the cards. We might do a technique from Roberto Assagioli's system of psychosynthesis[3] such as exploring subpersonalities[4] or working on a synthesis of opposites. Use of Tarot in a session can prove to be an energizing and rewarding experience for both client and counselor.

One of my clients had been concerned about her relationship with her boss and the value of staying at her present place of employment. We decided to use the Tarot to work with the situation.

We drew a central card to represent the relationship as well as a card each for my client and for her boss to represent their positions or attitudes within this relationship. The central card was the Major Arcana card Judgment. It seemed that there were strongly held opinions, and there was a call to both parties for a transformation in the relationship. This was further amplified by the two poles of the relationship. My client was represented as the King of Wands, indicating strong will and most likely strong use of counter-will as an employee. The boss was represented by the Queen of Swords, emanating strong control, judgment, and severity. The boss was a good but exacting teacher. My client's strong will tended to resist being controlled or manipulated.

We asked how this affected the working atmosphere and drew the Four of Cups, which seemed to indicate that many feelings remained unexpressed creating an atmosphere of withdrawal and avoidance. As the reading continued, the client became aware that most of the conflict between them lay on the personality level and that beneath the surface of conflicts lay a strong power-play. We drew cards for the "Persona" and "Shadow" of the relationship with, again, cards for both the client and boss. The Five of Wands in the Persona position indicated both personalities engaging in a battle of wills. My client was aware that there was also constructive potential in their ability to fight it out. Perhaps through their willingness to engage in conflict, the transformation indicated by the central card could begin to unfold.

The Chariot, a Major Arcana card, appeared in the Shadow position, emphasizing the power-play beneath the surface of personality conflicts. The Chariot, which represents the zodiacal sign of Cancer, can pertain to emotional energies relating to the solar plexus chakra.[5] This center is one of emotion and power, of power and submission. The individual cards showed my client as being worn down by the personality squabbles, feeling burdened, as represented by the Ten of Wands. Her aspect of the Shadow position was The Aeon and seemed to show a kind of deep naivete despite her own inner wisdom. Our attention was drawn to the wide eyes and the finger in the figure's mouth.

The boss' individual card of personality was the Queen of Cups, a deeply insightful woman offering a wealth of advice for my client's well-being. Her aspect of the Shadow was the Six of Pentacles and held a definite quality of one-upmanship in the relationship. She needed to keep my client in her learner position so that the boss could remain teacher and giver.

My client's frustration came from not having her growth and maturity acknowledged by the other. As we worked with the cards, my client's intuitions toward her boss were verified, and she began to have a better understanding of her boss' weaknesses and strengths.

My client asked what she was to learn from the situation. The card for this was the Nine of Cups. As we looked at this card and played with the imagery, she came to identify it as meaning that she was learning to rely on her own inner sense of self-satisfaction rather than on compliments and recognition from others, a problem that she had been grappling with for some time. Despite the conflicts with her boss, the outcome of staying at her present job was shown as the Nine of Disks. It seemed a very beneficial and supportive thing to do both in the practical sense, as indicated by disks, and in terms of her spiritual or transpersonal development as indicated by the unfolding wings surrounding the disks.

The most important result of this session was my client's ability to clarify vague feelings, verify intuitive insights, and to better integrate her own attitude in the situation. She realized that she needed to rely on her own will and her own sense of inner worth. As we completed the throw, she felt a great sense of satisfaction and clarification. The reading, to her, was right on target. I was able to discover again that even when I am not sure of the results, the client, who has directly felt the impact, experiences a very definite shift in awareness—an "aha."

There are at least two contraindications to using the Tarot in a counseling session. The first is simply when a client needs to stay within a more traditional periphery and would have an adverse reaction to the use of more avant-garde tools such as Tarot, astrology, or *I Ching* . The second is when clients are in such a negative state of awareness that they have a strong tendency to invert the energy of symbols, taking these into the negative vortex in which they find themselves trapped. This state is especially volatile if it is accompanied by a very active imagination, hallucinations, or a strong ability to visualize. Any image, however benign it may be seen by the therapist, may appear as ominous to the suffering individual. Because of the power of Tarot images as representations of primary or archetypal energies, I would hesitate to add their impact to an already overburdened, ungrounded, and usually frightful image-producing psyche. Therapists should use discretion in these instances.

SPECIFIC ENERGY TECHNIQUES

The 22 Major Arcana, as well as the Aces of the four minor suits, constitute the most powerful symbolic images of the deck. These are visual representations of archetypal energies, akin in purpose and impact to the yantras of Eastern traditions. Their use in creative-visualization exercises and as focal images in meditation can have a profound effect.

Symbolic identification with an archetypal representation aligns the conscious and unconscious fields of the individual with the universal creative field within which this image has its source. Eventually, the individual psyche becomes more and more tuned to its vibration. The channel between this energy and the individual opens. The individual can then draw on this energy, setting up the corresponding vibrations within the personal field.

This alignment and opening involves an awakening or transformation, the purpose of which is to bring the personal self into the larger matrix of the transpersonal Self. A more effective, purposeful, and harmonious functioning in the world is thus effected. Roberto Assagioli describes this process as being invoked by an act of will. Its essence is expressed in Law Number One of his psychological laws. Law Number One states that "Images or mental pictures and ideas tend to produce the physical conditions and the external acts that correspond to them."[6]

Symbolic identification can be used quite effectively in the therapeutic process. I'll use the example of a client who is experiencing a block in creative self-expressions. Working with the Empress card can prove quite effective in realigning creative flow.

I begin with a preliminary relaxation technique and then guide the client on an inner experience that follows this basic format:

Imagine yourself in a garden . . . in this garden, seated on a cushioned throne, sits a woman dressed in a forest-green gown . . . allow yourself to approach her. . . and as you do, begin to experience the energy of this woman . . . an incredible fullness radiates from her . . . the crescent moon resting under her foot reverberates, responding to her slightest movement . . . allow yourself a few inner moments to just be with this woman . . . let yourself experience whatever thoughts, feelings, images, or sensations emerge as you absorb the energy of her presence . . . and . . . as you continue to absorb this energy, begin to feel yourself merging with this image . . . until you feel yourself seated on a cushioned throne . . . becoming aware of the lushness surrounding you . . . the fragrance and freshness of grass, flowers, trees, filling your every cell . . . enjoy the sensation of your robe's texture against your skin . . .allow yourself to absorb the soft refreshing song of the brook at your side . . . its movement soothing and purifying your entire being . . . experience yourself as creatress, allowing your body to take the pose of this image . . . feeling the moon responding under your touch . . . open to the creatress energy flowing through you on a

liquid wave of green light . . . permeating every cell . . . and now begin to
express yourself as Creatress . . . . I am Creatress. . . through me, spirit
becomes manifest . . . nurture and guide it to fruition' . . . you are giving
birth to your own creativity.

After guiding the client back into a more conscious awareness, I have the client share the experience with me and perhaps write it down. Both of these help to ground or solidify the experience. I suggest that the client set aside a time each day until our next session to meditate on and identify with this image, to play with and express its energy as fully as possible. As the client practices experiencing the image, it is also important for him or her to become aware of the resistances that surface. The resistances serve as keys to discovering how the client blocks creative energy.

The four Aces of the minor suits offer the opportunity to align with and activate more fully the four primary elements. The Wand represents fire, will, and the archetypal plane. The Cup represents water, emotion, receptivity, and the creative plane. The Sword represents air, mental clarity, and the formative plane. The Pentacle represents earth, practical grounding, manifestation, and the material plane.

I have especially enjoyed using the following two exercises to help a client or group get in touch with the energies of the four elements. These exercises can be done individually or in sequence during the same session. I usually use a musical accompaniment as background for these experiences to enhance and more strongly activate the process. Albums and cassettes by many fine New Age composers and musicians are available. Their music is especially evocative for meditational and deep-relaxation states.

I call the first of these three exercises "The Magician's Garden." After a beginning relaxation and breathing exercise, I guide as follows:

Imagine before you a path . . . walk along this path . . . and notice the
scenery as you go . . . feeling the air touching your cheek . . . the freshness
and vibrance of nature as you walk along this path . . . and now . . . notice
ahead of you an enclosure . . . surrounded by a wall . . . with a wooden gate
. . . approach this enclosure, and as you do, allow yourself to open the gate
. . . and see a garden . . . enter this garden . . . explore it for a few inner
moments . . . and now become aware that in the center of the garden stands
a large grey cube . . . approach this cube and notice that there are four
objects lying on it . . . a Wand . . . a Cup. . . a Sword . . . and a Pentacle . . .
become aware of these elements more fully . . . and as you continue to look
at them, notice that one of them attracts you most strongly . . . pick up this

element and examine it, allowing yourself to experience its energy . . .
become aware of the thoughts, feelings, images, or sensations that emerge as
you hold this object . . . open yourself to its energy as much as you can
allow . . . and   now . . . when you feel ready, return this first
element to the cube . . . and begin to become aware of the element that you
are drawn to next . . . (repeat instructions as for first element until all four
elements have been introduced and experienced).

Then, the client or group is guided back into conscious awareness. Again, the experience should be shared and/or written down to ground the energy.

The second exercise is a ritual done literally with the four elements and a table. Placed on a table are representations of a wand, cup, sword, and pentacle. These can be household items serving as symbols for the four elements. For instance, a stick, a knife, a wine glass, and a coin or round stone are suitable objects.

My client, or group, and I stand around the table. After a centering and relaxation exercise, I begin by picking up one of the elements (objects) from the table. As I hold it, I begin to get in touch with the feeling and symbolism of the object and, as I do, start to express myself verbally and in body position *as* this element. For instance, "I am the Cup. I am a vessel of receptive plasticity. I flow and change, moving with the tides, my nature contains the reflection of the universe in its very depths." When I have finished, the object is passed onto the client or next member of the group, who spontaneously impersonates this element. The exercise continues until each element is explored and experienced.

Through each of these exercises, the client has the opportunity to get in touch experientially with these four basic elements. One or more of the elements may resonate easily and feel strong in the individual's experience, while others may feel weak and awkward or even bring up resistance to contact. The therapist and client may discover where greater integration of an element is needed in the client's life. To bring this integration about, the individual can meditate on the Tarot card depicting this element. After looking at the card, the client can close his or her eyes and concentrate on the image, holding it in imagination for three to five minutes to experience the thoughts, feelings, and sensations that emerge while visualizing, or thinking, or remembering this image.

I recommend a period of six to nine months of daily visualization on a particular image to bring about the desired result. This period acts as a gestation cycle for the image to become fully incorporated into the unconscious, allowing for a creative transformation within the psyche.

In an article on creativity, psychosynthesist James Vargiu explains the effect of symbols as follows, ". . . symbols have both a transmuting and a selective property. Jung, one of the foremost authorities on symbols, stated that 'The psychological mechanism that transforms energy is the symbol.' Assagioli talks about symbols as 'accumulators, transformers, and conductors of psychological energies,' and goes on to explain how, because of these properties, symbols are well suited as tools to foster creativity, personality integration, and expansion toward the transpersonal dimension."[7]

I have found the Tarot a powerful and versatile tool in my therapeutic work. Its images catalyze the intuitions of both therapist and client. Meditation and imaginative exercises using its visual symbols have a transforming effect on the psyche. The pioneering effect of transpersonal psychology can benefit greatly from the intelligent use of this therapeutic aide. Whether used as an assessment tool, map of the inner environment, yantra, or catalyst for communication with the deeper self, its legitimacy, potency, and effectiveness are undeniable. To dismiss Tarot, to relegate its image to that of a device of feeble-minded and eccentric characters in a Hollywood expose of sensational occultism, or to otherwise devalue its potential for legitimate use is to waste another valuable resource, to miss another opportunity to expand our understanding, to deny our willingness to bond with a larger matrix of existence.

NOTES

1. Paul Foster Case, *The Tarot, A Key to the Wisdom of the Ages*, Virginia: Macoy Publishing Co., 1947, p. 23.

2. In his book, *Realms of the Human Unconscious*, Stanislav Grof, M.D., developed the concept of coex systems (systems of condensed experience), which he defines as a "specific constellation of memories consisting of condensed experiences (and related fantasies) from different life periods of the individual." (See page 46 of the text.)

3. Psychosynthesis is a system of techniques and principles developed by Italian-born psychiatrist Roberto Assagioli to bring about a synthesis of separate elements of the personality around a new center. See his two main texts *Psychosynthesis* and *The Act of Will*. NY, Penguin Books, 1971.

4. Subpersonalities represent different roles we play, contradictions in our behavior, our various selves. The unveiling and exploration of these various "selves" can be quite revealing and helpful in developing a better understanding of our inner conflicts and personality contradictions.

5. *Chakra* is a Sanskrit term for a vortex of energy in a person's etheric (subtle-energy) body. There are seven of these vortexes. The solar plexus, or navel chakra, is a center of power, aggression, and various emotions.

6. Roberto Assagioli, M.D., *The Act of Will*, New York: Viking Press, 1973, p. 51.

7. James Vargiu, "Creativity", *Synthesis*, vol.3-4, "Realization of Self," California: Synthetic Press, 1977, pp. 42-43.

Tarot Clientele:
Who, When, Why?

Angeles Arrien, PhD, and James Wanless, PhD

O■O■O■O■O■O■O■O■O■O■O■O■O■O

In 1978, two Tarot consultants analyzed who, when, and why clients sought a Tarot reading. Each surveyed the data recorded for 600 clients. The results revealed that the following motivations and intentions were most common for seeking the guidance of the Tarot.

A friend has recommended that the client should have such an experience.

The individual is in a quandary and does not want to seek "professional" help yet trusts the insight or intuition of one purported to be "psychic."

The individual cannot accept personal responsibility and wants another perspective; unconsciously wants another, the psychic or the reader, to assume responsibility.

It's a fad, "in thing" to do; makes great conversation; the individual has a love for the sensational or unusual.

The individual believes symbols are a valuable tool for further growth and development; a means of gathering additional information about oneself to become more effective in using one's potential.

The individual has a distrust of the technical/clinical psychologies; but does trust the intuitive systems.

After these initial motivations have been satisfied, clients often state what their real personal concern or major issue is. This study reveals that clients seek a Tarot counselor predominately for relationship issues. In order of importance, these issues include:

Changes in the relationship and how to handle those changes

Separation/divorce/relationship ending

Questions surrounding commitment to engagement, marriage, living together

Issues surrounding children, family members, or relatives

Triangular relationships

Coworking relationships

Besides relationship issues, clients cited other key factors for seeking a Tarot consultation. These are listed in descending order of importance:

Career transitions or job/work/creativity issues

Finances

Health

Chronic problems and how to overcome or face them; e.g., problems with alcohol, drugs, or sexual identity

In all of these concerns, clients desired focus, direction, and possible alternatives for resolving these issues. The Tarot consultation provides a "safe" environment in which clients can reveal themselves to a "stranger" they will not see again; or if they have difficulty in accepting the information, they can call the consultant a "quack" or not really "psychic." The whole thing was just a card game—just chance—so it can be ignored. On the other hand, if the consultant is particularly well-skilled, the information cannot be easily dismissed. Typical statements include: "How did you know that? You don't know anything about me!"—and definitive credence is then given to the consultant without further reservation. The client may choose at this point to confront the issue and obtain as much information as possible.

Beyond the responses to the consultation itself, it is necessary to consider how people handle uncertainty and unpredictability in their personal lives. Some are fatalistic—"What will be will be." These individuals would not seek a consultation of any kind. Others try to manipulate unknown forces. When they request a deity to intercede on their behalf, we call it prayer; when they attempt to influence unknown forces through ritual or the use of charms, we call it magic.

In a study, George Gmelch and Richard Felson found a statistically significant correlation between the uncertainty of an activity and the amount of magic people will use or believe in. *The more uncertain the outcome, the more likely the individual will use unconventional resources or magic.* This leads to an interesting anomaly. As societies become more technologically advanced, people become more highly educated and, as a result, presumably less inclined to use magic. However, Gmelch and Felson have found that emphasis on achievement and success also increases with modernization. Since people use more magic when they care most about the outcome of performance, *the use of magic in some activities may increase with modernization, not decrease.* Perhaps, then, the external reasons for seeking an unconventional resource for information such as a Tarot, astrological, or *I Ching* counselor are that the outcome is very important and the client cares about the performance within the situation.

TAROT AS AN ARCHETYPAL GUIDE

Having considered the personal and societal reasons that attract individuals to Tarot consultations, let us now consider another possibility that may underlie all the possibilities considered. Psychologist Carl G. Jung proposed and discovered that underlying all of our most rational activities may be internal forces or "archaic remnants" know as "archetypes"—ancient symbols that motivate internal and external experiences. These primordial images channel or surface consciously as an individual experiences varied life events and relationships. Jung identified 50 mythic images that all humankind have in common, and as a result wrote *Man and His Symbols.*

Perhaps individuals are internally prompted to seek a symbolic system to mirror their own internal/external symbolic processes. Jung stated that "The psychological mechanism for transforming energy is the symbol." Of all the unconventional resources, the Tarot is preeminently a *visual/symbolic* process. The ritual of shuffling the card-symbols, laying them out, and reading them is a symbolic process in itself. It is this underlying symbolic process that creates situations of synchronicity or coincidence too profound to ignore as having happened only by chance. The symbolic process is responsible for the dreams, meditations, visions, and "mythic scripts" individuals play out.

When individuals cannot understand what is happening to them and need guidance, there may be a predominant archetype or archetypes that surface to facilitate change and growth. The Tarot is an archetypal guide or map during periods of enormous personal growth and change. During periods of transformation, individuals need tools that can adequately facilitate the process. If, as Jung suggested, the psychological mechanism for transforming energy is the symbol, then personal change is guided by visual symbols that correspond with internal and external experience.

A symbol is "meaningless" only because we do not know how to intepret it or at times do not understand it. Individuals seek a Tarot counselor, one versed in symbolic understanding to provide the clues to the primordial images they are experiencing. This reason may be consciously known, seldom given as a reason; or it may be the underlying unconscious motivation for seeking a Tarot consultation.

The ultimate motivation may be that which we do not fully understand, and which is eloquently stated by sociologist Robert Bundy: "Images of the future are mythological images of the past, and in a certain sense it is a case of them choosing us rather than us choosing them."

THE POPULARITY OF TAROT

This study is both a statistical and subjective analysis of the kind of people who patronize a Tarot counselor and their reasons. The conclusions are based upon data from 600 consultations given over a two to three year period by one reader. Although the findings show the nature of the clientele drawn to a particular reading style and personality, they offer meaningful insights into the attractiveness of Tarot in general.

The data support the conclusion that most individuals seek the Tarot as a tool for guidance for specific issues in their life such as love and career. Generally, these Tarot clients are not psychological cases with severe mental or emotional imbalances. Since these people are neither "sick" nor consider themselves psychologically unhealthy, they would not seek the help of a psychiatrist. Tarot is attractive because one can go to a Tarot reader for guidance without considering it an admission of a problem. Clients can seek Tarot counsel under the guise of curiosity.

Tarot is accessible to everyone. Unlike other forms of counseling, there is very little special terminology and psychological theory a client must learn over a period of consultations. The card-symbols say what they mean in everyday language and in pictorial representation. Tarot is a simple, direct, and rapid means of receiving guidance.

Although Tarot is a convenient alternative to psychiatric counseling, it is nevertheless widely perceived in this culture as occult and without credibility. Its popularity can better be understood, therefore, by a closer examination of the clientele. The vast majority of Tarot patrons in this study were found to be in their late twenties or early thirties. This age group is receptive to the Tarot, perhaps, because these are individuals who grew up under the social conditioning of the 1940s and 50s, but in the 60s became disenchanted with the conventional ways of viewing life and themselves. They have found the traditional ways of perceiving themselves to be unproductive and limiting, let alone false.

Dr. Roger Gould, in his study *Transformations: Growth and Change in Adult Life* (which is the research basis for *Passages* by Gail Sheehy), has identified this age group as typically undergoing serious reevaluation of their lives. Having established a career, marriage, home, and personal lifestyle in their early and mid-twenties, thirtyish people have found their life unsatisfying. They seek to express their emergent "real" feelings and desires, and start life anew with different relationships, occupations, and lifestyles.

The majority of the Tarot clientele is also female. That women are more responsive than men is probably the result of social conditioning. This culture more readily allows women to explore their lives in such "mysterious" and "irrational" ways. For men, such subjective, soft, and speculative self-exploration is not so acceptable.

It is interesting to note that in analyzing the male clientele by profession, the predominant occupation is business. This could indicate that men are more attracted to the oracular for reasons of fortune than for self-knowledge. Perhaps businessmen are more open to the intuitive process of Tarot because it is in business that men call upon their intuitive faculties—going by the "gut", trusting "hunches." In the highly competitive world of business, a businessman looks for any means of gaining an edge on his competition. Such an advantage is acquired through information. An "extra-ordinary" source of information, such as the Tarot, is therefore welcomed. Businessmen are also risk-takers and would thus be more willing than other males to risk the counsel of the cards.

TYPICAL TAROT CLIENTELE:
SOME ARCHETYPAL PORTRAITS

We can examine in greater depth the reasons people are attracted to Tarot and what they hope to receive by looking at the most typical kinds of clients as determined by their "life-time cards." The first step in the style of Tarot consultation used in this study is the determination of a person's life-time card-symbol, which depicts one's predominant archetypal energies, and thus one's basic personality type.

There are twenty-one possible personality profiles in this system. According to the data, three of these types patronize the Tarot with much greater frequency than others. The predominant type is the combination of the Sun (19), Fortune (10), and Magician (1). The second most common type is the Hierophant (5), followed by the Fool (22)/Emperor (4) combination.

Sun-Fortune-Magician Personality

Those people with the combination 19-10-1 are the archetypal magicians, the alchemists. This archetypal energy is expressed in their ability to transform. As the Magician, they can change nothingness into abundance. As the Wheel of Fortune, they are able to turn their lives around. As the Sun, they can convert darkness into light. The 19-10-1 archetypal combination desires a sunny, bright, golden, and glowing life of richness and abundance. In the possibly dark, unfulfilling, and unrewarding years of their late 20s and early 30s, they want to know how they can change that situation. They seek the Tarot as a vehicle for transforming their life into goldenness because of their attraction to the "magic" of the cards, Tarot's association with "fortune-telling," and because of their willingness to take a gamble by seeing what the cards have to say.

Tarot satisfies their desires by lending insight into the changes they are experiencing through their selection of the cards in a reading. The Tarot focuses on the mundane aspects of life that are undergoing change such as relationships, career, health, finances, home, sexuality; and it explains how one's mental (Swords), emotional (Cups), perceptual and character (Wands) qualities create these transformations. The Tarot provides 19-10-1s with the information that enables them to make the changes they seek.

The philosophy of this approach to Tarot is that negative cards depict lesson-learning experiences. Like the Wheel of Fortune, one can convert and turn a problem around into an opportunity. The lotus grows out of the mud; the garden blossoms from the compost heaps, the garbage. In acquiring this perspective from the Tarot, a client is better able to deal with problems and, in fact, even become thankful for them as they offer opportunities for personal growth and flowering through their resolution.

Also worth noting is the client's "growth card" for the year. (See pages 88-104). This card indicates the kind of archetypal energy or situations a person will experience for any given year. The data show that in a preponderance of cases, Tarot clients are experiencing, foremost, the Hierophant energy; second, the Chariot; and third, the Lovers.

Hierophant Personality/Year

It is interesting that both those with the Hierophant lifetime card and those in their Hierophant growth year are attracted to the Tarot. The Hierophant is the learner-teacher, a person of self-knowledge and wisdom. Those with the archetypal energy of the Hierophant desire to know, to learn of what is happening in their lives. Individuals whose Hierophant archetypal energy is highly activated would find the Tarot a particularly appropriate and satisfying means for learning about themselves. The Hierophant is the ancient sage within us, the possessor of old ways of learning and knowing. Hierophant types are drawn to the Tarot because it is an old body of knowledge and technique of self-knowing. Ancient man knew himself through the internalization of the symbolic meaning he gave to the natural world around him. Tarot is a symbolic way of knowing. The ancients consulted their priestesses for revelation. Those who strongly carry the Hierophant within their consciousness consult the modern priestess—the Tarot reader. Those of the past consulted their Delphic oracles. Tarot maintains the oracular tradition. The ancients asked their own inner priestess, their own inner oracle, the intuitive voice, for counsel. Tarot, as an intuitive medium of knowledge, maintains this tradition. Ritual, as well as symbols, priestesses, and oracles, gave meaning to the life of the ancients. The ritualism of the Tarot is attractive to those who carry strong seeds of the past within them. Hierophants, as people who want to know, are naturally curious. Feeling tugs toward the oracular, intuitive, and symbolic, they are compelled to investigate this ancient system of knowledge.

The Tarot offers an alternative to the modern rationalistic and behavioralistic way of learning and teaching. The Hierophant is an archetype: it permanently and universally operates within all of us. Thus, the Tarot's way of knowledge will always exist and be attractive. Consulting the Tarot fulfills an aspect of our human nature. As our world becomes more and more computerized and explained in terms of numbers and observable physical laws, a need to understand through intuition, symbolic imagery, ritual, and oracle will grow commensurately.

Those who have opened themselves up to the Hierophant energy within and who are experiencing the lessons and tests such as defeat, disappointment, worry, and strife (the number five card-symbols in the deck relevant to the experience of the number-five Hierophant) of one's reevaluation, transition, and expansion years would seek out the Tarot for answers on how to resolve those difficulties. As the Tarot contains negative card-symbols, problem areas in a client's life are often revealed in a consultation. This enables a person to see a problem which, as a result of being too close, too much a part of the individual, may have been previously unrecognized or deliberately unacknowledged. In seeing difficulties portrayed in front of oneself, the situation is objectified. A mental-emotional distance is created between oneself and the problem. The problem is thus perceived as not so bad and as resolvable because the hang-up is not oneself. Rather, there is the person and the problem—separate and yet connected. This distancing gives an individual a sense of control over the difficulty. If a person were to feel that he or she is the problem, then how could it ever be solved—how can the problem solve the problem?

Fool/Emperor Personality

The third most common personality type attracted to the Tarot is the Fool/Emperor combination of archetypes. The Fool symbolizes the pure spirit of life—whole and perfect. A person experiencing the archetypal energy of the Fool would seek to manifest the spirit, to realize perfection, in the sense of actualizing all of the potentials embodied in the spirit-essence. Through the Tarot, one can see one's potential, what one can do with one's life. That potential is primarily symbolized in one's lifetime and yearly growth cards, which come from the Major Arcana and depict the archetypal qualities that all of us as human beings possess.

Fool archetypes realize their potentials during periods of major change in their lives. The transformations associated with the transition-expansion years compel them to seek out their potentials, which are not usually defined and supported in our culture nor in traditional forms of counseling.

The Fool-Emperor is the archetypal energy that seeks to create new life. The Fool, as the spirit, is life-creation. The Emperor, as the archetypal male and Aries, the first sign of the zodiac, is the sower of seeds that bring new life. Both the Fool and the Aries Emperor symbolize the spring, the time of new life and growth. New life—that is precisely what those in their transition-expansion years are seeking to establish. Tarot is replete with symbols of creativity that support this quest: children, flowers, spring colors, phalluses, pregnant women, wheels, phoenixes, crocodiles, lions, and snakes. In providing individuals with knowledge of their potential and with the information that gives them ability to gain control or Emperor-like dominion over their lives, Tarot helps to engage them in the process of self-creation.

Fool/Emperor archetypes are attracted to Tarot as a vehicle for facilitating their creative drives because of their Fool or childlike trust in the spirit's ability to select the appropriate card-symbols. Strong like the Emperor and fearless like the Fool, who leaps into the abyss, they are unafraid to take a chance, to risk what the cards have to say. Like the Fool who follows his own spirit and marches to his own drum (which may be contrary to the traditional beliefs and conventions of society), they are willing to consult an unorthodox and, by society's standards, "foolish" medium such as Tarot.

Chariot Year

Those in their Chariot year are often clients. The Chariot archetype is the energy associated with movement— of setting new things in motion. The Chariot is a vehicle of change. It moves a person from one situation to another. In experiencing the energy of the Chariot, individuals need and seek change, and want to break out of any stagnating aspects of their life and get themselves moving again, as indeed are those in the transition-expansion period of their lives. Stifled, restricted, and bound by their lifestyle, they desire to become mobilized. The powerful symbolism of the Tarot is the catalyst. It energizes them to get their wheels in motion, create changes, and make breakthroughs.

If the archetypal energy of the Chariot has manifested itself strongly within a person, he or she may have already become mobilized and begun the process of self-transformation. Such people, however, need to know where they are moving, where the process of change is taking them. They want to master their fate, to become the driver of their life. Tarot is attractive to the Charioteer because through its fortune-telling quality of showing possible direction, the person gains a sense of self-control. This style of Tarot emphasizes that future probabilities are realized through present decisions, states of mind and perception—all of which can be controlled by the individual.

In experiencing the change and movement associated with the Chariot archetype, there is often a sense of insecurity. Charioteers, symbolizing Cancer (the home) want to feel comfortable, secure, at home. The Tarot provides a "chariot," a secure structure, by helping individuals acquire a conceptual grasp on their life. This is achieved by showing their probable future and how they can control it. Also, in depicting one's situation in life, the Tarot often confirms much of what the individual already knows. This validates a person's own self-perception and creates a sense of trust in one's judgment. This is a reassuring realization to a person in transition.

Lovers' Year

The third most common type of archetypal year in which a person seeks a reading is that of the Lovers. Activation of this archetypal energy drives a person toward a meaningful relationship in life, whether familial, friendship, occupational, and/or love. In this quest, a person experiences signficant transformations in relationships. In the Lovers year, a person undergoes, in particular, a consummation or disintegration, or both, of a love relationship. As people in their late 20s and early 30s typically experience expansive changes in relationships and as Tarot clients have readings because of relationship concerns, it is natural that those in their Lovers year and in that age-group would be clients. They may be attracted to the Tarot because of its general perception as a tool for divining relationships, the "You will meet a tall, dark person" stereotype of Tarot.

At a time of change and transformation in their lives, individuals often feel unbalanced and unintegrated. This would be acutely felt among those with an active Lovers archetype because the Lovers is Gemini, meaning the experiencing of dualities, dichotomies, and oppositions. Yet the Lovers archetype wants to integrate polarities, which are symbolized in the Lovers card, such as the child and adult within them, their masculine and feminine qualities (the marriage of Emperor and Empress); their rational mind (Gemini-air-mental sign) and their feeling heart (love); their animal passions (Scorpio and Leo symbols) and their humanness; their pursuit of independence (Hermit) and their desire for relationship (Lovers); their physical, worldly concerns (the marriage) and their spiritual quest (the hooded Hermit); self-love (the inner union of polarities) and love for others (the external union with others).

The Tarot consultation is a healing process; it helps a person become and feel more integrated. It accomplishes this by first breaking down the symbolic picture of the individual into separate attributes. In the "whole person" version of the Celtic Cross spread employed in this reading style, a client sees his or her state of being represented in the positions corresponding to the head (mental), heart (emotional), legs (physical and/or subconscious), and two sides (masculine and feminine). At the conclusion of the reading, the cards are rearranged by suit, so that the client can see the extent of integration and balance mentally, emotionally, and physically.

Moreover, the Tarot addresses itself to the individual's inner dualities. Many of the cards possess symbols that recognize the various kind of oppositions a person experiences. In confirming and objectifying the un-togetherness a person might feel, it becomes more manageable to the individual. Also, opposing tendencies that are often combined in the card-symbols catalyze the integrative forces within a person. This merging of dualities is best illustrated in the Crowley-Harris Thoth deck in the Major Arcana symbols.

One of the foremost manifestations of the Lovers archetypal energy is the desire to love oneself. In the standard Tarot deck, there are, in fact, only a few negative card-symbols. The preponderance of the symbols are positive, which accurately reflects the conditions of our lives. Clients feel wonderful when they see so many positive and beautiful cards reflecting themselves. In this culture of competitiveness, where the mind is trained to think critically, people often hold themselves in low esteem, particularly when changes bring a sense of loss or confusion. A reading, therefore, boosts self-love and esteem. Instead of being put down and torn apart, Tarot as an integrative process builds people up and puts them back together.

The zodiac sign most associated with Tarot clients is Aries. Aries is the Emperor and as such symbolizes male energy in terms of dynamic initiative, as contrasted to the symbolic femaleness of receptivity. The Fool/Emperor, the Chariot, and to a lesser extent the Hierophant are all masculine energies. Most clients consult the Tarot at a period in which they want to initiate and forge a new life for themselves, which is reflected in the Aries and male-oriented cards. Most clients are women and are thus experiencing the masculine side of their nature. This is consistent with the situation of women who are presently thirtyish—liberated, independent, and having to create their own life through their own initiatives. Feeling their male energy and living in a time in which it can and must be expressed, these women view the Tarot as helping them establish a new life.

SUMMARY

It is evident from the personality types that avail themselves of the Tarot and from the issues with which they are concerned that it is particularly helpful to those in dynamic, transformative, and creative periods of their lives. The Tarot is useful in such circumstances because it provides self-understanding and self-dominion through the knowing, as a result of the Tarot's diagnostic qualities, of one's realities, probabilities, and potential. For persons feeling, amidst changes, that their life is out of control, gaining some understanding of what is happening to them and feeling able to direct the changes is vital to their well-being. The Tarot provides an individual with a sense of stability and self-trust that are important in destabilizing and uncertain periods of transformation. Because of its integrative and positive qualities, Tarot prevents the personal disintegration and loss of self-esteem associated with the breakdown of relationships, careers, etc. The card-symbols, through their visual affect and connection with archetypal energies, empower the individual. By catalyzing decisions and actions, Tarot helps us to manage and direct changes creatively rather than merely survive them.

Epilogue

O■O■O■O■O■O■O■O■O■O■O■O■O

To practice Tarot is to experience the wheel of life. Like the wheel, Tarot takes us to our destiny. Grasping the Tarot steering wheel of illumination, we become aware of the universe that we are. Riding the transformative energy of the revolutionary Tarot wheel of life, we take a new turn. We are moved. Our universe revolves. Through the eye of Tarot we make changes that take us closer to the full circle of total being. Approaching universal being, we reach out to help others along the path. Tarot is our medicine wheel.

Practicing the Tarot, we become the archetypal Charioteer. Piloting our life on the chariot of Tarot, we move on its wheels to our destiny of *tota* total being. It shows us the "royal road" and empowers us along the way.

Our universal nature is symbolized by the mandala of Tarot. A mandala is a wheel of life. As Judith Rozhon and Twainhart Hill have shown, Tarot is a circular pattern of interrelated symbols whose structure shows the relationship between the many spokes of our being. Mandalas reveal the whole picture. Through Tarot we explore our universe in totality.

Like the universe, which is guided by laws that are a product of some underlying mental purpose and will, you steer your life through the wheels of your mind—your values, ideas, and decisions. Through the cards, symbolizing qualities of mind, the Tarot cultivates your role as the creator who manifests the physical-material world in which you live. Shiloh Turner show how you can recreate your reality by altering your beliefs and perceptions through the assistance of the Tarot.

The wheel is like the Pentacle or Disk in the Tarot. They symbolize your worldly, material, physical life. The wheel is a sun (health), a coin (wealth), a community circle (relationships), and a nest (home). Sharon Jeffrey illustrates how you can use the Tarot to create a wheel of worldly fortune.

Just as this physical earth-sphere shakes, your body flexes. As the rivers flow, your fluids circulate. Like the air which moves, you inhale and exhale. You are catalyzed by your own fire as the earth by its blazing inner core. Susan Cole demonstrates how the Tarot can improve your earthlike physical body so that you can move with more ease and energy.

Like the world, which moves from a parched desert and dry river bed to luxurious gardens and flowing rivers, you have your own moments of emotional scarcity and abundance. Open spheres, like cups and flowers, symbolize your emotionality in the Tarot. You are full or empty, radiant or closed.

The Tarot connects you to your world of feelings. Judith Bolinger demonstrates how Tarot symbolism elicits your hopes and fears, your joys and sorrows. The very act of feeling, whether good or bad, gives you a life vitality that completes the circle of mundane being along with mental thought, physical sensation, and worldly activity.

This life of thinking, feeling, sensing, and doing is the shell, the structure that houses the supra-mundane, the ineffable inner light of spirit or consciousness. You are often unaware of this metaphysical universe and its levels of consciousness. Through the process of consulting or "reading" the Tarot, you use your superconscious to reveal your subconscious. Mary Culbertson presents the Tarot as a tool for tapping into these hidden dimensions of consciousness.

The wheel makes a totality but also a zero. Zero is like your spirit—untouchable, omnipresent, limitless. It is your connection with all things and no things. By enhancing your awareness, the Tarot connects you with this primordial and infinite state of being, which is pure consciousness. This light of awareness, symbolized by the eye, is the core essence of the self and the universe. You are one with all in consciousness. This explains why, as Ralph Metzner theorizes and Jane English demonstrates through statistics, you possess psychic ability, the power to accurately discern the unseeable through extra-ordinary perception.

Humanity is the physical, emotional, and mental manifestation of original consciousness, the zero-spirit. Your human nature is archetypal, preexistent to physical being. As Anne Stine asserts, the Tarot's Major Arcana are archetypes, or universal personality types, of human being. They connect you with the "original source."

As everyone and everything is created from this spirit source, the worlds of the universe are one. All phenomena are interrelated. As Karen LaPuma and Gary Ross have shown, we are associated in consciousness with all the material forms on the earth as well as the extraterrestrial planets and constellations. These in turn are related to the archetypal energy patterns of our consciousness, which manifest in the mythological gods and goddesses of Tarot.

As the universe is an ever-evolving multi-faceted whole, so are we. The Tarot provides such a kaleidoscopic view of ourselves. Mary Greer demonstrates this in her permutative way of looking at ourselves through the Celtic Cross spread. In revealing our totality, the Tarot can be compared to a hologram. In this holographic map, each picture (card or layout) contains multiple time-space frames of our past, present, and future, for here and there.

The chariot of Tarot takes us on an explorative journey into our multidimensional universe. Like explorer-cartographers who bring the universe together, the Tarot bridges worlds within worlds: the inner self with the outer world, the physical with the metaphysical, the present with the past and future, the individual with the collective, the intuitive with the rational, the conscious with the subconscious. As we experience our universe through this unified structure, we automatically integrate our own worlds and become whole.

Dori Gombold and Charloe Wittine have shown that the symbolic imagery of the Tarot mandala possesses catalytic and psychodynamic properties evoking within us the qualities it portrays. In becoming aware of the universe that we are through the universal symbology of the Tarot, we assume universal dimension. We realize the objective of the Tarot—to become the total human being.

God of the Wheel, Gallo-Roman Period

Index

Axiom (continued)
    of probability theory, 29
    theory of probability based on, 24-26

Bahy, 195
Being chakra, 152
Being-specific synchronistic causality, 10
Beliefs
    dealing with, 170-71
    transformational, 182-83
Blocks, identifying, 205-6
Bolinger, Judith, 164, 215, 217, 290
"Book of life," 137
Book of Thoth (Crowley), 105
Breakthrough, transformation stage, 185-86
Buddhism, 238
Buddhist Tantras, 7
Builders of the Adytum (B.O.T.A.), 191-92, 201
"The Burial of the Dead" (Eliot), 233
Business
    organization assessment of, 258-60
    using Tarot in, 249-52, 255-56, 261-62

Cabalistic mysticism, Tetragrammaton, 62
Caduceus, 203
Cairns. *See* Monoliths
Calcination, 197
California Institute of Transpersonal Psychology (CITP):
    dream/tarot correlation, 34-37
Calligraphy, 187
Cancer, 285. *See also* Knight of Cups
Canyons, symbolism of, 119-20
Capricorn. *See* Knight of Disks
Case, Paul Foster, 192, 263
Causality principle, vs. synchronicity, 8
Caves, symbolism of, 122
Celtic Cross Spread:
    card make up of, 53-54
    experiencing the, 54-55
    Greer on, 48
    history of, 49, 51-53
    as holographic map, 291
    meanings of positions listed, 56-59
    "whole person" version of, 286
Celtic mythology, Grail legend and, 232
Chakras
    harmonizing the, 196
    keys and, 200
    listed, 151-52
Changer, symbolism of, 158-59
Changing Woman, 124
Chariot:
    as energy symbol, 256-57

skills, education, and training, 70, 72-73
    symbolism of, 96, 98, 139-40
Charioteer:
    symbolism of, 139
    Tarot and, 284
Chariot year, described, 284-85
Chi-squared test:
    in English experiment, 26
    used in CITP research, 36
    use of, 31
Citadel, symbolism of, 159-60
Cities, symbolism of, 122
Clairvoyance, 28
Closed book, 160. *See also* First chakra
Cloud, symbolism of, 116-17
Cole, Susan K.:
    on dance and Tarot, 205
    on flexing the body, 164
    on healing or transformative process, 203
    on physical tension, 247
    on self-improvement, 290
Color
    using, 195-97
    visualizing, 200
Communication, 160. *See also* Fifth chakra
Compassionate love, 156-58. *See also* Fourth chakra
Compassion chakra, 151
Composite relationship spread, 65-66
Consciousness, aspects of, 189
Controls, Tarot cards and, 21
"Cosmic consciousness," 38
Court cards:
    as Nature's Archetypes, 105, 123
    as symbols, 77
    Tetragrammaton and, 106-7
Creation, Tetragrammaton and, 122
The Creative Word (throat chakra), 151
Crowley, Aleister, 149
Crowley-Thoth deck, 85, 139, 286
Crucifixion, Celtic Cross and, 52-53
Crystallization, 113
Cups, 61, 106-7
Cycle of Completion, 93, 95-96
Cycle of Growth and Regeneration, 93, 95-96
Cycles:
    defined, 93
    energy and, 88

Dageh , 195
Damyata, teaching of, 238
Dance therapy, 205-6
Datta, teaching of, 238

ESP:
: and choice of Tarot cards, 23
: spatially distant events, 6
Euclid, parallel axiom of, 24
Evolution, 30
External, symbols, 90

Father Sky, 53
Feeler, symbolism of, 156
Feminine archetype, 200
Fifth chakra, creative word as, 158
Fire, symbolism of, 106-7
"The Fire Sermon" (Eliot), 237
First chakra, 152
Five, symbolism of, 81
Five of Swords, symbolism of, 81
Flow, symbolism of, 112
"Flying Arrow Spread," movement therapy, 207-8
Fog, symbolism of, 112-13
Fog Woman, 124
Fool:
: dual nature of, 128-29
: as life-creation, 283-84
: movement pattern and, 210-11
: Radical Potential, 69-70
: symbolism of, 81-82, 98, 148-49
Fool/Emperor personality, described, 283-84
Forests, symbolism of, 121-22
Fortune-telling, by gypsies, 187
Fourth chakra, compassion as, 156-58
Freud, Sigmund, 30, 188
Freudian school, 190
Fruition, as stage, 162

Galaxies, symbolism of, 118
Galileo, 31
Gematria, 195
Gemini, Lovers card and, 209-10
Gemini. *See also* Queen of Swords
Geomancy:
: defined, 10-11
: mantic procedures in, 13
Geo. *See* Princess of Disks
Gestalt:
: defined, 79
: of Tarot, astrology, alchemy and
psychology, 19
Gleichartigkeit , defined, 8
God-as-macrocosm, and man-as-microcosm, 7

Godhead:
: experiencing Absolute Reality, 182-83
: leading to the, 181
: nature of, 152
: seventh chakra and, 159-60
Gombold, Dori:
: on psychodynamic effects of Tarot, 185, 187
: on symbolic imagery, 291
: on transforming, 164
Grail legend, 231-32
Grasslands, symbolism of, 120
Gravity, symbolism of, 119
Greater mysteries, 69
Group sharing, process of, 257-58
Growth cards, 91-92, 281-82
Gypsies, use of Tarot by, 18

"Hander". \plain \i See\plain Hermit
Hanged Man:
: karmic pattern realized, 70, 73-4
: Neptune and, 83
: symbolism of, 99, 143, 156
Healing, 195-97
"Heavy" cards, 67
Hebrew, 192, 195
Hermaphroditic wholeness, 157-58
Hermit:
: movement therapy and, 206-7
: skills, education, and training, 72-73
: sstrength, skills, education, 70
: symbolism of, 93, 95-96, 98, 147
Hierophant:
: business symbolism of, 254
: Conditioning/Child Environment, 70-72
: peyote and psilocybin and, 122
: symbolism of, 98, 146
: as teacher, 255-56
Hierophant personality/year, described, 282-83
High Priestess, Primordial Masculine/Feminine, 70-71
Hills, symbolism of, 122
Hindu Tantras, 7
Hippocrates, 7
Holographic map, 291
Horary astrology, 11, 13
Horoscopes, 14
Human figures, 190
Human psyche, 105, 188
Humans, symbolism of, 114
"Hunch," 185
Hurricanes, symbolism of, 117

Huxley, Aldous, 234

Paracelsus, 7
Paradigmatic "clairvoyance" experiments, 12
Parapsychic, 6
Parapsychological phenomena, 8-9
Parzival. *See* Percival
Passages (Sheehy), 280
Past, present, future, premutation, 60-61
The Path of Hermes. *See* Yod he Vau He
Penatcles, symbolism of, 61
Percival, 231-32
Permutations:
    a composite relationship spread, 65-66
    defined, 49-50
    maintaining ambiguity, 55-59
    of Tarot reading, 55-66
    the turning of the wheel, 59-60
    variations through time-the journal
approach, 64-6
    the whole-person summary spread, 61, 66
    Yod He Vau He, 62
Personality profiles (Tarot), 281-88
Personality and Soul Cards, 90-91
Personal pattern, 64-65
Peyote, symbolism of, 122
Phenomena (synchronistic), 6
Philo, on man-as-microcosm, 7
Physics, synchronicity and, 6
Pineal gland, 152
Pisces:
    age of, 86
    Moon and, 112
    Neptune and, 83
    as Queen of Cups, 111-12
PK. *See* Psychokinesis (PK)
Planetary clock, analogy of, 14
Planets, as symbols, 78-80
Pluto:
    Ra kings and, 84
    role of, 80, 84-85
    in sextile, 86
    symbolism of, 84-85
Plutonian energy, 84-85
Postcognitive telepathy, 28
Power, 166. *See* Third chakra
Power chakra, 151
Power of the word, 195-96
Precognition, 13, 28
Premutations, past, present, future, 60-61
Preparatory meditation, 196
Priestess, symbolism of, 140
Primal Pain Pool, 112

Primordial Masculine/Feminine, 70
    High Priestess, 71
    Magician, 71
Principle of Creativity, 104
Probability and Scientific Inference (Brown), 28
Probability theory, 29
"Prologue," 219-20
PSI, 12-14
Psilocybin, symbolism of, 122
Psi-mediated instrumental response (PMIR), 9
Psyche, 105, 188
Psychic synchronicity, categories of, 10
Psychokinesis (PK), 13, 28
Psychological energy, 188
Psychology:
    development of, 30
    gestalt with, 191
    synchronicity and, 6
Psychosynthesis, symbols used in, 190
Psychotherapy, 246, 263-75
Purposive behavior. *See* Instrumental
behavior
Pythagoras' seven celestial beings, 104

"Qabalistic Doctrines on Sexual Polarity," 200
Qabalists, 107, 195, 197-98, 200-201
Qualities of life:
    external, 99
    internal, 98
    mergence, 99
Quantum mechanics, 29-31
Queen of Cups:
    described, 111-12
    as energy symbol, 260
    as image of consciousness, 209
    Neptune and, 83
"Queen of Cups to Prince of Disks," 226-27
Queen of Disks, 119-20
Queen of Swords, 115-16
Queen of Wands, 83, 108-9
Questioner, in Tarot reading, 12-13
Quetzalcoatl, 186

Radical Potential, the Fool, 69-70
Rain, symbolism of, 111
Rainbow, symbolism of, 109
Rainforests, symbolism of, 113
Ra kings, 84
Random choice, of Tarot cards, 22-23
Random numbers, production of, 28-29
Reader, role of Tarot, 13

Symbolism:
  Lifetime Progression Chart and, 89-90
  as nonthreatening, 250
  primitive man use of, 187
  as psychological tool, 189-90
  use of dynamic, 201
Symbols:
  abstract, 191
  animal, 190
  assessing strength and weaknesses in,
    256
  calligraphy developed from, 187
  identifying individual purpose in, 256
  identifying organizational purpose in,
    255-56
  individual and spontaneous, 191
  language of, 33-34, 44
  man-made, 191
  methodology for using, 250-51
  nature, 190
  power of, 181, 185-86
  as psychological machinery, 189
  purpose of, 261
  religious and mythological, 191
  Tarot as system of, 44
  transformative power of, 188-91
  transmuting property of, 274
  use of identification, 271-74
Synchronicity:
  dream/tarot correlation and, 37-38
  events of, 7-8
  Jung on, 6
  manatic procedures and, 14
  parapsychological and, 8-9
  vs. causality principle, 8
Synthesis, defined, 62

Tableau, Tarot, 193-95
"Tai Chi Chuana" spread, 59
Tammuz legend, 232
Tao, 6, 59
Tarot:
  in Ancient Egypt, 102, 104
  an introduction to, 192
  applications of, 88
  applying synchronistic phenomena to, 11
  archetypal experience with, 183
  as archetypal guide, 278-79
  archetypal symbolism of, 88, 167
  Aries symbol of clients, 286-87
  B.O.T.A. and, 191-92
  Charioteer and, 284-85
  consciousness evolution and, 87
  Court Cards of, 106

creation of "energy bank", 188
deck layout, 128
as diagnostic instrument, 245-46
dreams and, 16-18, 23, 34
element symbols in, 106
ESP process in choice of, 23
experiments, 16, 24-27, 29-31
Fool/Emperor personality, 283-84
fundamentals of, 192-93
gestalt with, 191
as guidebook, 125-26
healing through, 195-97, 247
Hebrew letters and, 192
Hierophant personality, 282-83
history of, 187
as holographic map, 291
importance of observer in, 30
internal and external meaning of, 89-90
interpretation of, 193-95
"intuitive reading" of, 126
language of, 68, 181, 183
as living wheel, 163-64, 289-91
Lovers and, 285-87
as map of consciousness, 78
as means of opportunity, 51
motivations for using, 276-77
movement patterns and, 209-13
permutations (rituals) of, 55-66
personality profiles in, 281-88
popularity of, 279-80
as positive archetype, 190, 287
PSI and, 12-14
psychotherapy using, 263-75
questioner in, 12-13
reader in, 13
reading the map, 133-36
of relationships, 65-66
science and, 16, 18
subjective data and, 18-20
Sun-Fortune-Magician personality, 281-
  82
symbolism of Major Arcana, 165
synchronicity theory and, 10-12
as system of logic, 249
Tableau, 193-95
to build self-esteem, 260-61
as tool, 47-48
tree as symbol of, 203
typical clientele of, 280-91
use of archetypal depth dimension of
  Major cards, 7
used to identify obstacles, 205-6
used to tap energy, 170-72
use of symbolic diagnostic media, 77

Victorious One, symbolism of, 153-54, 157-58
Virgin:
    as Pisces symbol, 86
    symbolism of, 157
Virgo. *See* Queen of Disks; Virgin
Virtue, value of, 145
Vision chakra, 152
Visual/symbolic process, Tarot as, 278
Von Franz, 7

Waite deck:
    divination provided by, 234
    signs of Zodiac in, 55
    use of, 50
Waking dream, 189-90
Waking symbols, 33
Wand of the Magician, 52
Wands, symbolism of, 61, 106-7, 185
The Wasteland (Eliot), 187
"The Waste Land" (Eliot), 231, 236-38
The Waste Land (Smith), 236
Water, symbolism of, 106-7
Water Bearer:
    the Star and, 82
    symbolism of, 86
Waterfalls, symbolism of, 111
Waves, symbolism of, 110-11, 116
Way-Shower, symbolism of, 159
Wheel of Fortune, 53

business symbolism of, 252
Celtic Cross and, 59-60
as creative energy, 207-8
as energy symbol, 257
signs of Zodiac in, 55
symbolism of, 96-97, 99, 145
Transpersonal Perspective, 70, 73
Wheel of life, 289-91
"Whole Person Spread," 61, 66, 173
Womanhood, symbolism of, 122-23
Word, power of the, 195-96
World:
    symbolism of, 146
    Transformation and Integration, 70, 75-76

Xeno, Goddness of Mystery. *See* Princess of Cups

Yeats, William Butler, 236
Yin-Yang, 107, 160, 201. *See also* Second chakra
Yod He Vau He, 62, 107

Zodiac:
    four fixed signs of, 55
    Keys and, 196
    as symbols, 78-80
    symbol of wheel, 78
Zrcanum X, 53